A NOT-SO NATURAL DISASTER

A Not-So Natural Disaster

Niger 2005

Editors

Xavier Crombé And Jean-Hervé Jézéquel

HURST & COMPANY, LONDON

in association with Fondation Médecins Sans Frontières

First published in 2007 by Editions Karthala, Paris,
as *Niger 2005: Une Catastrophe si Naturelle.*
This translation published in the United Kingdom by
C. Hurst & Co. (Publishers) Ltd,
41 Great Russell Street, London, WC1B 3PL
© Médecins Sans Frontières, 2009
All rights reserved.
Printed in India

The right of Xavier Crombé, Jean-Hervé Jézéquel and the Contributors
to be identified as the authors of this publication is asserted by them
in accordance with the Copyright, Designs and Patents Act, 1988.

A Cataloguing-in-Publication data record for this book is available
from the British Library.

ISBN
978–1–85065–954–9 *paperback*

www.hurstpub.co.uk

The Charter of Médecins Sans Frontières

Médecins sans Frontières (MSF) is a private international association. The association is made up mainly of doctors and health sector workers and is also open to all other professions which might help in achieving its aims. All of its members agree to honour the following principles:

Médecins Sans Frontières provides assistance to populations in distress, to victims of natural or man-made disasters and to victims of armed conflict. They do so irrespective of race, religion, creed or political convictions.

Médecins Sans Frontières observes neutrality and impartiality in the name of universal medical ethics and the right to humanitarian assistance and claims full and unhindered freedom in the exercise of its functions.

Members undertake to respect their professional code of ethics and to maintain complete independence from all political, economic, or religious powers.

As volunteers, members understand the risks and dangers of the missions they carry out and make no claim for themselves or their assigns for any form of compensation other than that which the association might be able to afford them.

Niger

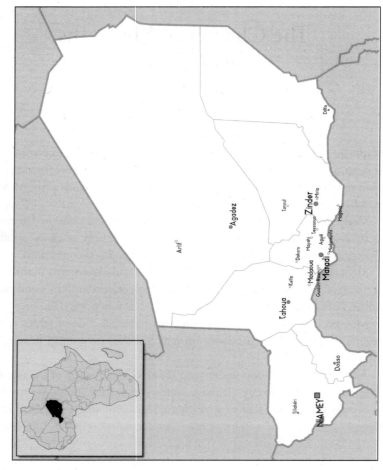

Contents

CONTENTS

Part III
MAKING CHILDREN LIVE

Acronyms

ACF	Action Contre la Faim (Action Against Hunger)
AFD	Agence Française pour le Développement (French Agency for Development)
CCA	Cellule de Crise Alimentaire (Niger's Food Crisis Cell)
CDC	Center for Disease Control
CFA	Communauté Financière d'Afrique (Africa's Financial Community, using the CFA franc as currency)
CILSS	Comité Permanent Inter-Etats de Lutte contre la Sécheresse au Sahel (Permanent Interstate Committee for Drought Control in the Sahel)
CMC	Commission Mixte de Concertation (Joint Consulting Committee)
DHS	Demographic and Health Surveys
DNPGCA	Dispesitif National de Prévention et de Gestion des Crises Alimentaires (National Food Crisis Prevention and Migration System)
ECHO	European Commission Humanitarian Office
FAO	Food and Agricultural Organization
FEWS-Net	USAID's Famine Early Warning Systems Network
GIEWS	Global Information and Early Warning System (on Food and Agriculture)
HKI	Helen Keller International
IMF	International Monetary Fund
IRAM	Institut de Recherches et d'Applications des Méthodes de Développement (Institute for Research and Implementation of Development Methods)

IRIN	United Nations Integrated Regional Information Network
LASDEL	Laboratoire d'Etudes et de Recherches sur les Dynamiques Sociales et le Développement Local (Laboratory for Studies and Research on Social Dynamics and Local Development)
MSF	Médecins Sans Frontières (Doctors Without Borders)
NASA	National Aeronauts and Space Administration
NGO	Non-Governmental Organization
OCHA	Office for the Coordination of Humanitarian Affairs
OPVN	Office des Produits Vivriers du Niger (Niger's Food Crops Office)
RUTF	Ready to Use Therapeutic Food
SAP	Système d'Alerte Précoce (Niger's Early Warning System)
CC/SAP	Cellule de Concertation du SAP (Niger's Early Warning System Consulting Cell)
SCN	United Nation Standing Committee on Nutrition
SNIS	Système National d'Informations Sanitaires du Niger (National Health Information System of Niger)
SOSA	Stratégie Opérationnelle de Sécurité Alimentaire (Food Security Operational Strategy)
UN	United Nations
UNDP	United Nations Development Programme
UNICEF	United Nations Children's Fund
USAID	United States Agency for International Development
WFP	World Food Programme
WHO	World Health Organization

Acknowledgements

Rony Brauman, François Enten, Vincent Foucher, Marc Le Pape, Judith Soussan, Milton Tectonidis, Claudine Vidal and Fabrice Weissman all read parts of the manuscripts of this volume and offered their thoughtful remarks and advice. Their contribution has been invaluable.

Roger Blein, Christian Captier, Jean-François Corty, Isabelle Defourny, Stéphane Doyon, Emmanuel Drouhin, Regis Ghesquier, Geza Harczi, Philippe Le Vaillant, Laurent Ligozat, Frédéric Mousseau, Vladimir Najman, Michael Neuman, Hugues Robert, Mahaman Tidjani Alou, Rémi Vallet and Anne Yzebe all contributed their support and expertise to our work. The information and the important documentation they made available to us have been invaluable.

The work of IRAM and LASDEL on the 2005 crisis has constituted an indispensable reference for most of the contributions to this volume. The various exchanges we have had with the members of these research groups have always been enriching. We are equally indebted to the IIED for authorizing us to reproduce in part the study conducted on their behalf by Marthe Diarra and Marie Monimart.

Bérengère Cescau, at the MSF Foundation, unfailingly supported us in dealing with many technical details involved in the production of this book. Kevin Phelan, of MSF-USA in New York, offered precious help in coordinating the translations for the English edition.

Finally, we are particularly grateful to Johanne Sekkenes, head of mission in Niger, her successor Thierry Clima, and the members of the Médecins Sans Frontières teams in Niger for sharing with us their daily experiences, their observations and questions. This book would not exist without them.

To all of them, we express our most heartfelt thanks.

INTRODUCTION

A Not-So Natural Disaster

Xavier Crombé and Jean-Hervé Jézéquel

On 29 April 2008, at the close of a two-day meeting of the executive heads of the UN and the Bretton Woods institutions, convened to design a common strategy in the face of the dramatic rise of food prices worldwide, the World Bank President Robert Zoellick made his point clear: "This is not a natural disaster. Make no mistake, there is nothing natural about this. But for millions of people it is a disaster."[1] On the same day the UN Secretary-General Ban Ki-moon, displaying an equal sense of urgency and determination, expressed nonetheless his confidence that "we can deal with the global food crisis. We have the resources. We have the knowledge. We know what to do."[2] A central theme in his approach was that, to deal with the crisis, the international community must display equal resolve in meeting emergency needs and committing itself to long-term reforms and action.

By contrast, when in July 2005 international media had started to report on an ongoing famine in Niger, there appeared at first to be little doubt that the disaster had natural causes—drought and locust infestation. Within

[1] Robert Zoellick, Statement on the global food crisis made after a meeting in Berne of the United Nations System Chief Executives Board for Coordination, 29 April 2008 (http://web.worldbank.org/WBSITE/EXTERNAL/NEWS/0,,contentMDK:21749013~pagePK:34370~piPK:34424~theSitePK:4607,00.html).

[2] Secretary-General Ban Ki-moon, "Opportunity in Crisis"—Inaugural lecture of the Geneva Lecture Series, sponsored by the UN Office at Geneva (UNOG) and the UN Institute for Training and Research (UNITAR), Geneva, 29 April 2008 (http://www.un.org/apps/news/infocus/sgspeeches/search_full.asp?statID=227).

1

Niger's government circles and the aid community, however, no one seemed to agree on the nature and extent of, and adequate responses to, the situation. Polemics between promoters of long-term development approaches and humanitarian agencies advocating emergency measures were particularly heated.

Although discussions of the global food crisis have occasioned only scant references to that which affected Niger three years before, ex post assessments of the latter[3] have shown that the economic dynamics behind the two crises in fact bear much in common. Drought and locusts only provoked a minor and localized production deficit and could not account for the food crisis in Niger. Instead, rising demand for cereals from neighbouring Nigeria—the booming regional economy, as are China and India at the global level—, speculation on grain and export restrictions imposed by cereal producers in the region resulted in a dramatic increase in the price of millet in Niger, making this staple food inaccessible for many rural Nigériens. In short, market dynamics, not nature or fate, played a central role in bringing about the Niger food crisis in 2005, as they have across the world in 2008. Why, then, should the interpretations and reactions to both crises differ so strikingly?

There is no straightforward answer to this question. One key factor, however, which economic analysis alone cannot grasp, has to do with widely shared preconceptions regarding people's ways of life and natural environment in a Sahelian country like Niger. To many—and not only in the media, which are too easily singled out for oversimplification or exaggeration—it simply made sense that in a land of poverty and overpopulation on the margins of the Sahara desert, famine would strike once in a while with no more complex causes than a lack of rain or an invasion of locusts, or that farmers would eat what they grow and depend on nature alone for their subsistence, as they supposedly always have done. Nor did it seem "unnatural" or abnormal to consider child malnutrition as a fact of life, aggravated by harmful feeding practices rooted in unchanging local culture. In essence, that Niger would undergo a food and nutritional crisis reflecting social and economic transformations and the effects of regional and global dynamics was for many observers, including some in the country, hard to fathom in 2005. These changes and dynamics—the "new face of hunger", in the words of the WFP's Executive Director Josette Sheeran—have apparently been more readily conceivable at the world level in 2008, although the concept of a "global food crisis" does not allow much attention to be given to local specificities.

[3] See in particular IRAM, *Evaluation du Dispositif de prévention et de gestion des crises alimentaires du Niger*, Niamey, February 2006.

It is the purpose of this book to account for some of the changes and dynamics that shaped the context of the events of 2005 in Niger, and to examine the preconceptions and logic that influenced how various actors, both national and international, played their part in the crisis and its response.

MSF was indeed a key player in the crisis, which in turn proved to be an unusual experience for this humanitarian organization. In 2005, MSF treated more than 40,000 children suffering from severe malnutrition—one of the most ambitious operations in its history. By comparison, in the most recent large-scale nutritional intervention prior to Niger—during Angola's famine in 2002—MSF treated 8,000 malnourished children. At the same time, MSF also found itself at the forefront of the controversies among the actors involved in managing the crisis over the summer of 2005. Finally, at the very moment it was straining to mobilize other actors to intervene in what it judged to be an emergency situation, MSF was undergoing in-house, heated arguments and questioning as to the exact nature of the situation it was attempting to manage. Public and operational involvement of this kind thus called for some form of reflection at a distance from the event.

MSF has already published several books to describe its experience and share its analyses concerning conflict situations, which constitute its predominant contexts of intervention. To this end its members have often called upon outside analysts and scholars to add their perspective to that of the humanitarian actor. We felt it was equally necessary to apply this method to a peacetime context, when humanitarian action seldom makes the headlines. We believe the social, institutional and political realities that formed the context for "Niger's emergency" and MSF's role in it do, in fact, deserve the same level of attention humanitarian agencies usually give to armed factions, militias and other rebel groups in conflict zones.

The present work makes no claim whatsoever to be comprehensive, or to provide a final, definitive version of "the truth" with respect to the 2005 crisis. Instead we have endeavoured to shed new light on a multifaceted crisis.

Crisis...which crisis?

While most commentators now recognize that a crisis indeed occurred in Niger in 2005, they find it more difficult to agree on the nature and substance of the event. A remarkable array of different labels has been attached to the crisis. It has been characterized, either at the same time or alternatively, as a food crisis, a nutritional crisis, an agricultural or a pastoral crisis, a political crisis, a media crisis, a demographic crisis...and, of course, as a famine.

How can one explain this profusion of perspectives? Is it symptomatic of the complexity of Niger's situation, in which several crises are juxtaposed or interwoven? Or does the diversity of labels rather reflect a deeper underlying conflict among different analyses? Should we, then, go about identifying which is the most adequate label for "the crisis" and what is the "right way" to analyze it? What (or which) crisis (or crises) does this book discuss?

In addressing these questions we have been guided by studies that view every crisis as essentially a construct of converging or competing forces, mobilized and driven by a number of actors.[4] Without these mobilized forces and the rhetoric that gives them shape and meaning, there is no crisis—which is not to say that a crisis consists of rhetoric alone.[5] Niger in 2005 was the theatrical setting for a number of "stagings" of the crisis, with different groups or institutions marshalling their knowledge and expertise, assembling their own interpretations, and striving to impose them or else articulate them with those of other actors, each according to its different interests. From this standpoint, the diversity of the labels cited above does not so much result from the complexity inherent to the event itself, or from conflicting analyses; it reflects, rather, the multiplicity of mobilizations that attempted to give this event meaning. Hence, in this volume, Mamoudou Gazibo analyzes how a range of Nigérien political actors, from government to civil society, positioned themselves by invoking a symbolic and historical language specific to Nigérien politics. Benedetta Rossi does the same with respect to the actors external to Niger—from "*urgentistes*" to "developers"—who all employed their own different interpretive lenses. In each case the goal for these various actors has been to impose a meaning or a diagnosis in order to advance a political agenda or to justify specific intervention practices.

By adopting a historical perspective, Kent Glenzer demonstrates how images portraying the Sahel as a highly fragile ecological space that periodically falls prey to scarcity are constantly mobilized not just to make sense of crises in this region, but also to render acceptable and understandable the fact that a number of deaths always occur before aid is provided. Analysts and

---

[4] Michael Dobry, *Sociologie des crises politiques*, Paris, Presses de la FNSP, 1986.

[5] Didier Fassin emphasizes the need to reconcile two sociological approaches when studying a social event such as a public health issue: a "constructivist approach" that focuses on how actors combine a health problem with political and social elements, and a "realist approach" that studies the material conditions of a disease and the concrete environment in which it is embedded (Didier Fassin, *Faire de la santé publique*, Rennes, Editions de l'Ecole Nationale de Santé Publique, 2005: p. 19). We believe the same approach is called for with respect to the crisis in Niger.

experts are mobilized precisely in this context. Their knowledge is selected, used, or rejected not so much for its power to enlighten decision-makers, but for whether it serves to legitimize their political agendas. This is something Barbara Cooper observes in her analysis of the prevailing narrative with respect to "bad mothers": shifting the blame to cultural taboos and poor mothering practices is a convenient way to evade discussion of the broader economic and political dynamics at play.

We have therefore called upon authors capable of analyzing the events of 2005 from distinctly varying perspectives (though we can by no means claim to have included every possible viewpoint). We have invited them to approach the crisis from whatever angle they thought most appropriate. As mentioned earlier, the crisis has already elicited several excellent assessments and analyses, to which this volume owes a great deal as well. We do not advance any one particular interpretation of the crisis in this book, but rather diverse approaches, in the belief that the 2005 crisis unfolded and was influenced very much according to how these various readings of the event interacted, were aligned, or were excluded. To be sure, the notion of a nutritional crisis is more prevalent than others in certain chapters of this book. Nonetheless, it is not the only analytical framework available to describe the dynamics affecting the situation in Niger at the present time. It is the framework MSF chose to apply, and it has unquestionably been one of the most prominent. In spite of this, as Mamoudou Gazibo shows, not all the actors have used it, and ultimately it has had very little impact on the debates that drove Nigérien politics during the crisis.

Before going any further, we feel it is important to stress here that no linear relationship exists between the crisis and those who intend to read and there-fore to construct it. The process is too complex to have been controlled or monopolized by any one actor alone. Xavier Crombé shows that MSF pro-duced one of the possible interpretations of the event, which prevailed in the summer of 2005. MSF arrived at this interpretation in connection with a medical project intended, well before the crisis struck Niger, to promote new forms of treatments for child malnutrition. Yet it cannot be concluded for this reason that MSF created the crisis in the pursuit of its own goals. Other actors influenced MSF's positions and contributed to shape alternative interpreta-tions of the crisis, beginning with the Nigérien mothers who flocked in large numbers to MSF feeding centres in early 2005. We must acknowledge that each group's own agenda and interests contributed to their vision of the crisis, but any oversimplification of the process should be avoided.

Development vs. emergency: At the core of intervention strategies

The conflict between development actors and emergency actors has been perceived as one of the fundamental cleavages of the crisis. The former argued that only long-term policies allow for a lasting and effective response to a crisis rooted for the most part in structural dynamics. They assailed emergency aid for measures that they saw as compromising the efforts made over the past twenty years to foster sustained development, thereby trapping Niger's rural communities in dependence. The latter emphasized the immediate human costs of long-term policies, maintaining that humanitarian operations had the capacity to save lives now. Some believe the disagreement has been an impediment to effective management and to understanding of the situation itself, though they otherwise admit that it has brought to light a good many flaws in the food security system.[6] Many actors now call for reconciliation, partnership and coordination rather than conflict between development policies and emergency operations.

In his contribution, Xavier Crombé revisits this conflict by shedding light on the tensions existing between several specific long-term policies (health policies and rural development) and several ways of conceiving an emergency. He shows that a central feature of the crisis has been the renegotiating of the boundaries between emergencies and development, and that these boundaries have been frequently crossed by various actors in one respect or another. Although MSF is perceived as the quintessential emergency actor, the Nigérien arena of intervention has, on the contrary, produced a phase of intense internal debates for the medical organization that may redefine the limits it customarily imposes on its sphere of intervention.

Benedetta Rossi, on her part, sees little difference between the "development" and "emergency" camps. She rather emphasizes how they each view the crisis according to their respective interpretive lenses, what she labels a form of "institutional thinking" that, in both cases, is disconnected from the dynamics that are impacting rural communities in Niger. She echoes Kent Glenzer's contribution, suggesting that the crisis has revealed the shared assumptions of these different methods of intervention—assumptions that invariably reduce population groups in Niger to the status of victims, as opposed to rights-bearing citizens. Both authors thus cast doubt on the notion that either "developers" or "*urgentistes*" can improve the current situation in

---

[6] IRAM, *Evaluation du Dispositif de prévention et de gestion des crises alimentaires du Niger,* op. cit.

any meaningful way. For Rossi and Glenzer the crisis is destined to recur as long as no sustained effort is made to give population groups in Niger the chance to establish themselves as political agents of their own food and nutritional security.

The debate has yet to be resolved. Other contributions, such as that of Mamoudou Gazibo, suggest that certain elements of Niger's society may take back control of the debate in order to press the issue of state responsibility and force government authorities to undertake reforms in food security and governance in general. In his contribution, Jean-Hervé Jézéquel emphasizes how the crisis is bringing politics back in as a central factor in the food security system. Death and suffering previously considered normal and/or inevitable in Niger are now unacceptable. The crisis has cleared the way for effective measures to treat child malnutrition. But other questions now arise: how durable will these changes be? Might the success encountered in the nutritional sector serve only to re-establish a lowest-common-denominator consensus among the aid system's principal players? Could justly celebrated advances close the window on reforms that are more ambitious, and more directly political?

The varying positions expressed throughout this edited volume are not necessarily mutually exclusive. It would be useful at this point to place the aid system in historical context, guided by the American historian Frederick Cooper's work on the concept of development.[7] Cooper refuses to limit the concept to a one-dimensional definition by portraying it as the exclusive instrument of "northern" domination. He shows that development is a malleable concept—its meaning is periodically redefined by the actors who reappropriate it, and its impact on African societies varies according to historical circumstances. Cooper demonstrates that, from the post-World War II years up to the emergence of the new independent states in Africa, development was used first as an ideological basis for reinforcing colonial ties, later as the basis of political demands that advanced struggles for national independence, and finally as a platform for intervention, used by the former European metropoles to negotiate their continued presence on African soil while simultaneously freeing themselves of the obligations their imperial role once imposed. In every case, development has served either to legitimize or to challenge power relationships that were themselves in flux at the time.

[7] See especially Frederick Cooper, *Decolonization and the African Society. The Labor Question in French and British Africa*, New York, Cambridge University Press, 1996.

Cooper's studies suggest that we view the 2005 crisis as a moment when intervention policies themselves may have taken a new direction in Niger. At the same time, his work also invites us not to lose sight of the shifting relationships of power and domination that the mechanisms of intervention generate. The crisis of 2005 may have allowed certain figures to emerge or become stronger in local and international political arenas, whether doctors, civil society, or the children themselves. But it did not bring about a radical reversal of status: some actors, who were equally marginalized and ignored and to whom the 2005 crisis could have presented new opportunities, remain permanently excluded (young dependents forced into migration, the most vulnerable groups of women, etc.).

The doctor, the mother, and the child

In the summer of 2005, media images of the crisis pushed three figures into the foreground: the emaciated child, the mother, and the doctor. It could be argued there is nothing terribly specific in this: this trio is a classic element in the iconography of humanitarian action. What is specific, however, is that each of the three elements in this relationship has in turn been touched by controversy. Weren't the doctor's efforts in vain in light of the structural factors behind malnutrition? What was the "white" doctor's role with respect to mothers: source of free food or provider of treatment for their children? What role, indeed, have mothers adopted towards their children? Aren't they largely responsible, whether through ignorance or negligence, for their children's malnutrition? Even more disturbing, how to make sense of the curious apathy observed in some mothers as their children die, or the cold calculation that arguably leads them to cause their children to lose weight in order to benefit in various ways from their admission to nutritional centres?

These debates are not simply an indication of the cultural gap aid workers encounter in African societies. In many respects, they play a part in the political changes that may ensue from the crisis. Another historical digression might be illuminating in this regard. The historian and demographer Catherine Rollet has shown that very similar debates characterized the first stage in bringing about Infant Welfare policies during the Third Republic in France. Although, like the rest of Europe, France espoused Malthusian notions of population growth during the first half of the nineteenth century, worries over falling birth rates began to surface in the 1860s. The inquiries and debates occasioned by this new concern exposed what many contemporaries described as a moral crisis. Elites were aghast at working class maternal practices in the cities, even more so at those of countryside wet-nurses, who stood accused of every conceivable evil from ignorance to negligence to greed. A moral and ideological theme thus emerged: rehabilitation of the family through the promotion of breastfeeding. In reaction, other arguments maintained that what was occurring was, rather, a social crisis: the industrial revolution was generating profound transformations in ways of life together with increasing social inequality; these were the determining factors, and they heavily influenced the behaviour of impoverished mothers. Doctors played a dominant role on both sides of these debates, which at bottom turned on the relative importance to attach to the various causes of infant mortality: "vice, ignorance, or misery", as contemporaries were putting it.

It was the reform-minded doctors who eventually imposed their views in the formulation of policies and concrete measures that were successively adopted from the 1880s onwards. Political actors of great stature under the Third Republic, they encouraged the state to become directly involved in matters of early childhood. They were also among the principal designers of major technical and scientific innovations that would significantly lower infant mortality from the turn of the twentieth century onwards, in particular the Gouttes de Lait—charities that distributed sterilized milk and provided medical supervision to babies, the first of what today are called "medical-nutritional centres". They forged a new link with families, undisputed to this day, as guarantors of their children's healthy development, and oversaw decisive changes in French society's commitment to its youngest members. Convinced of the rightness of their views and the "march of progress", they resorted to numerous material and financial incentives to persuade mothers to bring their children to their dispensaries regularly.[8] In a number of respects the food rations distributed to the mothers of children admitted to MSF's nutritional rehabilitation centres are directly descended from these practices, and medical humanitarian workers share certain features in common with their republican "ancestors".

Several contributions in the present volume revisit the issue of the "poor feeding practices" of rural mothers in Niger that have been all too commonly cited in support of criticisms of the supposedly pointless activism of "emergency" doctors. Here again, Catherine Rollet's exploration of maternal practices among the French peasantry and working classes at the end of the

---

[8] Catherine Rollet-Echalier, *La Politique à l'égard de la petite enfance sous la IIIème République*, Paris, INED-PUF, 1990.

nineteenth century offers striking parallels with ongoing debates in Niger, to which our book is intended as a contribution:

Taken together, aren't such descriptions above all else an acknowledgement of heightened imbalances and of the extraordinary gap in "development" and wealth between regions and social classes—with rhetoric about "ignorance" offered in the place of solutions to the problems of poverty? [...] there would later be speculation as to the reasons why practices changed towards the very young: was it the doctors' credibility, their power of conviction, or their moralizing will that altered attitudes— was it a matter of scientific culture successfully rooting out popular culture? Or did popular culture lose ground because of changes in the material conditions that had originally fostered it? Besides, do these two interpretations conflict, or are they complementary?[9]

In their chapter, Marthe Diarra and Marie Monimart describe the patterns of impoverishment and the profound upheaval in ways of life—and particularly exclusion from farming and land ownership—that affect a growing portion of the rural population in Niger. They show that women are the first victims of these changes. Migration, as well as searching for ways to generate alternative income, is a strategy available for alleviating a social crisis that is also a crisis of "gender", from which the people the authors interviewed appear not to see any way out yet.

Elsewhere in the volume, Barbara Cooper tries to place maternal practices back in the context of this social environment. In her detailed tracing of the complex interactions between societal norms and constraints, she exposes the oversimplification and implicit reasoning underlying the rhetoric about "bad mothers" and their practices. Like Marie Monimart and Marthe Diarra, she demonstrates that the social expectations associated with the roles of mother, woman and wife are quite often contradictory, forcing choices or trade-offs that clash with our own moral categories and implicit models of the "right" mother-child relationship which, we too frequently forget, is itself historically determined.

Finally, in their respective contributions Xavier Crombé and Isabelle Defourny explore the evolution of the role of the doctor that MSF, as a humanitarian actor, has embodied in Niger—in contrast to a general perception that it has acted solely as an emergency-oriented organization. For Xavier Crombé the crisis was a moment of reaffirmation for the role of the doctor in the social and political playing field of development and food security actors and Niger's authorities. Isabelle Defourny, who was involved in formulating

9. Catherine Rollet-Echalier, *op. cit.*, pp. 98–9.

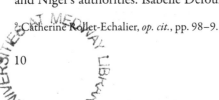

and implementing MSF's nutritional programme in Maradi, retraces how it evolved from its beginning in 2001. She sheds light on how the doctor's role in a new approach to nutritional treatment was defined step by step, through actual practice. For doctors, the challenges this posed to their customary practices and their very concepts of malnutrition itself aroused a great deal of hesitation and concern. Finally, she describes how interactions between doctors and mothers, misunderstandings included, helped to shape the programme and continually stretch its boundaries. The change in scale occasioned by the crisis has been one step in this evolution in the relationships between doctors, mothers and their children.

Making children live

Reducing mortality: Isabelle Defourny tells how much this goal continues to arouse reservations in MSF, when it is set for operations outside the circumscribed space that refugee camps represent. What is at play here is a perpetual tension between the self-imposed limits of humanitarian medical workers and the role of international public health actors that they have in fact assumed in the process of carrying out their missions. Campaigns for access to anti-retrovirals for AIDS patients in poor countries, lobbying—and even confrontation—with the health officials of individual governments in order to change ineffective therapeutic protocols for diseases with a high epidemic potential such as malaria or tuberculosis: MSF has more than once stepped outside the sphere of operations to become an advocate and a partner in establishing public health standards. In Xavier Crombé's view the effectiveness of the new method for treating malnutrition in Niger which was demonstrated on a large scale starting in 2004, and the will to see it recognized and adopted by other actors, were determining factors behind MSF's intervention in the 2005 crisis.

As several of the contributions in this volume point out, the crisis generated a fresh consensus on the need to treat malnutrition. Since the end of 2005, international organizations have produced a rising number of reports providing estimates of child mortality attributable to malnutrition in Niger, the Sahel, and worldwide. The change is substantial. As André Briend recounts in the introduction to his chapter, when international public health specialists had been invited two years earlier to propose the most effective measures for reducing child mortality in poor countries, none of the group had made any mention of malnutrition.

André Briend and Jean-Hervé Bradol, in his postscript, both emphasize that the response to the problem of malnutrition cannot rely on current scientific innovation alone, in the absence of political will to fund research and development as well as subsidy policies that would give the poorest parents access to the means to deal with their children's malnutrition. And a renewed political will has, in fact, emerged with respect to the need to treat severe acute malnutrition. But there the consensus ends. Isabelle Defourny believes that significantly combating mortality in one age group, by selecting zones where it is especially high, is only possible by treating malnutrition before it appears in its most severe forms. But at what stage should we intervene—at the level of acute malnutrition referred to as moderate, which in normal years would mean between 10 and 15% of Niger's children less than five years old? Or by supplying specialized food, such as MSF used in 2007, to the entire age group of children under three years old in a district where incidence of the disorder is highest? André Briend takes a different view. While he does not dispute the goal of treating malnutrition at an earlier stage, describing it as a necessary next step, he ponders how, and how soon, this can realistically be achieved. Mindful of the economic, social, and political obstacles such an approach would surely encounter, he proposes a few possible routes for the future. In his conclusion he emphasizes the limits of any approach based exclusively on nutrition. In his view, only an effort to significantly reduce poverty, including the use of social assistance programmes, can end malnutrition.

If we are to confront the "new face of hunger" described by Josette Sheeran, we should keep in mind that this "new face" is not only a reflection of new trends. It may likely seem new also because the lenses through which aid agencies, international institutions and policymakers have been used to look at food crises and malnutrition are at long last beginning to change. It is our hope that this book will contribute to this process.

Outline of the book

The book is divided into three sections. The first, entitled "The Politics of Crisis", shows how different actors seized upon the circumstances in Niger in 2005 to assert their own interpretations of the crisis over those of others and to argue for methods of action or intervention they believed were required to cope with it.

The second section of the book, "Contexts", gathers together contributions that seek to relocate the 2005 crisis in a series of specific contexts in order to shed light on its various aspects and offer revised or original approaches. The concern here is more with the structural factors that caused the crisis. But, in contrast to arguments often employed during and after the crisis, the authors of these four chapters dispute the primacy accorded to inevitabilities of climate and/or "bad cultural practices". The focus here is on patterns of social, economic and political exclusion, rather than cultural resistance to change. Without the political will to transform the structures those patterns represent, the authors of these chapters tell us, Niger is condemned to chronic emergencies.

The third section, "Making Children Live", explores the still tentative process of formulating a nutrition policy, for which the experience of the 2005 crisis could prove an important landmark. Increasing awareness, a search for new products, efforts to control their costs, decisive measures to make these products available to the poorest—the obstacles this policy approach faces are as formidable as its main ambition, that of preventing the avoidable deaths of millions of children in the world every year.

Translated from French by Richard Swanson.

Part I

THE POLITICS OF CRISIS

1

Consensus Reloaded? Niger's Crisis and Food Security in Policy and Practice

Jean-Hervé Jézéquel

In June 2005 an unsettling mixture of tension and uncertainty existed in Niger. There was discord among NGOs, donors, and the Niger government over the nature and severity of the country's crisis. Niger's Food Crisis Prevention and Mitigation System (*Dispositif de prévention et de gestion des crises alimentaires*—referred to below as the *Dispositif*), co-administered by the government and its major donors, was officially in charge of the matter. It had an impressive set of data-gathering techniques at its disposal but had come under fire over its handling of the situation. There was criticism of its obsessive focus on cereal production and market fluctuations, along with its neglect or ignorance of the genuinely troubling health and nutritional status of Niger's population. At the time only MSF was running a handful of therapeutic feeding centres in Niger and the number of its patients was soaring.

Two years after the crisis, in June 2007, the *Dispositif* appears in a very different light. Not only are the major actors now on relatively good terms, there is also a common focus on the nutritional conditions of Nigériens. Over the past two years studies have mushroomed, statistics have been released weekly, and it would seem that every food security policy or programme must now include a nutritional dimension. Feeding centres have spread throughout the country and tens of thousands of malnourished children are being treated annually with high rates of recovery.

Thus described, Niger would seem to be one of the finest, most rapid, and most successfully executed humanitarian interventions in recent years. The problem of malnutrition—responsible for the deaths of approximately 100,000 children each year, according to the UN (OCHA, 2007: 8)—was practically invisible in 2005. Today, nutrition is routinely incorporated into food security strategies. What happened? How is such a reversal to be accounted for? What is the actual scale and impact of the changes that have taken place since 2005?

This chapter examines the practices and policies of food security in Niger and their recent transformations. Inspired in part by James Ferguson's studies on development (Ferguson, 1990), it argues that, in essence, Niger's food security system is not what it appears (or purports) to be. There is far more to the *Dispositif* than a set of techniques for measuring and preventing food crises. Behind its outward rhetoric, the *Dispositif* operates according to a set of economic and political choices that are endorsed by a broad consensus, and are seldom debated. As the *Dispositif* operates on a day-to-day basis the decisive impact of these choices tends to be obscured—the consensus makes the hand of politics all but invisible. Yet, these choices are part of a wider process that shapes the relationships between international donors and local actors, the objectives of development policies, and the nature of the state in the Sahel region. By what it defines as food insecurity, this consensus implicitly maps out what level of suffering is acceptable and what is not, thus influencing actors to respond to crises with greater or lesser degrees of urgency, vigour and ambition (Bourdelais and Fassin, 2005).[1] In this sense, the 2005 crisis was not only a crisis for the Nigérien population. It was also a crisis for the consensus surrounding food security policies.

---

[1] Each society has its own history of what it sees as unacceptable, or "intolerable", as Didier Fassin and Patrice Bourdelais have shown in their collective work (2005). What is, and is not, acceptable—what elicits general indignation and calls for immediate action and what does not—evolves and changes over time, generating what is referred to here as a moral economy of the unacceptable.

Food security in Niger

Food security is a crucial policy domain in Sahelian societies. In Niger political authority is virtually inseparable from the capacity to manage food crises; after the 1973–74 famine Hamani Diori, independent Niger's first president, was overthrown by a military coup d'état. But local communities of Niger long ago lost a major portion of the control they once held over their own food security.

A brief history of food security. During the colonial era French administrators instituted compulsory food security measures in rural agricultural communities, criticized at the time for lacking foresight and planning. Grain reserves— "White Man's Millet"—became mandatory. But for Nigériens the perceived reality of this policy was one of confiscations and abuses, not food security. In the years after independence Niger government authorities moved aggressively to retake control. After eliminating the notorious "grain reserves", Presidents Diori and Kountché used the Nigérien Office for Food Products (OPVN) to enforce tight government control over the cereals market. This system of authoritarian control over stocks and prices proved inadequate, however, during the two massive famines that struck Niger in 1973–74 and 1984.

From the 1980s food security policy reforms were designed largely in reaction to past failures. One reformist trend under the influence of structural adjustment policies (SAP) rejected the interventionist model dominant in the 1970s. Government supervision was viewed as an obstacle to market growth, which it was believed would ensure food security in the long run. Other reformers drew lessons from emergency operations organized in response to the massive famines in the Sahel at the time. These were thought to be poorly coordinated and supervised, making it possible for criminal networks to divert and appropriate resources (Egg and Gabas, 1998). It was also believed that such operations made it impossible to deal with the structural causes of famines, and even proved counterproductive because they trapped rural communities in dependency on aid. In response, rural development experts advocated merging food security goals with those of long-term development. Emergency relief aid, while not entirely ruled out, was to be reserved for exceptional circumstances; in any event it should not be permitted to disrupt ongoing development efforts.

The privatization movement of the 1980s began with extensive modifications in Niger's food security policy. The food security apparatus was dismantled under structural adjustment policies and the government lost most of the levers at its disposal for intervening in the market for staple goods. The various state-run companies—Coproniger for imported mass-market products, Sonara for export crops (groundnuts, black-eyed beans, etc.) and the OPVN for cereals—lost their monopoly power.[2] The Niger government formalized its withdrawal from the cereals market in a 1985 structural adjustment agreement with the World Bank (Grégoire, 1990).

Although many government structures were dismantled during the 1980s, a food security system was reassembled towards the end of the 1990s. Anxiety over yielding complete control to private economic actors was doubtless a factor in the creation of a mixed system that, in part, restored an active role to government.[3] But this did not mean returning to the old methods: in 1998, Niger had to ratify a food security system developed by international experts and jointly administered by donors and the country's government. Drafted in August 2000 by the prime minister's office with European Union advisory and financial support, the Operational Strategy for Food Security (SOSA) provided a guiding framework for Niger's food security policy. Although it came more than two years after the food security system was created, it was a form of political charter. This document declared that food self-sufficiency, the old "pipe dream" of former regimes, would no longer be the goal of food security. In line with the new course charted by the International Monetary Fund (IMF), the World Bank, and major donors, the foundations of genuine food security would now be based on trade and new sub-regional economic complementarities. Nonetheless, "while acknowledging that privatization is an appropriate step for the Nigérien economy", the document's authors identified food security as a public service: "market forces alone cannot guarantee food security for the population as a whole" (SOSA, 2000: p. 19). SOSA set sharp limits on government withdrawal from an area as vital as food security.

The document identifies two overall objectives: sustained improvement in food security and crisis prevention on the one hand, and on the other, mitigation of cyclical food crises. Though the two goals might conceivably come into conflict, under no circumstances should one be accorded priority over the other:

Up until now, policies for preventing and mitigating food crises have been poorly coordinated with mid- and long-term policies, particularly when it came to evaluating

---

[2] The OPVN did so in 1983.

[3] A number of analysts did, in fact, warn of the risks of allowing the market to fall under control of the big trading companies (Grégoire, 1990). On how the World Bank's position on the role of government has evolved in general, see Hibou, 1998.

Chart 1: National Food Crisis Prevention and Mitigation System as of 2005 (*Dispositif National de Prévention et de Gestion des Crises Alimentaires, DNPGCA*)[4]

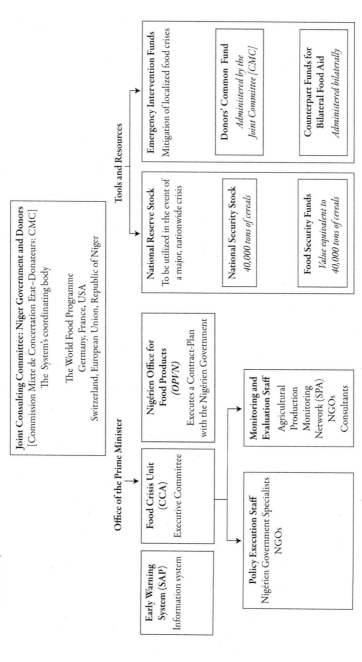

Joint Consulting Committee: Niger Government and Donors
[Commission Mixte de Concertation Etat–Donateurs: CMC]
The System's coordinating body

The World Food Programme
Germany, France, USA
Switzerland, European Union, Republic of Niger

Office of the Prime Minister

Early Warning System (SAP)
Information system

Food Crisis Unit (CCA)
Executive Committee

Nigérien Office for Food Products (OPVN)
Executes a Contract-Plan with the Nigérien Government

Policy Execution Staff
Nigérien Government Specialists
NGOs

Monitoring and Evaluation Staff
Agricultural Production Monitoring Network (SPA)
NGOs
Consultants

Tools and Resources

National Reserve Stock
To be utilized in the event of a major, nationwide crisis

National Security Stock
40,000 tons of cereals

Food Security Funds
Value equivalent to 40,000 tons of cereals

Emergency Intervention Funds
Mitigation of localized food crises

Donors' Common Fund
Administered by the Joint Committee [CMC]

Counterpart Funds for Bilateral Food Aid
Administered bilaterally

[4] Source: *GRET* presentation by Christophe Besacier (SCAC Niger) on crisis prevention and information systems in Niger.

the causes of food insecurity and the content of aid initiatives. [...] Conversely, mid- and long-term development initiatives do not always take sufficient account of house- hold food vulnerability, though this is one of the factors that discourage technological upgrades, investments, [...] (SOSA, 2000: p. 19).

In the wake of the 2005 crisis, a good number of assessments, it might be noted, now argue for the need to coordinate long-term initiatives and emer- gency relief: in doing so they are merely reviving a principle familiar to the food security systems established in the 1990s.

Before 2005, however, the principle of non-priority established by SOSA was not observed in the routine operations of the Niger food security system: through its selection of policy tools and priorities the *Dispositif* was making political trade-offs that clearly favoured long-term over immediate goals, and market privatization over the public sector. Hence SOSA's secondary objec- tive 2.4 specifies that "any emergency or short-term initiative must be consist- ent with a goal that offers a long-term solution to the targeted problem" (SOSA, 2000: p. 19). This implicit hierarchy of priorities, in contrast with SOSA's general statement, introduces the idea that aid policies rank below long-term development goals. This downgrading would come under scrutiny in the course of the 2005 crisis.

The Dispositif's *limitations.* The limitations of Niger's food security policies and instruments before the outbreak of the crisis become clear when we exam- ine the *Dispositif* in detail. The problem begins with a warning system geared towards monitoring the health of cultivated fields, not people.

The food security system is based on an early warning system—outwardly quite efficient—that relies on information gathered by a number of actors. There are no less than five institutions charged with gathering information on food security. Although they remain independent these different entities work with the CC/SAP (Early Warning System Consulting Cell), under the Prime Minister's authority. In theory, this diverse range of high-quality contributing sources ensures effectiveness. Some institutions even use high-tech tools such as satellite photography. FEWS-Net[5] uses NASA data to create maps that measure rainfall or locust threats. But the *Dispositif* has several significant operational flaws.

The actors in the information network have taken a common approach to measuring food insecurity in Niger. It focuses primarily on cereal shortages, leaving other key factors unexplored. As a result there is a great deal of data

---

[5] The food surveillance network under USAID's direction.

available on the status of the cereal and livestock markets, harvests and rainfall, etc. By contrast, until 2005 data on the nutritional status of Niger's population are scarce. For instance, FEWS reports on food security show a clear preference for analyzing production and markets, rather than the health status of the population itself.

The CC/SAP's monthly reports should, theoretically, include data on the population's health status as well as nutritional status. The data are to be supplied by the National Health Information System (SNIS) working under the Health Ministry. But at the time the crisis erupted this data-gathering agency had been in a state of advanced atrophy for a number of years. It was no longer able to supply the yearly report on the population's health status—its main mission. Before 2005 it was hardly in any position to furnish the CC/SAP with reliable data.[6]

As a result, assessments of food insecurity in Niger rely on measuring market conditions and agricultural production, which explains the occasionally absurd discrepancies between reports by the agencies in charge of food surveillance and conditions on the ground for Nigériens. For example, during the 2004 lean season that followed the exceptional harvests of 2003, FEWS-Net and other CC/SAP actors demonstrated satisfaction with a situation of "very limited food insecurity"—while in that same year the Maradi region nutritional stabilization centre alone treated 10,000 children with severe malnutrition. If a food security system is not responsive in a situation such as this, we might reasonably ask how useful it actually is.

The *Dispositif* also works in a way that eliminates political dimensions and favours a consensual approach to food security. Outwardly, the *Dispositif* projects the image of a vast, coordinated apparatus geared to finding consensus and the best technical solutions. It carries out the recommendations of the 1990 Food Aid charter to the letter: "There can be no real solution to the problems posed by food aid unless donors reach a consensus among themselves, in agreement with the beneficiaries, to coordinate efforts and actions."[7] Similarly to development institutions with which it is intimately connected,

---

[6] Generally speaking, child malnutrition was a neglected issue in Niger as of 2005. To be sure, things had begun gradually to change shortly before the crisis; in 2004 malnutrition was featured in the National Health Development Plan, classified as a health problem of high priority (see Isabelle Defourny's contribution). But the document had no operational impact on the food security system.

[7] 1990 Food Aid Charter (http://www.fao.org/GIEWS/english/otherpub/Food%20 Aid%20Charter.pdf).

the *Dispositif* functions as an "anti-politics machine", in James Ferguson's phrase.[8] Indeed, food security is critical in the Sahel, yet the food security system monopolizes this sphere with neither discussion nor debate as to the many political dimensions inherent in this responsibility—issues concerning the relationships between local communities and international organizations, political responsibilities towards the beneficiaries, the priority accorded to markets, etc. This does not mean the choices made are necessarily wrong— only that they are not, or are no longer being discussed. And it would be hard to argue that the supposed beneficiaries themselves have endorsed them.

The *Dispositif* operates as though the priority it accords long term development is self-evident, or a matter of common sense, rather than a political choice. But choices are indeed being made, and they shape a political-economic framework for what is acceptable and what is not. For instance, high rates of malnutrition and child mortality are explicitly considered to be "normal" for the present and priority is given instead to the more long-term, effective protection of future lives—child malnutrition and mortality rates are to be cut in half, according to the Millennium Goals. The claim here is not that this consensus excludes any possibility of discussion or debate inside the *Dispositif* itself. Rather, it frames and compartmentalizes the discussion in terms of primarily technical and scientific goals. And, at that point, it eludes the control and understanding of the target populations, who are either excluded from or lack access to this knowledge. Ultimately, the search for consensus and technocratic fixes for food security means avoiding central political issues behind food security in Niger. In this sense, the food security system routinely operates as an anti-politics machine. The process is not a new one: Michael Worboys describes how it was already at work in the colonial era at the time malnutrition was "discovered". Scientific discourses expunged the role of specific forms of colonial domination by ascribing malnutrition to endemic, cultural, essentially ahistorical processes (Worboys, 1998).

It is frequently lamented that the food security system is politically exploited in the interests of Niger's elites, or international donors. The criticism is not entirely invalid. But the *Dispositif* is far more than a mechanism for redistributing resources to the politically well-connected. It contributes more broadly, though less visibly, to defining the moral economy of the acceptable

---

[8] That is, a combination of institutions that have the power to define what the fundamental problems of the "developing world" are, and generate primarily technical solutions to these problems. A relatively unconscious, routine, automatic process, it suppresses the ideological or political aspects of problems and their solutions (Ferguson, 1990).

and the unacceptable, and imposes political choices that profoundly impact the present and future of Nigérien populations. These choices and this moral economy would come under scrutiny in the summer of 2005.

Summer 2005: Food crisis, nutritional crisis…political crisis

When the Niger crisis hit the headlines during the summer of 2005, the West was condemned for its neglect and ignorance of the plight of peoples in the Sahel region.[9] But the situation in Niger at that time was no more a product of hypocrisy or disinterest on the part of the Western powers than it was a result of fate or climate. Western donors were anything but absent from Niger. Contrary to what has been claimed, they called very early on for the food security system to respond.

If the major actors within the *Dispositif*, and food security actors in general, bear any responsibility for the situation in the summer of 2005, it is not due to their indifference but to the political choices they imposed in Niger—in short, a food security apparatus for which "food security is more important than food aid"[10] and a *Dispositif* which, in its routine procedures, essentially placed less priority on protecting populations at risk than on preserving consensus among all the parties involved.

This second section will discuss the 2005 crisis as a moment when politics re-emerged and the consensus underpinning the food security system was, for a time, shattered.

Poor forecasting? The food security system had been activated for the first time during the summer of 2004 as locust invasions swarmed over West Africa. It was reactivated that October, and the task force run jointly every year by the WFP, the FAO, the CILSS, FEWS-Net, and the SAP readied a preliminary assessment of the food situation. The assessment, which at the time was still based on cereal production totals alone, viewed the situation with concern: almost 1.6 million people were at risk of food insecurity. At that point the steps planned in response were no different from the customary range of mitigation measures the *Dispositif* prepared nearly every year in Niger. The volume of resources was of course higher than in prior years, but the

---

[9] See, for example, Action Contre La Faim, "Mali/Niger: Un Silencieux Scandale", press release, 1990.

[10] Louis Michel, "La famine peut être vaincue", *Libération*, 1 August 2005.

measures adopted were the same (food made available at reduced prices, community cereal banks, etc.).

After the crisis there was much conjecture as to why the situation had been underestimated to such a degree. It was accurately pointed out that statistics released a few weeks before Niger's presidential elections had been politically tainted.[11] Other observers, again with good reason, have stressed the inadequacy of the data, their inconsistencies, or their over-dependence on cereal production totals (IRAM, 2006; WFP, 2006). But the shortsightedness of the food security system should be judged in context. To a certain extent, the *Dispositif* did not underestimate the scope of the problem: at the beginning of October, the WFP/FAO interim report estimated that 1.6 million people were at risk; the figure nearly doubled in the final version released in December. The *Dispositif*'s inability to cope with a rapidly deteriorating situation cannot be ascribed simply to political interference and technical shortcomings. If the *Dispositif* failed to anticipate the situation it was also because, paradoxically, it performed very well. Indeed, the *Dispositif*'s effectiveness should be measured not in terms of what it appears to do, but also—in fact primarily—according to its real purpose. And, despite its overt aim of protecting Nigériens from food crises, the *Dispositif* is not a purely technical apparatus. It is also one mechanism, among others, that organizes relations between international donors and local governments, a mechanism that preserves and perpetuates a consensus surrounding political and economic choices made—not in the Sahel, but elsewhere—in the cause of development (an order of priorities that favours long-term development; priority given to nurturing markets, etc.).

Regardless of how relevant the system-generated statistics of late 2004 may or may not have been, the fact remains that the prospect of three million persons exposed to food insecurity—in a country known to have high rates of child malnutrition, for that matter—triggered no reassessment of the *Dispositif*'s customary practices. Nor did any debate occur over policy measures that placed less priority on mitigating suffering than on accommodating market forces. As the summary report prepared in 2006 at WFP's request observed, "the initial strategy [based on selling 75% of food aid at reduced prices] occasioned no debate" (WFP, 2006: p. 11).

The food security system was not, then, simply a victim of appalling shortsightedness which in the future can be remedied with corrective lenses. It

---

[11] The total figures for cereals released by the Ministry of Agriculture were less disturbing, for example, than those contained in the WFP mission's October report.

viewed the onset of a crisis affecting nearly three million people in the same manner that it had viewed the onset of a scenario, every year, in which over one million people find themselves at risk of serious food insecurity.[12] And it was satisfied with applying, at slightly higher levels, the same measures it uses every year to "mitigate" this food insecurity—measures whose effectiveness went unquestioned because they were in tune with the fundamental choices that frame the food security process in Niger. This value structure would, indirectly, come under scrutiny at the height of the crisis.

The consensus is shattered. 2005 was not the first year of crisis the *Dispositif* had faced. A similar crisis had struck the country in 2000–1. Niger's Food Crisis Unit (CCA) meets to formulate a mitigation strategy even during productive harvest years. In 2005, however, this routine process was upset by data on the nutritional status of Nigérien population groups produced by actors outside the *Dispositif.* In April 2005 the NGO Helen Keller International (HKI) released disturbing data on the nutritional status in the regions of Maradi and Zinder. The study had been commissioned by the WFP, whose leading officials were beginning to grasp the seriousness of the situation (see Xavier Crombé's chapter). The data were reinforced shortly thereafter when MSF released its admission figures for the Maradi region. What would have happened if WFP had not commissioned a nutritional survey by HKI and MSF had not publicly released its admissions data for the Maradi centre? Perhaps the crisis would have remained invisible. Or it may simply never have existed at all. The *Dispositif*'s mitigation initiatives would probably have gone into effect on a routine basis—no doubt at higher volume levels than in previous years, but still unable to come to grips with the severe nutritional crisis sweeping through Niger.

In any event the release of these data, along with increasingly troubling reports of rising millet prices, bred tension inside the food security system. Increasing attention was turning to agricultural zones not centrally featured in the food vulnerability maps the *Dispositif* routinely generated. And an increasing number of actors were beginning to focus on a problem—the nutritional crisis—to which the food security system, preoccupied with cereal production totals, had given scant attention.

---

[12] The February 2007 FEWS-Net report estimates that "nearly 30% of Nigérien households currently face food insecurity. Among them, 9%—or 1,100,000 people—face food insecurity classified as severe" (FEWS-Net report, 27 February 2007).

Tensions mounted between MSF and both the government and the WFP—between actors outside the *Dispositif* and those within it. The former group called for free food distribution, something the latter group considered not only inappropriate but also counterproductive because it bred a dependency that would wreck the country's future; they in turn were accused of sacrificing Niger's youth on the altar of the free market and sustainable development. Some observers, including Benedetta Rossi in her contribution to the present volume, view this period as a clash between two interpretations of the crisis—one from the perspective of development, the other from that of emergency relief. She argues that it was also a clash between two forms of "institutional thinking", both driven more by internal dynamics than by close observation of the situation as it actually was. The analysis is accurate but the clash did, nevertheless, make it possible to bring politics back in: to reopen discussion of what had ceased to be discussed.

The consensus endured for some time, however. At a CMC meeting in June 2005 the participants made a show of unity, signalling that all was under control. Unaware that therapeutic feeding centres were overflowing with children, the ambassador of France, which had contributed to the creation of the food security system, publicly congratulated Niger's Prime Minister on measures "...consistent with free market rules".[13]

In the end it was the media's coverage of the crisis, beginning in June and July, that shattered the consensus. Much has been said about the excesses of the media, suggesting that journalists hunted sensationalism and/or were manipulated by certain NGOs, and thus produced a highly simplistic view of the situation in Niger. The criticism is legitimate: intended to arouse compassion, the images of drought and famine drew from the classic visual lexicon of suffering in Africa but corresponded only faintly to the real situation Niger faced in 2005. Heavy-handed coverage of this kind would afterwards be blamed for panicking the *Dispositif*'s member agencies into taking measures of doubtful utility in order to appease public opinion abroad; this occurred in the case of free food distribution. But the media's impact should be assessed in a more qualified manner. Their emotional discourse unquestionably provoked fresh scrutiny and revision of the economy of the unacceptable in Niger. Is there not a certain hypocrisy, then, in condemning media excesses or calling for greater control over the media, when it was this very coverage that yielded the changes in practice we now applaud? Exactly why are the media

---

[13] Quoted by the author.

criticized—because they produced an over-simplified, dangerous portrayal of Niger's crisis, or because their message threatened to upset the economy of the unacceptable underpinning the consensus? The media carved out an opening, in effect, that was exploited by individuals and institutions that had previously been deterred, by the established consensus, from speaking out for alternative policies.

Other factors, apart from media coverage and the pressures exerted by certain NGOs involved, played a role in shattering the consensus. For example, difficulties and interruptions in cereal supplies for regional markets provoked considerable panic among international actors, who then bypassed the *Dispositif*'s customary supply channels (WFP, 2006). Most important, though, was the WFP's unilateral decision in July 2007 to launch blanket distribution of free food—a bright red line the food aid system had previously refused to cross. In a matter of a few weeks, management of the crisis passed from national to international hands. The food security *Dispositif* was swiftly relegated to the sidelines owing to "the combined impact of several factors: the shifting of resources to free food distribution; the decision of most donors to use the WFP and NGOs to deliver emergency relief; the unsynchronized arrival of numerous humanitarian relief actors on the scene; the sheer volume of resources at the command of the UN and the large NGO" (IRAM, 2006: p. 10).

A façade of harmony was, of course, maintained when the WFP and the CCA returned to meeting on a regular basis during August to co-administer the free distribution plan. In reality, however, the Nigérien *Dispositif* was almost completely bypassed by a massively-scaled operation beyond its control. Tensions peaked among the one-time partners. Open expression of policy disagreements had previously been discouraged by the consensus approach, but in the summer of 2005 a flurry of opinions, analyses and recommendations issued forth that defied simplification in terms of two opposing points of view. For example, the WFP was assailed by the Niger government and by MSF simultaneously. The government essentially believed it had been stripped of most of its instruments of control over relief operations: the WFP's unilateral decision to act had exposed the government's relative weakness in contrast to these international actors. MSF, on the other hand, criticized the UN agency for planning its food distributions using food vulnerability maps produced by the Nigérien food security system and poorly suited to the situation.

USAID, which was not part of the *Dispositif* in 2005, also increased its aid to Niger during this media-saturated crisis. At the same time, however, it circulated a memo from the FEWS-Net network that downplayed the severity of the situation. In particular, the memo decoupled food security from nutritional security as a way of criticizing emergency operations based on blanket distribution of free food. It also pointed out that the high levels of child mortality at the time were normal for Niger. It is precisely this structure of the normal and acceptable that would be condemned over the summer of 2005: the crisis transformed "'normally' high levels of infant mortality" (USAID, 2005: p. 1) into avoidable—hence unacceptable—deaths.

Although there was indeed a crisis in Niger in 2005, we could well ask whether it was not primarily a crisis of the food security system itself. As the summer ended a troubled mood lingered amongst aid and development actors alike. From an operational point of view, the level of response and the success in treating malnutrition were highlighted positively in post-crisis reports. A report by IRAM noted, "more than 600 therapeutic feeding centres have been opened by some twenty national and international NGO; it is estimated that more than 210,000 children have been treated". The operations of the summer of 2005 did save lives, undeniably. But a state of extreme tension has existed among aid actors ever since the consensus split apart. Nothing has yet occurred to restore the confidence that once reigned. The overriding objective of the post-crisis period, from the outset, has been to refashion a common approach.

Towards a new consensus?

What is the situation in Niger now, two years after the crisis? Did the crisis really mark a political turning point? If so, in what direction are we headed? It would be hazardous to attempt any kind of definitive assessment. There is no question that in the space of a few months Niger's food security system underwent sweeping change, but it is too early to assess the full breadth of these changes or, more important, how durable they will be.

Reforms in food and nutritional security. In August 2005 Niger began its reform process by adopting an official national protocol for treating malnutrition. Prepared by a group of partners that included UNICEF, HKI, WHO, and the Niger government, the document establishes principles for monitoring, detecting and treating malnutrition by Niger's public health actors and all NGOs. In particular it identifies measures to be taken in cases of emergency, for which the threshold is 15% of children under five suffering from overall, acute malnutrition. The protocol was allied with a national food and nutrition policy and a national action plan for nutrition for 2007–13; these set the parameters for determining goals, along with their practical implementation. Moreover, they securely establish the importance of fighting malnutrition by making it a central goal of Niger's economic and social development.

But the reforms did not only generate new documents—practices have changed as well. In concrete terms, a network of therapeutic feeding centres was established in the wake of the crisis. More than twenty local and international NGOs are running nearly a thousand feeding centres—there were only a few at the beginning of 2005. A total of 382,400 children suffering from acute malnutrition—314,667 with moderate and 67,733 with severe acute malnutrition—were admitted into nutritional stabilization centres during 2006 (UNICEF, 2006). The average rate of recovery, for all participating organizations combined, was over 75% for moderate and severe acute malnutrition. The treatment of malnutrition has improved in terms not only of quantity, but also of quality. The use of therapeutic foods, Plumpy'Nut in particular, is spreading throughout Niger, and ECHO and UNICEF now support plans for a Plumpy'Nut production plant in Niamey,[14] which would reduce costs. UNICEF, the UN agency that oversees action against malnutrition, believes that "treatment efforts have contributed greatly to reducing the prevalence of malnutrition, which declined from 15.3% in October 2005 to 10.3% in October 2006" (UNICEF, 2007).

In May 2006, moreover, the Niger government made the decision to provide free medical treatment to children under five, along with free family planning.[15] Developed in collaboration with partners such as WHO and UNICEF, the recently begun programme appears to be a great success with beneficiaries. If the initiative goes well it could point the way to the resumption of control over nutritional affairs by the country's government. But the considerable financial burdens imposed by measures of this kind make it hard to predict how long such a policy can last.

Nutritional surveillance has greatly expanded over the recent months, as well. The SNIS, something of a poor cousin to the food security system in 2005, is now well-financed thanks to WHO support. It releases a "Weekly Morbidity, Mortality and Nutritional Status Report", with statistics that are now featured in the SAP's monthly report. This is a striking contrast: before

[14] "ECHO and UNICEF promote Plumpy'nut production to improve child nutrition in Niger", 18 May 2007 (www.unicef.org).

[15] Caesarian sections would also be provided free of charge as of October 2005.

2005, the SAP report contained only agro-economic indicators. At the same time, several surveys have been undertaken to measure and better understand child malnutrition in Niger (the UNICEF/CDC/Niger government survey of October 2005, the MICSIII survey of May 2006, the UNICEF/WFP/ Niger government treats survey of October 2006). In the two years since the crisis, more statistics have been generated on the nutritional status of Nigériens than in the fifteen years that preceded it.

Beyond the single case of Niger, donors and UN agencies have focused renewed attention on food and nutritional security across the entire Sahel belt. The 2007 Consolidated Appeals Process (CAP) for West Africa has requested more than $102 million to cope with the food and nutrition situation in the region. Since 2005 a group representing West African divisions of NGOs and UN agencies has been meeting monthly to design new policies and tools for combating chronic hunger. Free medical treatment of children under five years old in cases of nutritional emergency was, for example, one of their first recommendations.

The 2005 crisis was not the only factor behind these reforms. In a wider sense they are the product of an international climate that favours a more proactive approach to treating malnutrition. The Millennium Goals—especially Goal 4, which directly targets the reduction of child malnutrition—have prompted the creation and funding of international programmes such as the Global Alliance for Improved Nutrition (GAIN, created in 2002), the International Alliance Against Hunger (IAAH, also created in 2002) and, more recently, the Ending Child Hunger and Undernutrition Initiative (ECHUI, created in 2005) of the WFP and UNICEF. Medical advances have also brought about new practices with respect to child malnutrition, as the contributions of Isabelle Defourny and André Briend in this volume point out. The 2005 crisis can also be interpreted from another perspective: the sudden emergence, or resurgence, of medical actors and medical approaches to issues in an arena dominated until now by development advocates. André Briend shows furthermore that this change should be seen in the context of dynamics in the medical field that go far beyond the single case of Niger.

An unpredictable process. There remains a good measure of uncertainty, however, about the scale of these developments. Nigériens, to begin with, are concerned over the avalanche of resources devoted to malnutrition, a volume that ultimately raises doubts as to how permanent current practices will be. MSF, which treats malnutrition in one section of Niger, has a budget for this equivalent to 15% of what the Ministry of Health spends to cover the entire country, with a mandate far beyond the problem of malnutrition alone. The WHO estimates that Niger spends an average of five dollars per inhabitant per year on its population's health. At a time when the Niger government is still obliged by international financial institutions to enforce financial discipline, it is hard to see where it will be able to find the resources on its own for an ambitious public health policy. Up to now the bulk of government and NGO activity has been financed with emergency aid, which has grown so rapidly since 2005 that it outstripped development aid. How long can that level of assistance continue?

It is also worth considering how these large-scale programmes are currently justified. There are two types of arguments. The first cites gross mortality figures: the 2007 CAP estimates that in West Africa 56% of deaths of children under five years old are associated with problems of chronic hunger. By fighting this, the CAP estimates that 300,000 lives could be saved every year (almost 100,000 in Niger). The ability of UN agencies to generate figures such as these when programmes need to be funded stands in contrast to the peculiar absence of—or disregard for—such data before 2005. It is not the greater availability of child mortality figures that has motivated current programming and operations. Rather, it is the political decision to tackle the problem of nutrition in the Sahel region that has led to production of figures such as these.

The second argument associates malnutrition with development. And, in fact, action against malnutrition has come to be a central goal of Niger's economic and social development. The reasoning is actually somewhat circular: in recent documents on development projects in Niger, one finds the notion that fighting malnutrition will contribute to development and, later, that development itself will lead to reduced malnutrition. But the core of the argument lies elsewhere: it is to show that nutritional goals are compatible with development programmes. This would then justify funding aid programmes that, until now, might have been considered inconsistent with the philosophy behind long-term development goals. It is a little ironic to see action against malnutrition justified by the very principle of development invoked by opponents of the emergency response of the summer of 2005. Irony aside, however, this evolution in attitude may be viewed in two ways. We could first of all take great satisfaction in seeing food security actors speak enthusiastically of the possibility, even the necessity, of reconciling emergency relief with the goals of development. This position is not new—it can be found in documents like

SOSA—but it lends legitimacy to genuine changes in practice that will lead to more effective health-care for children. No longer do we neglect the children of today for the sake of the children of tomorrow: there is an authentic effort to reconcile short- and long-term goals. In this sense the moral economy of the unacceptable was transformed between 2005 and 2007. On the other hand, the underlying objective of these attempts to reconcile malnutrition with development is to restore consensus, that key mantra of the post-crisis period. Scars remain from the disputes of 2005, and several post-crisis reports have highlighted the need to restore consensus and improve coordination among food security and nutrition actors.

When developing the revision at hand, humanitarian actors have taken into consideration the difficulties encountered in trying to establish a consensus on the humanitarian situation in the Sahel in 2005 which ultimately impacted the quality of the response, its timing, and the way in which targeting was decided upon. To avoid a similar situation in 2006 it was felt that the largest possible range of experience and expertise should be drawn upon and a wide consultation take place to allow for a better dialogue and less discrepancies in readings of the situation (OCHA, CAP 2007 West Africa).[16]

The Niger government's May 2006 decision barring foreign journalists from entering the country to cover the food situation was, in a certain sense, consistent with this intent to refashion a consensus. And the silence of the major aid actors in response to that censorship was no doubt a signal of their readiness to restore something of a united front after the dissensions of the summer of 2005.

There is, undeniably, a need for coordination and harmony among the partners. But this cannot be at the cost of suppressing debate and differences of analysis. After all, differences of view—even conflict—ushered in the changes we welcome today, however much remains to be done. In this respect the crisis of 2005 marked a kind of comeback for politics in a food security system all but numbed by its obsession with consensus. Since then, a process of critical stocktaking has taken place with respect to the crisis and the food security system. A number of reports have stimulated reflection among actors inside the food security system, giving them a chance to absorb the lessons of the crisis. This excellent work is nonetheless limited to technical analysis of shortcomings during the crisis, without touching on disputes of a more political nature over how suitable present food security systems are. The WFP report,

---

[16] Executive Summary, Consolidated Appeal for West Africa 2006, Revision, 28 March 2006.

for example, very correctly emphasizes the inadequacy of the standard interpretive frameworks that are applied to crises in the Sahel; but it thereafter
confines itself to primarily technical considerations regarding the failures of
the WFP and other actors in their initial response. To address the structural
aspects of the crisis, it recommends more vigorous policies geared to specific
sectors, along with more investment and development aid. But it does not
venture to reflect more broadly on the political dimensions of the development choices underpinning the *Dispositif*. Indeed, these organizations seldom
allow room for debate over central issues concerning the assumptions behind
the aid and development systems, government-donor relationships, the
responsibilities of intervening organizations towards local people, or the marginal role allotted to these same people in food security systems. The 2005
crisis signalled the unexpected resurgence of political factors in food security
management, which had been reduced to its purely technical aspects. The
post-2005 period, on the other hand, looks more like an era of depoliticization—an effort to purge the food security system of politics as expeditiously
as possible.

Lastly, on a more general note: even as we stress that very real progress has
been made in the "right to life" for early childhood in Niger, a final comment
might be in order with respect to precisely how Nigériens are gaining such
rights, in the wake of the crisis. In fact, it was physical illness, and illness alone,
which made it possible for them to obtain rights like these. Other vulnerable
groups, such as young dependants and women, are not included in the benefits
of this progress, even though the crisis presented an opportunity to acknowledge and decisively address their circumstances as well. In this respect the
Niger case would appear to share certain features with the cases explored by
Miriam Ticktin (2006) in her work on undocumented immigrants in France,
or with Didier Fassin's (2005) work on children suffering from lead poisoning.
The advances in treating malnutrition in Niger force us to consider, along with
Didier Fassin, "...the meaning and implications, in terms of the social contract
that binds the members of our societies together, of a growing tendency to use
suffering or illness as a justification for granting rights to citizens" (Fassin,
2005: p. 54).

Conclusion: opening a window, shutting the door

Today, in 2007, the aid system is required to take into consideration, and to
act forcefully against, the 100,000 annual deaths associated with chronic

hunger in children (OCHA, 2007: p. 8). Yet it is once again possible for the food situation to be to termed "generally good" when "nearly 30% of Nigérien households face food insecurity" and "1,110,000 people face food insecurity classified as severe."[17] Here is where the changes in the economy of the unacceptable brought about by the 2005 crisis show their limits. In a sense, by adding a nutritional dimension to current intervention efforts, the institutions involved in the food security systems give themselves the chance—at a price, but a relatively acceptable one—to refashion a consensus and preserve the current *Dispositif* for managing problems in the Sahel, in spite of its inadequacies, amply illustrated in several contributions to this volume.

The manoeuvrings of the post-crisis period are also a way of coping with the sudden emergence—or resurgence—of political factors in the food security system, and development policy in general for the Sahel. Politically, the crisis represented an opportunity, an interlude when new alternatives emerged. For MSF the crisis opened the way for a new treatment for malnutrition. But this was not the only alternative to surface in 2005: beyond the issue of malnutrition, there were some who spoke out to accuse development and relief advocates of being in the same boat; they condemned any intervention mechanism that serves the interests of its designers better than those of its beneficiaries (see contributions by Benedetta Rossi and Kent Glenzer). Others took advantage of the opening the crisis provided to expose the dynamics of economic and social exclusion that victimize rural populations, and the inability of development policies to respond to these dynamics (see the chapter by Marthe Diarra and Marie Monimart). In Niger itself some are speaking out, as well, to protest against conditions that remain unchanged despite promises from government and development agencies alike (see the chapter by Mamoudou Gazibo). In the final analysis, what hangs in the balance during the post-crisis period is how these alternatives will be dealt with—an ongoing, implicit process of negotiation to determine which windows will be open and which doors will remain shut.

It now appears that the major actors have agreed, in the end, to leave the "malnutrition window" open. Food security actors have marked out the path to a new consensus which, though it comes at a price (bringing doctors and nutrition specialists into the process), nevertheless marginalizes more radical actors and more far-reaching ideas for reforming current intervention practices. Taking genuine responsibility for the nutritional problems of children

---

[17] FEWS-Net report, February 2007.

under five years old represents solid progress on the part of very many actors. But it also represents a middle ground for reassembling a post-crisis consensus that conveniently expunges a number of other categories of vulnerable people. To put it even more directly: for children under five years old an apparently effective system of surveillance and protection is now up and running, but there is far less concern over what happens to adolescents, women, the elderly or adults in general. The retort to this might be that medical organizations cannot do it all—they are each responsible only for what is within their own purview or field of expertise. It is nevertheless an open question whether the medicalization of this crisis opens the window for useful reform of nutritional security in Niger and the Sahel, only to shut the door indirectly on more ambitious, more straightforwardly political, reforms.

Translated from French by Richard Swanson

BIBLIOGRAPHY

Bourdelais, P. and D. Fassin (eds), 2005. *Les constructions de l'intolérable. Études d'anthropologie et d'histoire sur les frontières de l'espace moral*, Paris, La Découverte.

Egg, J. and J.-J. Gabas (eds), 1997. *La prévention des crises alimentaires au Sahel. Dix ans d'expérience d'une action menée en réseau*, Paris, OECD Publications.

Fassin, D., 2005. *Faire de la santé publique*, Rennes, Éditions de l'Ecole Nationale de Santé Publique.

Ferguson, J., 1990. *The Anti-Politics Machine. Development, Depoliticization, and Bureaucratic Power in Lesotho*, University of Minnesota Press.

Gado, B.A., 1993. *Une histoire des famines au Sahel*, Paris, L'Harmattan.

Grégoire, E., 1990. "L'État doit-il abandonner le commerce des vivres aux commerçants?" *Politique Africaine*, n° 37, Paris, March.

Hibou, B., 1998. "Economie politique du discours de la Banque mondiale en Afrique: du catéchisme économique au fait (et méfait) missionnaire", *Les Etudes du CERI*, 39, Paris, March.

IRAM, 2006. *Evaluation du Dispositif de prévention et de gestion des crises alimentaires du Niger*, Niamey, February.

OCHA, 2007. *Consolidated Appeals Process (CAP), West Africa*.

République du Niger, 2000. *Stratégie Opérationnelle de Sécurité Alimentaire (SOSA)*, Niamey.

Ticktin, M., 2006. "Where Ethics and Politics Meet: The Violence of Humanitarianism in France", *American Ethnologist*, 33 (1): pp. 33–49.

UNICEF, 2007. *Réponse à la situation nutritionnelle des enfants. Niger. Bilan annuel 2006*.

USAID, 2005. *Niger: an Evidence Base for Understanding the Current Crisis*, Washington, 28 July.

WFP, 2006. *Evaluation de la réponse du PAM à la crise alimentaire au Niger en 2005*, Rome, May (2 volumes).

Worboys, M., 1988. "The Discovery of Colonial Malnutrition Between the Wars", in David Arnold (ed.), *Imperial Medicine and Indigenous Societies*, Manchester University Press.

2

Famine or Food Crisis? Views from Niger's Political Scene[1]

Mamoudou Gazibo

During the summer of 2005 the crisis in Niger, a country classified as one of the poorest in the world, suddenly caught the attention of the media. This media coverage produced a variety of images, depending on whether it was provided by international or local journalists. Although it was unbearable images of starving children and the urgent need for aid that dominated the foreign press, the domestic media mainly focused on the semantic quarrel between the political stakeholders. In fact, the debate polarized between the position of President Mamadou Tandja, who supported the argument that Niger was not facing a famine but rather a food crisis, and that taken by his Prime Minister, who spoke more willingly of famine. That second position was relayed by the opposition and civil society. Initially, this battle appears paltry, even a cause for anger as it concerned a tragedy affecting a major segment of the population, particularly in the regions of Zinder and Maradi and, to a lesser extent, in Tillabéri.[2]

---

[1] I would like to thank Tidjani Alou Mahaman, Jean-Hervé Jézéquel and Xavier Crombé for their documentary contribution and their critical reading of this text.

[2] Tillabéri traditionally receives particular attention as a result of its proximity to Niamey and its electoral weight for the party in power, the MNSD, Mouvement National pour la Société de Développement (National Movement for the Development Society).

It is argued here that this semantic debate raged because the stakeholders in Niger's political space[3] realize that describing problems also involves imposing a meaning on them, specifically with regard to their causes and the subsequent political blame. The convergence of a cluster of phenomena such as historical memory (the famine of 1974 and the coup d'état which it served to justify), the symbolical dimension (the famine indicates the leader's misfortune falling on his fellow citizens) and the personal variable (President Tandja was one of the instigators behind the 1974 coup) explain why both sides insist on imposing their interpretation, whether it is political or not, of the phenomenon. So behind the quarrel over words, we must identify a political issue and particularly a contest over the definition of political responsibility.

In this chapter, we primarily use sources taken from the local press, which provided broad coverage of the phenomenon, which has been described, in turns, as a food crisis or a famine. It should be noted that, of the newspapers quoted in this text, *Le Sahel Horizon* and *Le Canard Déchaîné* are deemed to be close to the government, whereas *L'Enquêteur, L'Expression, La Griffe, Le Soleil*, and *Le Démocrate* are deemed to be relatively neutral and *L'Évènement, Alternative, Le Républicain* and the *Roue de l'Histoire* are deemed to be close to the opposition. *Libération* and *La Différence* are both new and have limited audiences. Obviously, these positions influence the coverage which these local media provided of the crisis. First of all, we need to review the semantic debate in order to demonstrate that, above and beyond official discourse, the crisis that occurred in Niger in 2005 can be explained primarily by political factors. We will do this specifically by illustrating the shortcomings of the process for making decisions and implementing public policies within the context of a

---

[3] Since the presidential and legislative elections of 2004, Niger's political landscape has been composed of two alliances structured respectively around the MNSD (48 seats) headed by President Tandja and the former Prime Minister Hama Amadou, and the Parti Nigérien pour la Démocratie et le Socialisme (PNDS, Nigérien Party for Democracy and Socialism, 23 seats), headed by the leader of the opposition, Mahamadou Issoufou. With 88 seats out of 113, the coalition supporting the government brings together, in addition to the MNSD, almost all of the other political powers in the country: the Convention Démocratique et Sociale (CDS, Democratic and Social Convention, 22 seats) headed by former President Mahamane Ousmane, the Rassemblement Social Démocrate (RSD, Social Democratic Rally, 6 seats), headed by Amadou Cheiffou, the Rassemblement pour la Démocratie et le Progrès (RDP, Rally for Democracy and Progress, 7 seats), founded by the late President Baré Mainassara, and the Alliance Nigérienne pour la Démocratie et le Progrès (ANDP, Nigérien Alliance for Democracy and Progress, 4 seats) of Adamou Moumouni Djermakoye.

food crisis that also struck other countries in the Sahel region, though not on the same scale. Then, we will analyze the political issues of the debate concerning the crisis, to cast light not only on the political agendas pursued by the various stakeholders but also on the deeper characteristics of Niger's political system. Finally, we will demonstrate that a favourable result of this crisis was a reconfiguration of the political arena with a renewal of actors, especially "civil society" organizations that used the situation to assert themselves and impose new standards of governance.

A crisis with complex causes, but essentially political in nature

A local newspaper stressed that if there is a topic that angers Niger's President, it is the use of the word "famine" and, above all, any report or any statement alleging that the country could be affected by problems of this nature. For President Tandja, "There is no famine in Niger, just a slight food-producing deficit."[4] Since he is "allergic to the word [...] and flies into a rage whenever it is used,"[5] it is this line that he officially imposes when invoking both the historical vulnerability of the country and the classical analyses of food shortages.

From the official explanation of the food crisis...

The government focused in particular on two explanations: first, food shortages caused by natural factors and, second, the political instrumentalization of this shortage by internal stakeholders (the political opposition) and external stakeholders (international agencies and NGOs).

First, the President's argument involves demonstrating that what happened in Niger is not new, but rather represents a recurring phenomenon as a result of the particular situation of a landlocked Sahelian country that is regularly threatened by climatic variations. In fact, generally in the Sahel region, perhaps more often than anywhere else, famines are explained, and not without justification, by structural causes of a natural order, principally climatic in nature. This is one reading that the official discourse, particularly that of the President and his advisers, tried to impose. It is supported by a rich

---

[4] Agence France Presse, "'Il n'y a qu'un léger déficit vivrier' au Niger, insiste le président Tandja", press release,11 August 2005.
[5] "Le jeu de l'autruche du président Tandja", *L'Enquêteur*, No. 222, June 2005: p. 6.

scientific literature and analyses made by many organizations and experts specializing in the Sahel region's developmental problems. Numerous authors, in fact, feel that certain regions are particularly exposed to famines as a result of their geographical locations, climatic variations, sudden cessation of rain and other natural catastrophes.[6] From this perspective, what happened in Niger in 2005 seems to have been the result, above all, of a combination of natural factors, both structural and conjunctural, and specifically a lack of rainfall, which was made worse by a devastating locust invasion during the summer of 2004.

This vision is backed by research that highlights the argument that there was nothing exceptional about the 2005 crisis. Thus, in his *Histoire des famines au Sahel*, Boureima Alpha Gado lists nine droughts and eight locust invasions since 1900.[7] The French researcher Jean-Pierre Guengant adds that "for 20 years, Niger has been in a period of chronic grain deficits."[8] With this in mind, the government's spokesman, who was close to the President, explained to a journalist that "there is no famine in Niger. It would be preferable to speak of a food crisis. This crisis is a result of the poor rainfall combined with locust infestations. More than 50% of our crops were destroyed by locusts. Niger is a Sahelian country and lives a precarious existence on a daily basis. It is a country with cyclical droughts. As a result, drought is not a new phenomenon for us. To put things simply, the international media distorted the information. They gave this crisis a scope that was too unsettling. There has been no adult death in the country, no village in Niger has been depopulated, no shanty-town has been set up near large urban centres."[9]

The President and his entourage used similar rhetoric to neutralize the idea of a nutritional crisis among children, a notion put forward by certain humanitarian stakeholders to replace that of famine. Once again, childhood malnutrition was presented as a structural element of the Niger landscape, so that there was nothing exceptional about the situation in 2005. Interestingly, there

---

[6] David Arnold, *Famine. Social Crisis and Historical Change*, Oxford, Basil Blackwell, 1988: p. 29. See also the contribution by Kent Glenzer in this work on the history of discourse concerning the Sahel.

[7] Boureima Alpha Gado, *Une Histoire des famines au Sahel: étude des grandes crises alimentaires (XIXᵉ–XXᵉ siècles)*, Paris, L'Harmattan, 1993.

[8] "Niger: combien de famines encore?" *Le Monde*, 19 August 2005, reprinted by *L'Évènement*, No. 103, 23 August 2005: p. 6.

[9] David Cadasse, "Entrevue avec Mohamed Ben Omar, porte-parole du gouvernement nigérien", 5 October 2005. See www.afrik.com/article8844.htlm.

is barely any place for the idea of a nutritional crisis, which was progressively taking root among the external stakeholders, in the Nigérien debate. The latter continues to focus on the alternatives of food crisis and famine as if childhood malnutrition were a fact to which the national stakeholders have, in fact, become accustomed. Thus, it is revealing that this issue has not truly been debated in Niger's media.

The presidential points of view have, moreover, been supported by a report written by the French Senators Michel Charasse and Adrien Gouteyron, who went to Niger to evaluate the French reaction to the crisis. Using official terminology, the two senators "deliver their analysis of the 'nutritional crisis' in Niger, recalling that it is related to a cluster of conjunctural causes (lack of rainfall and locust infestation) and structural causes (exponential population growth, exorbitant infant mortality, expansion of the desert into arable surfaces)". They also supported the argument put forward by a government representative, who stated that the complexity of the crisis "seems to have largely escaped the media."[10]

The official interpretation imposed by the President is also based on discontent at the intrusion of stakeholders intervening in the management of the crisis. It is known, in fact, that in numerous food crises, particularly during conflicts, political stakeholders instrumentalize the phenomenon and use it as a weapon.[11] Although Niger was not a conflict zone during this crisis period, the idea of instrumentalization was still used by the authorities to denounce bothersome stakeholders. At a domestic level, the attack was essentially directed against the media, who were charged with being anti-patriotic. Thus a local journalist, who wrote the first report on the crisis, was suspended. The authorities also denounced the manoeuvres of the opposition, which it accused of using the crisis to destabilize the government. Finally, at an external level, the authorities did not hesitate to accuse numerous NGOs and certain UN agencies, particularly the World Food Programme (WFP), of working with the opposition and exacerbating the crisis in order to attract financing which Niger would in the end not benefit from. In October 2005, shortly after the crisis peaked, a government spokesman expressed the following regret: "Forty-four billion CFA francs were promised by the international community, including 24 billion from the various UN system organizations.

---

[10] Thomas Hofnung, "Au Niger, la France bonne humanitaire?", *Libération*, 6 October 2005.

[11] Sylvie Brunel, "Des famines qui n'ont plus rien de climatiques", *Cahiers Français*, No. 278, October-December 1996: p. 20.

To date, the national agency for managing and preventing food crises has only received four billion and that only from the 24 billion CFA francs promised by the UN."[12] The comments of the government spokesman undoubtedly reflect in this case the malaise of a state whose sovereignty was impinged on by the international institutions surrounding it at the peak of the crisis. Although, at the start of the summer, people were still denouncing the international community's lack of interest in Niger—Niger was the indirect victim of the Asian tsunami, Charlotte Cans and Philippe Perdrix wrote in *Jeune Afrique/L'Intelligent*—by the autumn it was no longer the absence of aid but rather its channelling by international agencies and NGOs that aroused the government's ire. The government was particularly angry with the WFP, which was accused of bypassing the authorities and contributing to discrediting of the regime.[13]

Although the government camp's rhetoric is not baseless—whether regarding the structural causes of the famine or encroachments on Niger's sovereignty—it would be reductionist to stop the analysis here. The crisis that occurred in 2005 was also the result of internal political dysfunction and reflects the current state of the political institutions and democracy in Niger.

... to a reading in public policy terms.

In fact, the official explanation does not provide a full answer. As Sylvie Brunel pointed out, "although natural problems can in fact result in real difficulties for certain populations [...], the famine was in no manner unavoidable, to the extent that, today, there are means to disseminate information and provide assistance. The moment that a situation of food shortage is allowed to 'rot' [...], that means there was a human will to allow it to do so."[14] There is no question here of supporting a conspiracy theory or insinuating that the authorities consciously starved their fellow citizens. However, an analysis of government policies indicates that the scope of the crisis can also be explained by shortcomings on the part of the Niger authorities who did not anticipate the situation as well as their neighbours had, and who, once the problem was acknowledged, attempted, for reasons that were essentially political in nature, to downplay the seriousness of the crisis and even deny that it existed rather than address it.

[12] David Cadasse, "Entrevue avec Mohamed Ben Omar", *op. cit.*
[13] "Après la famine, le gouvernement traîne le PAM dans la boue", *Le Républicain*, 6 December 2005.
[14] Sylvie Brunel, *Famines et politique*, Presses de Sciences Po, Paris, 2002: p. 35.

First, as we know, the 2005 crisis did not occur suddenly. Starting in 2003 and throughout 2004, the movement of flocks of locusts toward the Sahel was observed by the various early warning systems and the authorities knew about it. Of course, the problem largely exceeded the capacities of the Niger government and "the failure of the international community to mobilize during a period of remission was one of the causes for the scope of the current crisis, observed since September 2003".[15] According to a senior FAO official in Niger, the Niger government did ask for international aid as of November 2004, but the responses were slow in coming.[16] Nevertheless, numerous signs also show the failures of the authorities in Niamey, who reacted late. In particular, it appears that the pre-election situation of the last quarter of 2004 focused the government's attention and means on the presidential campaign. As written in a local newspaper, viewed as neutral, there was no response to the early warnings and "the government remained as still as marble, concerned as it was with electoral deadlines. Mamadou Tandja was re-elected President of the Republic and re-appointed Hama Amadou as the Prime Minister [...]. While our leaders were concentrating their energy and their intelligence on sharing post-victory cake, and preparing conventions for their respective political parties, the famine progressively expanded."[17]

Going beyond a simple accusation of negligence, certain articles denounced the government's determination to hide the problem. In particular, it was alleged that the President so fiercely denied the existence of a famine in Niger that "it was not until after the visit of Mohamed VI, the King of Morocco, on 19 July, that he finally went to see for himself first Maradi, then Tahoua and Agadez," and that the Prime Minister, Hama Amadou, only launched publicly "an anguished appeal for international aid" on 28 May, in his general policy speech.[18] The rapid reaction which could have been expected, particularly since Niger has an early warning system, clearly did not take place and, under these conditions, the timidity of the international stakeholders is not surprising.

---

[15] "Le criquet pélerin, plus petit qu'un haricot, plus dévastateur qu'un éléphant", *La Lettre du Sahel*, No. 90, February 2005: p. 3.

[16] "Interview with Helena Maria Semedo", Afrik.com, reprinted in *L'Évènement*, No. 93, 8 June 2005: p. 6.

[17] "La famine declarée au Niger: l'embarras du gouvernement", *Le Démocrate*, 7 June 2005: p. 5.

[18] Charlotte Cans and Philippe Perdrix, "La faim et les moyens", *Jeune Afrique*, 13 July 2005.

The lack of rainfall, the locust infestations, and the threats of a food crisis were not specific to Niger and affected almost all the Sahelian countries. Since the same factor—the locust infestation—did not result in a crisis of the same scope as that experienced in Niger, it is a good idea to look for explanations arising from within. From this point of view, the hypothesis concerning the shortcomings of the decision-making process and the ineffectiveness of the system for dealing with food crises makes sense. The crisis was also the result of the political authorities' poor management of the situation. The 2004 locust infestation also struck Mali, Burkina Faso, Mauritania and Senegal without turning into a national catastrophe there and focusing the spotlight on those countries. The data available even indicate that the challenge was not greater for Niger than for its neighbours. Thus, following the locust infestations, it is estimated that Niger's grain production dropped by 12% (depending on the region, 10–50% for millet and sorghum, the two principal staples) compared to 2003. At the same time, production dropped by 14% in Mali, 22% in Senegal and 44% in Mauritania! Mali, which was congratulated by the local WFP representative for its "discourse of truth", reacted more effectively—by starting to distribute food supplies to people in January 2005, removing taxes on imports of food supplies[19] and supporting both operations through a procedure similar to a war headquarters to track the changing situation and the impact of public policies, on a day-by-day basis and with a great degree of accuracy. Niger, on the other hand, preferred to concentrate its activities on "selling food supplies at modest prices" in keeping with its partners in the food security system. Even in 2005, the Prime Minister discounted the idea of distributing food supplies free of charge, preferring the formula of grain advances to be repaid after the 2005 harvest.[20]

Not only did these measures not go as far as those taken in Mali, but the impact of the government's policy was insufficient because of the gap between the needs, the forecasts and the means available. Thus, while the national reserve stocks should have amounted to 110,000 tons, Niger had only approximately 20,000 tons at the start of the crisis. At the same time, the grain deficit was estimated at 223,000 tons.[21] Obviously, it could be said that Niger's government shares sovereignty over food security, which cannot be managed

---

[19] *Ibid.*

[20] Abdou Seydou, "Rencontre État-donateurs: les difficultés alimentaires des populations seront atténuées", *Le Sahel*, 7 June 2005: p. 3.

[21] Thomas Hofnung, "Au Niger, la France bonne humanitaire?" *op. cit.*; Charlotte Cans and Philippe Perdrix, "La faim et les moyens", *op. cit.*

without the approval of the international authorities that impose obvious limits on the type of response Niger can make in times of crisis. In neighbouring countries such as Mali and Burkina Faso, however, it appears that the state exercises its sovereignty with greater vigour and is not so much a prisoner of the co-management of food security with international organizations.

Obviously, the 2005 Niger food crisis was complex and had many causes, some structural and others dependent on conditions. But, as demonstrated by the brief comparison with other countries in the region as well as the decision-making process and the hesitations of the authorities in Niamey, the scope of the crisis cannot be dissociated from political causes to be found at the highest level of the state. If this is so, it means that there are major political issues behind the food crisis.

Political issues behind the crisis

At this point it is reasonable to ask, above and beyond the considerations of sovereignty and national pride invoked by officials,[22] why the authorities persisted in portraying the food crisis as a slight grain deficit when even the Department of Animal Resources acknowledged—perhaps because it considered the information less sensitive—that the 2004 animal feed deficit was the worst it had been in the last 20 years. Why did other stakeholders insist on denouncing this attitude, especially the media which attacked the President as the "leader of negationists"[23] and the opposition leader, Mahamadou Issoufou, who asked "if the head of state had a stone instead of a heart?"[24] The principal satirical newspaper of Niamey spoke of elites taking advantage of the situation: "People don't need to be a link in the aid distribution chain to take advantage of the famine. All it took was for Tandja to deny its existence to draw the opposition out of its silence and toot its own horn. As for civil society, it took advantage of the opportunity to make stars, leaders, to add to the ranks of the privileged and the rich." During this time, the starving populations were "turkeys".[25] Of course, this type of interpretation tends to reduce

---

[22] David Cadasse, "Entrevue avec Mohamed Ben Omar", *op. cit.*

[23] Ibrahim Elhadj Hima, "Crise alimentaire: controverse autour de la question de la famine", *La Roue de l'Histoire*, No. 261, 16 August 2005: p. 7.

[24] Diallo Mahamadou, "Crise alimentaire: Mahamadou Issoufou s'insurge contre les propos de Tandja", *L'Évènement*, No. 3, 16 August 2005: p. 4.

[25] Okam, "La famine, les politiciens et les dindons de la farce", *Le Canard Déchaîné*, No. 185, 18 August 2005: p. 3.

the stakeholders to purely self-centred players. But it has the advantage of encouraging us to scrutinize the food crisis more closely, by emphasizing that something other than acts of compassion were at stake. The famine was, above all, a political issue.

Famine and risks of political instability

For those in power, particularly the President and his entourage, the idea of famine posed a threat to the stability of the regime. This perception is not baseless when one recalls the country's history and the personal career of President Tandja. In fact, when the military, led by Lieutenant-Colonel Seyni Kountché, overthrew the authorities of the first Republic 30 years earlier, they used the pretext of the "arrogance" of an "oligarchy that was indifferent to people it claimed it would guarantee happiness" to justify their coup d'état. At that time, Niger was experiencing a crisis similar to that of 2004. The new President, Kountché, promised that no citizen of Niger would die from hunger or thirst again, even if the entire national budget had to be used. For Mamadou Tandja, who was involved in the 1974 coup d'état, there was no question of acknowledging a famine in the country. As the newspaper *Le Soleil* remarked, "A famine! That provides grounds for overthrowing a regime!"[26] In this case the focus is on political responsibility. Yet, according to the same newspaper, "Tandja and his government neglected the work of the technicians in the field who had, however, done their work before the situation became chaotic."[27] This idea of responsibility is not solely political. It takes on a particular symbolic dimension in a Niger context in which good and poor harvests are generally interpreted as events related to the "head" (fortune or misfortune) of the leader. That is why the President stressed on several occasions that since the 1960s no real policy had been implemented to ensure food security in the country.

The entire semantic polemic on the "famine" also involved ministers, presidential advisers, regional governors and department prefects. A portion of the local media viewed it as a diversion and preferred to focus on government responsibility instead. The government was said to have miscalculated the results of the 2004 cropping season, underestimated the locust effect, been late in reacting to the situation, and adopted unsuitable means for

---

[26] "Crise alimentaire. La famine: Parlons-en...", *Le Soleil*, No. 119, 16 August 2005: p. 3.
[27] *Ibid.*

intervening.[28] Some people went even further, calling for the head of state to be taken before the High Court of Justice in keeping with Article 118 of the Constitution since "the words of the President of the Republic are an offence constitutive of high treason, an attack on civil rights and a questioning of aid to famine victims." The person who launched this appeal concluded by calling on elected representatives to legislate on the President's behaviour, while wondering if he could "continue to preside over the destinies of a country".[29]

Faced with this charge, and considering the historical link between famine and instability in Niger, the presidential strategy systematically involved minimizing the scope of the problem. At the same time, the presidential camp defused efforts to establish a link between this problem and the governing methods of the leadership.

Famine as a political battlefield

Contrary to the presidential camp's view, the opposition and a portion of the private media spoke clearly of famine. Moreover, they openly established a causal relationship between the regime's governing methods and the prevailing situation in the country. Thus, one opposition newspaper wrote that "when the President of the Republic noted that children between the ages of 0 and 5 are dying, it must be of even greater concern to him since the generation of his regime, the children born between 2000 and 2005, are disappearing in massive numbers..." The author continued that "since President Mamadou Tandja has been re-elected, the people have harvested an extreme deterioration in their living conditions..." before attacking the regime with the same criticism which the military—including Mamadou Tandja—had launched against the government they overthrew following the 1974 famine: "Despite everything, since the leaders of the regime continue to grow wealthy and eat to their fill, they are no longer concerned that international and national solidarity comes to the aid of dying Nigériens."[30]

---

[28] "Crise alimentaire au Niger: fondements institutionnels et administratifs", *La Différence*, No. 3, 23 January 2006: p. 5.

[29] Salifouize Ibrahim, "En niant l'existence de la famine: Tandja est justiciable de la Haute Cour de justice en vertu de l'article 118 de la Constitution", *La Roue de l'Histoire*, No. 261, 16 August 2005: p. 11.

[30] Laoual Salaou Ismaël, "Le magistrat suprême sème le doute et le désarroi", *La Roue de l'Histoire*, No. 261, 16 August 2005: p. 6.

Even the party of the first President of Niger overthrown in 1974, the Parti Progressiste Nigérien (PPN, Nigérien Progressive Party), did not stay on the sidelines. Recalling that President Tandja was involved in the 1974 coup d'état, it stated that "the reason why the President obstinately denies the existence of the famine can be found in history..." At that time, the military had found it humiliating that the country had to look to international assistance and had solemnly declared, "We have made a firm resolution to never see such a humiliating spectacle again". As if to encourage the authorities to recognize the situation while making them responsible for a national failure of which the famine was merely one manifestation, the PPN statement ended with these words: "May the President of the Republic rest assured: the spectre of famine will not be a threat to his power in Niger in 2005, which ranks last,[31] since it is no longer the Niger of 2004, united and desired."[32]

But, of course, the position of Mahamadou Issoufou, the leader of the principal opposition party, the PNDS, best illustrates how a political fracture was caused by the food crisis. Initially, the stand Issoufou took had two components: on the one hand, he interpreted the famine as a result not only of climatic problems, but also of five years of catastrophic mismanagement of the country. On the other hand, he criticized Tandja's position in an effort to discredit the President and present himself as a better statesman.

On the first point, he initially stressed the government's inability to predict the crisis and plan adequate means for dealing with it. According to Issoufou, "The state did not give the departments that have jurisdiction in such affairs the means they needed [...]. We are dealing with incompetent leaders [...] who do not care about the situation in which our people find themselves."[33] The Chairman of the PNDS then said he had noted during visits to the affected areas that up to 40% of food aid was being misappropriated, before accusing the "head of state and the government of complicity in the misappropriation of food aid intended for the people of Niger."[34] Finally, he described what had happened as a problem of poor management. Under these

---

[31] A reference to the UNDP's ranking of countries. It should be noted that, in 2005, Niger was ranked last, that is, poorest, which increased the embarrassment of the government, as well as the resentment of the leaders against the United Nations agencies.

[32] PPN-RDA, "Déclaration du bureau politique du PPN-RDA", *La Roue de l'Histoire*, No. 261, 16 August 2005: p. 6.

[33] Diallo Mahamadou, "Crise alimentaire: Mahamadou Issoufou s'insurge contre les propos de Tandja", *op. cit.*: p. 4.

[34] *Ibid.*

conditions, "only good government of the country and the definition and implementation of a modern agricultural policy can protect the people of Niger from insecurity."[35]

On the second point, the leader of the opposition clearly wanted to give the impression of "replacing" the President of the Republic and sought to position himself as a true statesman in the eyes of the international community, which Mamadou Tandja had accused of following an agenda harmful for the country's image. Addressing the external partners directly, he described the President's words as sabotage before declaring: "We, as those with political responsibility, apologize to the United Nations system on behalf of Niger; we ask the United Nations system to continue working for the people of Niger [...] and we ask Kofi Annan not to take account of the words, which I would deem irresponsible, of the President of the Republic, and to continue with his plans to visit Niger on August 22 and 23."[36] This declaration echoed—in a more offensive manner—the initial position taken by Hama Amadou who, while speaking about the famine and calling on the international community for aid, also wanted to position himself as a responsible statesman, playing the card of transparency.

This provides a clear view of how external stakeholders, particularly the UN and donor agencies, are used by the local political stakeholders, to an extent that depends on the situation, for purposes of internal and external legitimization: one side (the President) denounced their interference, invoking national sovereignty, while the other side (the leader of the opposition and, for a while, the Prime Minister) encouraged them in an effort to create an image of a man of the people. However, these differing strategies produced different benefits for those who developed them. The policy of relative transparency adopted by Hama Amadou earned him a reprieve from the ordinary newspapers that were most critical of him, while the President's denials resulted in anger within the country and a lack of understanding externally. The rivalry between the President and his Prime Minister, highlighted by their different stands on the famine, was related to the adoption of the parliamentary motion of censure that overthrew the head of government on 1 June 2007.

---

[35] PNDS, "Le PNDS se prononce sur la situation alimentaire", *Le Républicain*, 26 May 2005: p. 5.

[36] Diallo Mahamadou, "Crise alimentaire: Mahamadou Issoufou s'insurge contre les propos de Tandja", *op. cit.*

The food crisis reflects the limitations of a formal democracy

How can this semantic quarrel concerning the food crisis and the manage-ment of the crisis be interpreted, beyond the mere expression of partisan dif-ferences? According to Sylvie Brunel, denied famines are above all famines of an ideological order which are noted "in totalitarian and dictatorial regimes or in territories controlled by guerrillas".[37] Obviously, Niger does not corre-spond to any of these situations. The current regime resulted from democratic elections and the government had no problem with respect to its legitimacy. Moreover, a private press exists—and even includes about 40 titles—and, as the extracts cited here clearly indicate, it does not necessarily side with the government. Despite this, the situation was denied at the highest levels of government.

This may seem surprising. Literature on democratization generally postu-lates that, in a democratic regime, the stakeholders tend to prefer short-term decisions that satisfy their electorate over long-term policies that are unpopu-lar with the electorate even if they are propitious for economic success in the long run.[38] For other authors, even in a context in which the economic situa-tion requires urgent structural reforms, governments tend to imperil such reforms in order to satisfy their electorate.[39] Certain authors even think that famine is impossible in regimes that are truly democratic because their open-ness means they have early warning systems for crises[40] or media favourable to the implementation of anti-famine strategies.[41] In keeping with these posi-tions, those who hold power should have rushed to resolve the problem even if that meant taking funds from longer-term development projects.

This suggests that what happened in 2005 is for all intents and purposes an indicator of the weakness of Niger's democracy. Although the management of the crisis does not indicate a dictatorial character of the regime, or a desire to

---

[37] Sylvie Brunal, *Famines et politique, op. cit.*: p. 39.

[38] Walter Galenson, *Labour and Economic Development*, New York, Wiley, 1959.

[39] Stephan Haggard and Robert Kaufman, "Economic Adjustment in New Democracies" in Loan Nelson (ed.), *Fragile Coalitions: the Politics of Economic Adjustment*, Oxford, Transaction Books, 1989.

[40] On this subject, see Athar Huaasin, "Introduction" in Jean Drèze, Amartya Sen and Athar Hussain (eds), *The Political Economy of Hunger. Selected Essays*, Oxford, Claren-don Press, 1995: pp. 30–1.

[41] On the role of the media, see also Narasimhan Ram, "An Independent Press and Anti-Hunger Strategies: the Indian Experience", in Jean Drèze, Amartya Sen and Athar Hussain (eds), *The Political Economy of Hunger, op. cit.*

starve people, the shortcomings noted in the decision-making process and state policies point to deficits in the political system in terms of efficiency and accountability. The 2005 crisis resulted first from a refusal on the part of informed political stakeholders to place the situation at the top of their national political priorities. It also reveals the limitations of a formal democracy like those found in many countries that recently joined the wave of democratization. In these countries, a gap has been noticed between procedures that may be completely democratic and the practices of the stakeholders who are not subject to standards of accountability. This observation has led specialists in the "new democracies" to propose various descriptive terms for the nature of these new regimes, which some refer to as "hybrids".[42] The concept of "delegative democracy"[43] seems particularly suited for referring to Niger, in the sense that it refers to regimes which were elected following a transparent vote, but then function as if elected officials were not accountable. These regimes are very unreceptive to the signals and demands from the people and pursue their own agendas. In response to any protests from civil society or other organized groups, they tend to raise the issue of their popular legitimacy, although the electors whom they rely on—often captive electors for regional, ethnic or clientelistic reasons—have little control over the policies adopted. This description applies to the Niger political system: the MNSD, heir to the former single party, is a partisan structure in the hands of the elites whose socialization to politics dates back to the period when the party personified the state. Although it proclaims determination to develop the country from the ground up, its methods of government have always been developed by the elites and not the general public. As for the CDS, the other heavyweight in the power coalition, the media accuse it of being primarily concerned with conserving the positions it has at all levels of government and international parliamentary assemblies while its Chairman travels around the world.

This state crisis, which became particularly acute in 2005, cannot however be attributed solely to the poor management of the political elites.[44] It is, rather, the combined result of local management and the country's

---

[42] Larry Diamond, "Thinking about Hybrid Regimes", *Journal of Democracy*, Vol. 13, No. 2, 2002.

[43] Guillermo O'Donnell, "Delegative Democracy", *Journal of Democracy*, Vol. 5, No. 1, 1994.

[44] This is obviously the case of the leader of the opposition, Mahamadou Issoufou. See PNDS, "Le PNDS se prononce sur la situation alimentaire", *op. cit.*

dependence on those who provide funding for food security, all of which was aggravated by the policies supported by international financial institutions. This combination led to policies of privatization and a withdrawal of the state from its essential social functions such as the free distribution of food, which had, however, been practiced by previous regimes. These policies, too, are not unconnected with the abandonment of past policies concerning state regulation of the food market or the quasi-closure of the installations of the Niger Office of Food Products (Office des Produits Vivriers du Niger, OPVN) where national security supplies—found to be insufficient in 2005—were stored throughout the country.[45] As has been noted, "the situation in Niger was sufficiently critical when famine struck".[46] All of these factors combined to reveal the relative powerlessness of the state in the matter of food security. However, unlike those interpretations which view the powerlessness of the state as a mere reflection of subordination to a neo-colonial or liberal order, we think it is important at this time to highlight the role of internal shortcomings specific to the manner in which Niger's democracy is being shaped. Considered from all these strategic, political and institutional angles, the scope of the crisis is no longer a surprise.

Towards a reconfiguration of Niger's public sphere?

Despite situations of chronic shortages, what could even be referred to as the cyclical character of food crises in Niger, the 2005 crisis came as a true shock and produced a reconfiguration of the political landscape and the balance between authority and society. The reason for this was that the crisis occurred in an environment that was much more democratic than during the crises in the 1970s and 1980s. This new environment favoured the emergence of a public space in which speech and criticism could no longer be stifled. In exchange, this criticism seemed to force the state to redefine its relationship with society.

The emergence of a much more vocal "civil society"

It is too early to say if this reconfiguration is durable, but several signs clearly indicate that it has taken place. Specifically, an increase in the power of the

---

[45] Thomas Hofnung, "Au Niger, la France bonne humanitaire?", *op. cit.*
[46] Yahaya Garba, "L'urgence du retour à un partenariat plus sain", *La Roue de l'Histoire*, No. 261, 16 August 2005: p. 5.

organizations claiming to represent civil society has been noted. These organizations have managed to force the authorities to be more receptive and demonstrate that they will adopt new standards of good government from now on.

In support of the mobilization generated by this crisis, a reconfiguration of the national political landscape and the stakeholders seems to be underway even if—and we emphasize this—it is too early to determine if it will be sustainable. The new stakeholders who seem to have established themselves through the crisis include the private media. Whether they were independent or linked to the opposition, journalists did not hesitate to focus on three themes throughout the crisis: the denunciation of silence, intimidation, and misappropriation of aid.

On the first point, numerous journalists denounced "the temptation of silence [which] is the easiest path", but which, according to them, indicates "a totalitarian vision of the state and management of public affairs."[47] Very quickly, other journalists called for the debate to be moved to the public arena "considering such lack of concern."[48] Moreover, they did not refrain from denouncing harsh actions by the authorities—for example, the suspension of Maimouna Tchirgni, a journalist with the public media, and the campaign conducted in the state media against Donaig Ledu, a reporter for Radio France Internationale who was criticized because of her reports on the famine. They even commented on the "expulsion" of expatriates of MSF and Plan International.[49] Journalists' associations also denounced "acts attacking the freedom of the press [...], threats, sanctions and intimidations used to shape information..."[50]

In addition to this defence of freedom of expression, the media made a large contribution to denouncing and probably limiting the misappropriation of aid. For example, the media denounced the fact that "in Agadez [...] a total of 199 bags were misappropriated: 32 bags offered to a floating population, 20 bags given to the neighbourhood leaders, 15 bags to the sultanate, 15 bags

[47] M.S. Sanda, "Famine au Niger: crise silencieuse selon l'ONU", *L'Évènement*, No. 92, 31 May 2005: p. 3.

[48] Moussa Tchangari, "Famine et négationnisme", *Alternative*, No. 309, 27 May 2005: p. 1.

[49] Oumarou Keita, "Que s'est-il passé entre MSF et le gouvernement?", *Le Républicain*, 30 June 2005: p. 4. In fact, it was MSF that recalled one of its volunteers after an altercation with a member of the government in a nutrition centre in Maradi.

[50] Press release issued by several journalists' associations and reproduced in *Libération*, No. 102, 31 May 2005: p. 4.

given to the marabouts, 15 bags to the National Armed Forces (FAN), 10 bags to the National Intervention and Security Forces (FNIS), 5 bags to the police, 5 bags to the gendarmerie and 2 bags to the environment department..."[51] Far from merely denouncing these misappropriations, the media called on the head of state to make a commitment to prosecute those behind the misappropriations. By doing this, they demonstrated that the press can, by making such matters public, contribute to reducing the harm caused by them. By the end of the crisis, the media had grown stronger and were less subject to self-censorship.

A similar conclusion also applies to the other organizations that claimed to represent civil society and now serve as the flag-bearers of social issues. This is especially the case for Coalition Qualité/Équité contre la Vie Chère and the Coordination Démocratique de la Société Civile Nigérienne (CDSCN). These groups were among the first to organize walks "against hunger", walks "against expensive lifestyles", and "dead city operations", in order to obtain a series of measures like the free distribution of food to the starving people or a decrease in the price of consumer products, particularly those deemed essential. For these associations, when faced with the government's denials, "only our mobilization can lead the government to respect the people and assume its responsibilities."[52] These mobilizations effectively helped force the government to make concessions on several issues pertaining to the food crisis: acceptance of the principle of free distribution of food in certain zones, a decrease in the prices of several products, and the involvement of civil society organizations in the management of the food crisis. In this way, the group coordinating civil society obtained the right to sit on the ad hoc committee responsible for managing the food crisis. Participation in this committee gave civil society a right to examine the policy of appealing to the international community, the delivery, consignment and distribution of food, and the assessment and checking of all operations undertaken as part of emergency aid.[53] If there were any need to demonstrate the impact of this citizen movement, it would be sufficient to think of the institutionalizing of a dialogue between these organizations and the government on social issues and, above all, the creation—during the ministerial reshuffle of March 2007—of a new

---

[51] Yayé Nassamou Djibril, "Détournement de l'aide alimentaire destinée aux populations démunies", *L'Expression*, 30 November 2005: p. 5.

[52] "Déclaration de l'association Timidria, l'ONDHP et la CDSCN", *La Griffe*, No. 108, 30 May 2005: p. 4.

[53] Moussa Douka, "Coordination et supervision des aides d'urgence: le comité ad hoc se dit satisfait", *La Griffe*, No. 120, 22 August 2005: p. 5.

ministry, the Ministry of National Competitiveness and the Fight against the High Cost of Living, which was maintained under the government of Seyni Oumarou, Hama Amadou's successor.

Of course, it is possible to wonder whether, given their generally urban character, these civil society groups are really in touch with peasant realities. However, their action led the government to decrease the price of many products like oil, sugar, millet, and even fuel. In a country where almost everything is imported, decreasing prices of these products does not just benefit urban dwellers. On the other hand, in a country where the state is the principal employer and where, for sociological reasons, any civil servant (or any successful individual) is responsible for his family in the broad sense (with ramifications for villages), any action that serves to reduce the cost of living, even in urban zones, has beneficial repercussions everywhere. Now we need to see if the actions of these organizations will have lasting effects. In Niger, as in other African countries, the very existence of civil society is questioned. Some feel that at best there is a "precarious balance between the state and society",[54] and at worst, a fragile civil society tends to be absorbed by the state or the political parties, in keeping with various interests.

Towards a balance between state-society relations and new standards of governance?

The crisis is over now, but its repercussions go beyond the issue of food. It weakened executive power and possibly made way for a new era in matters of governance. Major cracks did, in fact, appear within the executive, corresponding to the different interpretations by the President and his Prime Minister. What the media referred to as the "President's anger" did not take long coming. Mamadou Tandja pointed out that he was the President elected by the people and that those who spoke of famine were involved in "false propaganda" with "political motivations or economic interests".[55] That was enough for some to claim that "the conflict between [President] Tandja and his successor (with respect to the 2009 elections) has entered a critical phase" and announce the "imminent departure of the Prime Minister",[56] which in fact took place in June 2007.

[54] Naomi Chazan, "Patterns of State-Society Incorporation and Disengagement in Africa" in Naomi Chazan and Donald Rothchild (eds), *The Precarious Balance: State and Society in Africa*, Boulder, Westview Press, 1988: pp. 121–48.
[55] Agence France Presse, "La crise alimentaire déclenche une crise au sein de l'exécutif", press release, 28 August 2005.

Since that time, the unsettled authorities have been criticized and forced to account for their actions. The food crisis created a precedent for increased involvement of the media, civil society and, of course, external stakeholders in the conduct of public affairs. As a result, it seems that the authorities, knowing they are being watched, are attempting to convince both external partners and internal opinion that they are now totally committed to planning and "good governance". First, this can be seen through the President's race against time to reconstitute the 111,000 ton food security reserve (including 50,000 in physical products and 60,000 in financial reserves) and put the OPVN's entire vehicle fleet back into commission so that the authorities can intervene quickly. This increasing influence of non-governmental stakeholders can also be seen through the so-called "Meba affair" (named after the Ministry of Basic Education) concerning the misappropriation of aid from the European Union to the educational sector. For the first time, two active ministers (the Education Minister and his predecessor, who had been put in charge of Health) were relieved of their posts, accused by a parliamentary commission dominated by members from the parties in power, and imprisoned for several months while awaiting trial. Since then, a "clean hands" campaign has been announced by the President and numerous people have been arrested: mayors, civil administrators, managers of public companies, traditional chiefs, former ambassadors...no one seems to escape from Mamadou Tandja's new battle against corruption.

A number of observers have remained wary, convinced that this is either a policy to save face, as suggested by the conditional release of the two incarcerated ministers in June 2007, or a selective and opportunistic campaign to get rid of rivals—including Prime Minister Hama Amadou, who was ousted by a motion of censure which, it is said, was organized by the President—in preparation for the 2009 elections. Under the constitution, the President cannot run again unless constitutional amendments are initiated to change restriction of the number of terms a President can serve.

Conclusion

The 2005 crisis was largely political in terms of the scope it assumed as well as the debates it raised and the consequences it had. These include the awakening

---

[56] Ibrahim Elhadj Hima, "Crise politique: le PR Tandja évincera-t-il le PM Hama Amadou?", *La Roue de l'Histoire*, No. 262, 23 August 2005: p. 3.

of organizations claiming to represent society and the incontestable reorganization of political power. Several measures clearly indicate that this crisis has left deep scars: the involvement of non-governmental organizations in all the steps in the management of the food crisis, the creation of a ministry to fight the high cost of living, the implementation of a framework for cooperation with civil society to deal with social issues, the regular communication between the head of state and the leader of the opposition, the reconstitution of the security reserve and the OPVN vehicle fleet in record time....All that remains is to determine if the re-balancing of forces and the reconfiguration of state-society relations that occurred during the 2005 crisis are sufficiently institutionalized to guarantee the accountability of the government and create a public sphere that is governed by sounder standards of governance.

Translated from French by Sheryl Curtis.

3

Building the Case for Emergency: MSF and the Malnutrition Factor

Xavier Crombé

"Lies" for the President of Niger, "a media coup" based on "outrageous simplifications" according to the representative of the World Food Programme (WFP): in 2005, Médecins Sans Frontières (MSF) was the direct and indirect target of numerous critics denouncing what they saw as a fabrication or, at the very least, an exaggeration of the crisis. In large part, these accusations reflect the cleavage, heightened by the events of 2005 in Niger, between "developers" and proponents of "emergency" relief, the former commonly charging the latter with mobilizing disproportionate resources in a counterproductive way unable to address the deep-seated causes of primarily chronic crises. Criticisms also pointed to the central role of legitimacy and sovereignty issues in the controversies accompanying the national and international responses to the Niger people's plight.

While most commentators now agree that 2005 was a particularly difficult year for many in Niger, including their children, suspicion hanging over MSF has not been entirely dispelled. There are several reasons for this. For the crisis to be recognized, it needed to be made evident and to some extent "constructed"; MSF played a leading role in this process. Moreover, many of the actions and public positions taken by MSF in 2005 derived in fact from a strategy worked out late the previous year. Its aim, however, was not to fabricate a crisis, but to construct an object of public health concern: infant-child malnutrition in Niger.

Didier Fassin has shown, through the example of lead poisoning in children in France, that to be recognized as worthy of a public health policy, an illness must be constructed socially and politically. It is often actors outside the legitimate field of public health who initiate this process. Thus, for the French authorities to recognize the scope and seriousness of a condition regarded as rare for the reason that only its most severe cases were identified in hospital setting, it was necessary for other individuals and institutions—doctors, associations, social workers, local government bodies—to mobilize. By campaigning for epidemiological studies and the definition of critical thresholds and by appealing to the press, they helped establish the statistical and social reality of lead poisoning. By pointing out the part played by immigration policies and social housing, they achieved the relocation of families living in substandard housing when the initial measures were limited to providing advice on hygiene to mothers of African immigrant families. In short, they made a political issue out of a little-known disease (Fassin, 2005).

The chapter that follows is based in large part on this analysis. In Niger, in the face of apparent lack of interest on the part of health authorities and international financial donors, the objective that MSF set for itself at the end of 2004 was to expose child malnutrition and the need to address it medically. In this regard, the 2005 food crisis constituted an "opportunity" to "bring the disease into social existence", to borrow Yannick Jaffré's expression (Jaffré, 1996), and put it on the political agenda.

The cards were shuffled, though, by the sheer number of severely malnourished children flooding into MSF treatment centres, the pattern of the emergency itself, and the interplay with other actors in the crisis. Lively discussions and questioning took place throughout the MSF movement and within its various sections[1] concerning the delay in taking action and the problem of understanding a "non-war-related" food crisis. In fact, what was at stake for MSF in Niger in 2005, together with its fight for the survival of the children whom it treated, was the renegotiation of legitimate areas of action for a

---

[1] MSF is composed of a number of operational sections based in different countries. Until July 2005, only the French section of MSF, MSF-France, was present and active in Niger. It was joined successively by MSF-Switzerland, MSF-Spain, MSF-Belgium and MSF-Netherlands during the course of the summer. For convenience, MSF will here refer to MSF-France or to the entire movement. The full name of the sections will be used only when it is necessary to distinguish between their respective actions.

humanitarian medical organization. This issue was already present in embryonic form in the definition of the nutritional programme started in 2001 in Maradi. It was this medium-term programme and its achievements that would lay the foundations for MSF to build the case for emergency in 2005.

A humanitarian, development, or public health issue?

The history of MSF in Niger began in 1985 with an initial emergency nutritional operation in the context of the great Sahel famine. This experience was typical of those that would follow: the organization's emergency nutritional programme was reoriented towards technical assistance to health structures in Niger, including the training of personnel and provision of equipment. It also reflected a time when under-availability of medical care and poverty, outside crisis situations, was on MSF's agenda. This vision changed in the 1990s, when conflicts multiplied in Africa and became priority areas of intervention. Nonetheless, several "Niger missions" followed one another, in response to epidemics or food shortages, as in 1997 at the request of Niger's *Système d'Alerte Précoce*[2] (SAP). The programme put in place on that occasion was initially defined as strengthening nutritional recovery centres in the Zinder region because "the chronic emergency, the responses to it and the existing structures d[id] not allow for tackling the problem of malnutrition through an emergency approach."[3] The "hidden" and chronic nature of malnutrition and the social stigmatization surrounding it were clearly identified by the team working on this project. Nevertheless, MSF was not convinced of its sustainability or the effectiveness of the current methods of treatment over the long term, and shut down the project 18 months later. The next emergency, a measles epidemic in 2001, seemed to justify the pessimism of the previous years since it served to demonstrate that health structures in Niger no longer offered curative treatment for severe malnutrition.

The emergency department, which coordinated the response to this epidemic, nevertheless proposed to implement a new medium-term nutritional programme in Maradi. It is important to recall arguments made for and against this project when it was presented to MSF's Board of Directors, as they reveal areas of tension associated with defining what constitutes a legitimate action for humanitarian medicine outside situations of conflict or, more generally, of crisis. For some, the chronic nature of malnutrition and its link

[2] Early Warning System.
[3] Internal MSF report, April 1997.

with underdevelopment and poverty ruled out using the criteria for emergencies or crises to justify an operation. Advocating a public health approach, these people questioned the curative option, a costly one in terms of Niger's limited resources, without an associated prevention approach. For their part, supporters of the project pointed out that a preventive approach was already in place but was used to justify the lack of curative treatment for the most severe forms of malnutrition. At the top of the aid system, prevention had to do with food insecurity and famine. At the bottom, preventing malnutrition consisted of promoting breast feeding and providing nutritional advice to mothers in rural areas.

It was no longer a question of building on what existed, as in the past, but of filling a vacuum associated with high mortality. For the project designers, this constituted a legitimate humanitarian concern and one that was not, in itself, new. Showing that death from severe malnutrition was not inevitable, that it was preventable, was already a part of previous projects. It was the chances of achieving this goal that seemed to have changed. Based on the development of an innovative therapeutic approach, potentially more effective than those carried out previously, the programme was presented as being complementary to the existing preventive approach. But a more political reading was already outlined: "prevention only" actually amounted to excluding from care a large number of children whose probable death was regarded as "normal". According to this reading, implementing the project meant agreeing to possible confrontation with the institutional nutrition officials in Niger: the health authorities, the WFP, and UNICEF. Thus, most of the issues that would be at the heart of the controversies characterizing the crisis of 2005 were already exposed within MSF internally.

Why, despite the expressed reservations, was this programme finally adopted? On the one hand, treating malnutrition has always had an important, indeed obvious, place among the medical activities of MSF in an emergency situation.[4] The possible development and validation of a new protocol that would result in more effective treatment of this pathology could therefore eventually benefit MSF's more classical medical relief activities. In addition, the issue of malnutrition lay at the crossroads of emergency relief and of another type of activity carried out by MSF since the second half of the 1990s:

---

[4] Obvious to such an extent that in some situations of conflict, as in Congo-Brazzaville or the Democratic Republic of Congo (DRC), it took several months for MSF to abandon this nutritional focus and redirect operations towards more pressing humanitarian concerns, beginning with women victims of sexual violence (Salignon and Le Pape, 2001).

the development of pilot projects to improve treatment of major endemic diseases such as AIDS or tuberculosis. Despite these motivations, the project's progress between 2002 and 2005 was marked by isolation in two ways.

To gain room for manoeuvre, MSF withdrew in 2003 from the hospital in Maradi and built an autonomous therapeutic feeding centre (TFC). The programme officers in Paris insisted on keeping their distance from any public health approach and focusing on demonstrating the effectiveness of the project itself. As a result, no nutritional survey and no evaluation of the programme's coverage of the region's population were undertaken. The only indicators considered were adherence to treatment and the recovery rates of children admitted to the project upon voluntary presentation by their mothers. Finally, the programme was not promoted pro-actively to Niger's health and nutrition officials, starting with the department responsible for public health. For the latter, MSF's legitimate role was limited to the support it provided in response to epidemics of measles and meningitis. The discretion surrounding this nutritional project on the ground in Niger reflected the relative isolation of its promoters within MSF. Niger, a country at peace, attracted little attention from the organization as a whole and the project, while it seemed promising, was largely perceived as experimental.

This relatively marginal position had a number of implications. It led to some frustration on the part of successive teams in the field that suffered from not being able to measure the impact of their efforts and worried about the continuity of the programme. Their dealings with local researchers and other NGOs prompted them to highlight the social, cultural and economic dimensions of malnutrition, which they felt were neglected by headquarters in Paris. In fact, the accumulated knowledge of the environment and the factors that explain malnutrition is clear from reading the various reports produced by staff in the field and the specialists at headquarters. This knowledge, however, remained individual; it was not capitalized upon by the institution and was largely lost with a change in the personnel in charge of the programme, both in the field and at headquarters. Thus, many of these inputs, which would prove decisive in developing MSF's public positions and operational choices during the 2005 crisis, would only be brought to light belatedly, and would even, in some cases, have to be rediscovered under the pressure of events. This was true both of the speculation affecting the price of millet and of the greater prevalence of malnutrition in southern Maradi. These two factors explaining the crisis and its impact on malnutrition were already mentioned in the final report of MSF's head of mission in Niger in the fall of 2004. He pointed out that the reason why "the prevalence of malnutrition is paradoxically greater in areas where agricultural production is higher: the threat that demographic pressure represents to the transmission of land. [...] In fact, overpopulation results in a social revolution in which women are the biggest losers."[5]

It would be tempting to see a typical emergency aid bias in the difficulty of capitalizing on past knowledge. This, however, does not excuse development agencies or the local administration. At the end of 2004, in fact, the nutrition department of Niger's Ministry of Public Health had been without a director for a year, while the position of nutritionist at UNICEF was filled on an interim basis by the official in charge of AIDS. These vacancies are revealing: for UNICEF, for the Ministry of Health and for many others, malnutrition had ceased to be a health problem and was regarded as a social and cultural problem or a result of lack of education. The focus on "poor feeding practices", however real they might be, revealed this, and determined the choice of measures, which did not include any curative approach. Conversely, MSF's programme officers narrowed their attention to their medical mission. The problem that concerned them was the lack of treatment for acute malnutrition in a context of insufficient access to healthcare, particularly for young children. Social data were not denied, but constituted, in the words of the head of mission, factors over which "we have no control [...] and no reason to think that the situation has a chance of improving in the years to come." In addition, the lack of recent regional or national surveys of the incidence of this pathology no doubt encouraged prudence.

In 2004 a new dynamic emerged. First, the results achieved by the programme proved exceptional when compared to MSF's previous experiences, including those in famine situations. Nearly 10,000 children were admitted to nutritional centres with an unheard of recovery rate of more than 80%. Moreover, the five-year health development plan developed by international donors on behalf of Niger's Ministry of Health recognized malnutrition as a priority health problem. The plan stated that half the annual deaths of children under five years of age were related to undernourishment. This acknowledgement did not lead to any concrete measure but nevertheless presented a new opportunity. Above all, the WFP, representing international donors in the food crisis prevention and management system and hence a stakeholder in

---

[5] Internal report, October 2004. This aspect is developed in the chapters of this work by Marthe Diarra, Marie Monimart and Barbara Cooper. This analysis of the social determinants of malnutrition in Maradi in fact owed much to the regular discussions between the head of mission and Marthe Diarra.

the preventive approach, showed renewed interest in nutrition. Its local representative was willing to build on MSF's experience and the results of its programme to commit to this focus in the years ahead. He also expressed interest in the local production of ready-to-use therapeutic food (RUTF), a project that MSF helped to put in place to reduce the cost of the product on which its protocol was based. Finally, he announced his intention to conduct nutritional surveys in the following months and to organize regular meetings on malnutrition involving the Ministry of Health, donors and NGOs, an initiative MSF had previously called for in vain. The WFP therefore appeared as a partner of choice, likely to bring the issue of malnutrition to the attention of international donors and authorities in Niger with more impact than MSF could have.

For all these reasons, the objectives set by the new programme officers of the Niger mission for the year 2005 assigned a large place to activities designed to "inform local actors and have them take on the responsibility" for child malnutrition. The strategy, finalized in February 2005, was in no way emergency-oriented. While working to improve the quality of the programme, it was designed to increase its visibility and document the phenomenon of malnutrition outside the context of the programme itself. The objectives included conducting a nutritional survey, strengthening outpatient centres, examining a method to provide care to children suffering from moderate malnutrition and, finally, working out a lobbying strategy to promote the project at the national level. In other words, MSF set itself the goal of helping to produce epidemiological data that would give statistical reality to the scope and gravity of acute malnutrition, identifying its causes (or more accurately, determining those which would warrant collective, medical-nutritional measures and not just action on individual behaviour, notably that of mothers) and making the availability of a curative response known.

This strategy was to be carried out throughout the year, with emphasis on the annual seasonal peak of cases of malnutrition, during the lean pre-harvest period. It was therefore defined without anticipating a specific nutritional emergency for 2005. An "emergency component" was incorporated into the objectives, but it was concerned with the response to infectious disease epidemics. Nonetheless, initial information on the poor harvests resulting from drought and locust invasions was taken into account and, in February 2005, the idea of opening new ambulatory nutritional centres, which was floated in the spring of 2004 as a way of increasing the programme's visibility, was again advanced and proposed for the northern Maradi region. According to data from Niger's early warning system, it was there that the harvests had been most affected.

The involvement of the WFP and the prospect of an increase in the number of undernourished children, together with the deterioration of the food situation and the opportunity it offered for advancing the issue of malnutrition, would influence the geographical orientation of MSF's strategy. In the first months of 2005, the new team in charge of the Niger mission was not expecting to come into confrontation with the institutional actors responsible for food security. A complementary rather than a confrontational approach was envisioned, while the possibility of a food crisis was becoming apparent. The goal was to emphasize the need for a specific medical and nutritional response in areas where the official food security system would address the shortage with food aid. The view expressed by a nutrition doctor during a visit to evaluate the Maradi programme in the spring of 2004 is revealing of MSF's initial appreciation of its role: "While we can rely on the government and its partners to intervene quickly in terms of mass distribution, as long as Niger's health policy does not make it a priority to treat severe malnutrition, children will continue to experience excessive and unacceptable mortality."[6]

However, contrary to what was anticipated, and to the assurances that MSF would receive in the first months of the year, the government and its partners did not intervene quickly and rejected the principle of free food distribution. Although they are interconnected, there are a number of differences between a food crisis and a nutritional emergency regarding children, in terms of both diagnosis and alleviating measures. At the political level, however, it would soon become clear that for the worsening nutritional situation of children to be taken into account by Niger policy-makers, they should first be made to acknowledge the seriousness of the food situation. This understanding would weigh heavily on MSF's policy in 2005 and would set in motion the inner dynamics of the crisis in Niger.

Constructing the nutritional emergency

To construct does not mean to fabricate. The actions taken by MSF until the summer of 2005 consisted in seeking to organize the facts that would gain recognition for the nutritional dimension of a new food crisis. They can be summarized as follows: producing figures, making noise and, finally, giving

[6] Internal MSF report, March 2004.

meaning. It was the final—belated—step that would take the organization from a *de facto* complementary position with those working in food security to confrontation. For MSF the production of figures—number of children admitted to its centres, rate of prevalence, rate of mortality—and the first press releases were designed to mobilize people. It was in this mobilization effort that MSF would measure the scope of the emergency that it cited in its first public position. When mobilization failed, confrontation ensued as MSF's political interpretation of the crisis and of the social and economic dynamics playing a part in child malnutrition was set against the reading of the food security institutions. Without this "frontal" opposition, to borrow the phrase used by IRAM (IRAM, 2006: p. 62), would it have been possible to change policy and actions? Contrary to what has often been said, this debate was not so much between situational factors and structural factors as between two conceptions of what "structural" meant in the context of the crisis. For MSF, it meant the "inhospitable medicine" (Jaffré and Olivier de Sardan, 2003) as represented by Niger's health system and the economic and political ideologies determining development strategies. For its opponents in this debate, it meant climatic and geological factors or "cultural practices". Different actions were warranted depending on the weight given to one or the other set of explaining factors.

The first attempts to raise awareness of the crisis, however, did not come from MSF. The first appeals for international assistance were launched by Niger's authorities in November 2004, while in January 2005 the WFP said it would conduct a nutritional survey in the agro-pastoral zones of Maradi and Zinder. A number of NGOs made proposals for programmes combining food security and nutritional support. MSF saw this as confirmation of the trend towards greater recognition of malnutrition, and informed donors of the results of its programme, without sounding an alarm. In February and March 2005 the government of Niger, together with the WFP and UNICEF, issued alerts based on social and economic indicators such as the availability of animal feed and early migrations. These various indicators of an upcoming food crisis persuaded the MSF programme officers that the large increase in the number of malnourished children admitted to the centres in Maradi was evidence of a related nutritional crisis.

Considering the lack of reliable nutritional data from outside its centres, the rapidity with which MSF developed the various components of the "nutritional emergency in Niger" suggests that public communications by the WFP and others about the food shortage prompted MSF's programme officers to implement, early and more ambitiously, the strategy they had outlined in broad terms a few months earlier. An internal report in May indeed points to a tactical intuition:

In view of this increase [in the number of children admitted to the TFC], the choice we have made has been to regard this as a nutritional emergency and to change our operational response. [...] This has a twofold objective: to save more children, because we know that many of them will die if we do nothing, but also to make everyone aware of the scope of the situation and stop accepting malnutrition as something "normal" in Niger.[7]

While the initial project was limited to opening a few new outpatient centres in the Dakoro region north of Maradi, programme officers decided to create three new TFCs and, for each one, several outpatient centres. The choice of sites—in Dakoro district and then in Keita and Tahoua in Tahoua province—was based on a food security survey that was itself largely determined by the vulnerability maps established by Niger's early warning system. By treating a large number of severely malnourished children in the agro-pastoral zones where MSF expected the attention of international donors and the government to be directed, the problem of malnutrition was to be brought to light. The initial contacts in February with institutions in charge of health in Niger—the World Bank, Belgian Cooperation, and the state health authorities—probably convinced MSF's representatives of the need to revise the coverage objectives upward. Representatives of these institutions had all expressed scepticism towards the message of alarm presented to them by MSF's head of mission based on the number of children admitted to the programme in Maradi. The medical approach recommended by MSF did not correspond to their view of the problem, either. It was therefore all the more necessary to document and above all provide figures on the situation. The volume of activity of the increased number of centres was one way to give tangible reality to malnutrition. The goal of treating 20,000 children over the year, set in March, reflected in fact the initial estimate of the programme's maximum capacity rather than an anticipation of especially high rates of severe malnutrition.

The nutritional survey conducted by Epicentre[8] was also a component of MSF's crisis policy. Planned in 2004, it was undertaken only at the sites where the new centres were being opened, but had no influence on their location. The survey was conducted at the end of April 2005 and was conceived as a

---

[7] MSF internal report, May 2005.
[8] An epidemiological survey agency affiliated with MSF.

crucial element in a communication strategy designed to give reality to the nutritional emergency associated with the food crisis. The first press release was issued on 26 April—several days after a January 2005 WFP-Helen Keller International (HKI) survey was published, revealing severe malnutrition rates of 2.2% in Maradi and 2.7% in Zinder. The MSF press release gave added impetus to this first statistical report on the problem by producing its own figures of the number of admissions to its initial programme south of Maradi. It also explained the operational measures put in place to respond to what was now publicly described as a "nutritional emergency". Finally, MSF stated that additional figures would be forthcoming: those from the Epicentre nutritional survey set to begin shortly in Tahoua and Maradi. Headquarters immediately planned a second press release to be based on the survey results. Pending the production of these data, however, MSF's communication remained prudent and no explanation of the "emergency" was given. The press release, like the initial interviews given to the press, spoke only of a deteriorating situation, as shown by the continued increase in the number of severely malnourished children admitted to MSF centres. On the MSF website, only a photo of a desert landscape accompanied by the caption "drought" suggested a possible cause, whereas in internal meetings, programme officers kept stressing that "drought and locusts do not explain everything."

As a matter of fact, many questions were left unanswered. An assessment conducted by MSF-Belgium in the Tanout district in the north of Zinder region had not identified a nutritional emergency, contrary to what the WFP-HKI survey and food vulnerability data had led many to assume. The Epicentre survey, in addition, did not dispel all doubts about the scope and gravity of the crisis. The mortality rates for children under five exceeded the internationally recognized emergency threshold of 2/10,000 people per day. Rates of global acute malnutrition[9] supported the diagnosis of a rapid deterioration in the nutritional status of young children, rising from 13.5% in January, according to the WFP survey, to more than 19% in the areas covered by the Epicentre survey. However, the rates of severe acute malnutrition identified were not higher than those recorded by the WFP three months earlier. Moreover, the mobilization expected from the initial press release never materialized. Not that the food crisis was entirely ignored: the Coalition contre la Vie Chère,[10]

---

[9] Global acute malnutrition includes severe and moderate forms of acute malnutrition. See André Briend's chapter in this book for a detailed presentation of the various types of measurements of malnutrition.

[10] Coalition Against High Cost of Living.

a civil society movement in urban areas, had successfully organized several "dead city" days and linked its calls for a lower Value Added Tax (VAT) on common consumer products to the food shortage in rural areas. As early as February, the local WFP representative, in a meeting with MSF's head of mission, had compared the 2005 situation to the 2001 crisis, but felt there was better preparation in terms of the quantities of food available, which he believed should permit targeted free distribution. The measures adopted by institutions in charge of food security, however, were limited to sales at moderate prices and grain banks. None of these measures showed official recognition of a food emergency, and they made it even more unlikely that donors and health authorities would acknowledge a nutritional emergency among Niger's children.

Hence, finding ways to pressure stakeholders in Niger's aid system into adopting emergency measures would from then on become a top priority for MSF. Since the data from the nutritional survey did not in themselves justify a reading of the crisis that would "change the course of things", to use the expression of the programme manager, MSF called upon additional resources to document the situation. A new food security survey was conducted with the specific objectives of "showing the inability of the compensatory systems put in place to respond to the food shortage experienced by some populations and prompting a review of this aid system." It was also designed to identify the most vulnerable pockets in order to strengthen the call for free distribution by helping to target them or, failing that, to identify areas where MSF could carry out its own activities to assist families.

The second press release, issued by MSF on 9 June, combined the results of these two surveys to reiterate, in a more insistent and constructed manner, the message of the emergency. It mentioned the lack of treatment available for moderately malnourished children, the mortal danger that seasonal infectious diseases posed to them, the fact that money was charged for medical care, and the inadequacy of the measures taken in terms of quantity, modes of delivery and accessibility to the poorest households. MSF's demand for "free and direct access to food" for the most vulnerable sections of the population was addressed to international food security and nutrition officials in Niger: the WFP, UNICEF and international donors. However, the emergency described remained a stated fact, like the inadequacy of the responses to it, and no explanation of the situation was given. Coming after a statement in May 2005 by Jan Egeland, the UN Under-Secretary-General for Humanitarian Affairs, who said the crisis in Niger was "the most forgotten and neglected humanitarian emergency", and the call by Niger's Prime Minister for international aid in response to a "famine", MSF's press release only reinforced their appeals by lending them the credit of its nutritional data.

Still, finding reasons for the crisis other than those usually cited—drought and the previous summer's locust invasion—had preoccupied the MSF teams for several months. Many explanatory factors had been gathered since the recognition of an abnormal situation through the increase in admissions to the Maradi centre, and doubt had soon been cast on drought as a decisive factor. As early as April, one of the programme managers, during a field visit, had noted the relative modesty of the grain deficit, the regional dimension of the problem, and above all—following her discussions with a researcher from Niamey—the problem of accessibility faced by rural dwellers having to cope with speculation and the withholding of millet stocks by merchants in Maradi. She had also pointed to the merchants' connections with members of Niger's government, possibly accounting for the official refusal to engage in free distribution. Finally, she had emphasized the "obvious lack of donors' interest in Niger". All these reasons, however, were not seen as providing meaning to the overall situation until the decision was made, given the initial absence of mobilization, to construct a political reading of the crisis and thus of malnutrition. This political intuition was eventually backed up by sending a researcher (co-editor of this book) to the field. His analysis enabled MSF to formulate a new discourse at the end of June: the aid system was no longer seen as simply late or out of tune with the emergency; its very logic led it not only to deny the emergency could exist but also to aggravate it more surely than any natural cause.

By attacking the logic of development policies practiced in Niger, which made it possible to link the rejection of free aid during a crisis and the structural exclusion from medical care of families who could not pay for it, MSF was able to reintroduce child malnutrition as a public health issue into a broader perspective than that of the emergency. By calling for access to free healthcare for children under five and free food distribution, including specialized food for malnourished children—measures that MSF decided jointly to implement in its own programme—the NGO set out milestones in that regard. However, the emergency had its own requirements and its own impetus because of the number of actors intervening, which would grow along with the media's increasing focus on Niger.

Tensions and reactions: an unfolding crisis

Among the themes most widely used by the media covering the crisis in the summer of 2005, that of "a crisis foretold" no doubt resonated the most. In press interviews MSF representatives, too, commonly cited it in support of their message about the delay in providing relief. Yet the crisis seemed also to be full of surprises. In its evaluation report, IRAM noted from an economic perspective that "unlike a classic supply crisis, this one was not readily foreseeable". Internally, MSF also had a feeling of losing its points of reference. To emphasize the paradox facing the organization, its president advanced the idea of a "free-market famine" as opposed to "war famines" or "totalitarian famines", whose rationale was well understood. Upon returning from Niger, many MSF aid workers questioned their ability to understand a food crisis not associated with a conflict situation.

A quick look back at MSF's experiences in "familiar" famine contexts, however, leads to a more nuanced view of this finding. During the great famine in Ethiopia in the mid-1980s, it took nearly a year and a half for the MSF members to piece together the web of events and the practices of the Ethiopian regime and to understand the role humanitarian aid workers were playing in the government's strategy of rounding up and deporting famine-affected populations. In the Bahr-el Ghazal region of southern Sudan in 1998, it also took many months for MSF teams to understand that food aid was systematically diverted for the benefit of the rebel army and thus not reaching the most vulnerable displaced people. Only in February 1999 did MSF denounce the complacency of UN agencies towards the predatory practices of their "partners", the representatives of the parties to the conflict.[11] Finally, in Angola, responding to the discovery of starving populations emerging from war zones thanks to the ceasefire in the spring of 2002, MSF struggled to raise awareness of the urgent situation at a time when the international community was congratulating itself on the peace. An internal memorandum evaluating MSF's communications strategy pointed to the initial lack of understanding of the context, the lack of figures for the territory as a whole, and MSF's prudence in using the word "famine."

Belated understanding, the emphasis on the political interests at play as against a general consensus on the natural origins of a food crisis or famine, the responsibility of the aid system for the delay and inadequacy of relief—these narratives of crises that MSF has responded to, including Niger's crisis,

---

[11] Philippe Biberson, "Soudan: un renoncement mortel", *Le Monde*, 26 February 1999.

repeat similar themes. Yet each crisis has its own story, following the provision of aid, and this has to do with more than simply the inherent uniqueness of each disaster. A crisis is also the outcome of interactions among its many actors and of the inevitable confrontation between their multiple rationales. Thus, although in the course of the Niger food crisis MSF's decision-makers implemented a strategy whose outlines were defined in advance, they did not control the dynamic of the emergency they helped to shape, and had to adapt to and react to the behaviour of others intervening.

The interaction between MSF and the WFP, in particular, reveals this dynamic, which placed them successively in a relationship of partnership, tension, and then confrontation. The ambivalence that characterized their relationship has to do first of all with the ambiguous link between the area of food security and the curative approach to malnutrition. Presented as complementary at the opening of the nutritional programme in Maradi in 2001, these two areas separated from one another in the years that followed, in view of the lack of interest shown in malnutrition by donors who supported the food crisis prevention system. The WFP's interest in nutrition, as we have seen, once again opened up a complementary possibility. Statistics from the FAO and WFP survey were used by MSF to construct its message about the crisis and broaden its programmes. The report of the nutritional survey conducted by the WFP in January 2005 was, in fact, in complete accord with the message that MSF was preparing to send: the rates recorded "four months before the lean period are comparable to those seen in countries at war or in the most severe food crises or lean periods faced by Niger. The rates will surely rise in the coming months." (IRAM, February 2006: p. 48). The report notes the permanent nature of malnutrition in Niger and its particular seriousness during 2005. In return, the initial MSF press releases and its nutritional survey were used by the WFP and other UN agencies to mobilize international donors and obtain funds to respond to the crisis.

The WFP itself, however, held an institutional position that would place it between two poles throughout 2005. The agency's mandate typically includes both the distribution of food aid in emergencies and the provision of specialized foods to treat acute malnutrition. This explains the initial interest of its representative in joining with MSF to reinstate malnutrition as a priority in Niger. It would also warrant the WFP being the principal actor in response to the food and nutritional crises. In Niger, however, the WFP was also the institutional representative of the donors backing the country's food crisis prevention system, and was therefore bound by that institution's logic of long-term market stabilization. The measures that would be dictated by its mandate as an "emergency" intervener were not compatible with the consensus among the partners in food crisis prevention. Thus the WFP's attempt to mobilize backers on the international level went hand in hand, until mid-July, with preserving the consensus within Niger's prevention system. Indeed, no high-level debate was initiated by the WFP to convince its members to undertake free food distribution (WFP, 2006: p. 16).

Nothing better illustrates the WFP's delicate position in managing the crisis than the successive statements of its local representative as MSF increased its pressure on the food aid system and the UN's emergency specialists voiced rising concern about the situation. On 27 May, in connection with a statement by Jan Egeland, the WFP representative in Niamey felt that "the probability that the situation will improve is practically nil".[12] On 21 June he told a reporter for *Le Figaro* that "the system is no doubt insufficient, but it works."[13] On 23 June he expressed satisfaction with the mobilization of aid, but said, "We must redirect the emergency response to the medium and long term."[14] On 28 June, the date of a press conference organized by MSF to denounce the *de facto* embargo on free distribution, his position was quite different: "It is a very serious situation that requires action immediately, not tomorrow."[15] He reiterated this position the following day, speaking of a "race against the clock".[16]

This institutional tension between the requirements of the crisis prevention system in Niger and the growing pressure on WFP headquarters in Rome for the agency to carry out its humanitarian mandate no doubt explain its change of strategy on 14 July. At the meeting of the food crisis cell (CCA) the WFP announced its intention to carry out free food distribution. The decision was adopted unanimously—evidence that representatives of the donors supporting the system were probably under pressure from their governments, as well. As early as June, the Prime Minister of Niger had issued an "anguished appeal" for international aid. In early July, the G8 Summit in Gleneagles (Scotland) saw the French President publicly refer to the "famine" in Niger. Following this decision, most of the institutions and agencies which had been insisting

---

[12] "La famine menace mais les fonds tardent à arriver", *IRIN*, 27 May 2005.
[13] "Le Niger menacé par la famine", *Le Figaro*, 21 June 2005.
[14] "Habitué aux crises structurelles, le Niger est sous le coup d'une crise conjoncturelle", *IRIN*, 23 June 2005.
[15] "Infants die of hunger as world watches", *Reuters*, 28 June 2005.
[16] "Relief workers scramble to find food aid for Niger", *Reuters*, 29 June 2005.

on a development approach to the food issue became, in the course of the summer, "emergency-minded". WFP emergency officials, dispatched from Rome, took over the UN agency in Niger and directed distribution operations. Similarly, the French ambassador, who a month earlier at the meeting of the CCA had expressed satisfaction that the system had resisted demands for free distribution—a statement that helped trigger MSF's message of 28 June, "Pay or die"—had to accompany the French political figures coming to bring emergency aid in response to the crisis.

The various assessment reports on the crisis all emphasized the role played by the international media in the change of direction forced upon the institutions responsible for development policies, pointing out both the role of emergency aid workers in their mobilization and their many "excesses" (Sénat, 2005; IRAM, 2006; WFP, 2006; LASDEL, 2006; LASDEL, 2007). The consultants responsible for evaluating the WFP's activities in 2005 stated that media coverage "took off from the MSF press release in late April and reached its peak in July and August" (WFP, 2006: p. 15). This cause and effect relationship needs to be qualified. While the first international reports on the food crisis in Niger do date from April, they were the work of journalists whose attention was drawn by the protest movement led by the Niamey-based Coalition contre la Vie Chère. It was, moreover, on the advice of the WFP representative and that of the CCA that MSF was contacted to give its opinion on the food situation. These reports, like MSF's initial press release, were to have little influence. Without the results from its nutritional survey, MSF, being prudent about its message, was not in a position to actively solicit the media. Nevertheless, MSF's communications director took advantage of a contact with the Arab Al-Jazeera network to accompany one of its reporters to Niger. This report resulted in the first widely broadcast television images of severely malnourished children being treated in an MSF centre, and led to the first international food donations in June from several Arab states. MSF, however, was not an isolated voice. The Prime Minister of Niger used this media report to issue his first appeal for international aid. It was also at this time that Jan Egeland expressed indignation about the forgotten humanitarian crisis in Niger. These images and statements, however, did not change the nature of the response or lead to a meaningful international mobilization to cope with the crisis.

MSF's second press release, on 9 June, attracted more attention in the French media than the first. Although the "emergency" was becoming news, few reporters went to Niger. Above all, the media reports on the food crisis were very far removed from the message that MSF was trying to convey. The natural origin of the catastrophe—drought and locusts—was always emphasized, but nothing was said about the responsibility of the aid system for the delay and inadequacy of aid. This attitude no doubt led MSF to adopt a more offensive posture and to elaborate a message based on denouncing the rationale of development aid in response to the emergency. But that strategy alone does not suffice to explain the pattern of media mobilization.

When the G8 Summit, devoted in particular to the fight against poverty in Africa and debt reduction, opened in Gleneagles, the food crisis in Niger provided the press with an ideal counterpoint to the messages of solidarity it produced. Prime Minister Tony Blair took the opportunity to call for a repeat of the large-scale concerts for Africa of the 1980s, whose 20th anniversary was being celebrated. Unusually for a country in Francophone Africa, it was English-speaking and in particular British reporters who first went to Niger. A 1 July article in the *Daily Mirror* was revealing: "As the *Live 8* artists prepare to take to the stage and the leaders of the world's richest nations consider their options, three million desperate souls in Niger once again walk hand in hand with famine."[17] It was not until the BBC report of 20 July that MSF's nutrition centres found themselves the focus of intense media coverage triggered by images shown by this major international news network. MSF found itself in this position primarily because the dying children, evidence of the "famine" that reporters were looking for, were concentrated in its centres. The BBC's coverage of the crisis had a considerable impact on how the situation unfolded by putting Niger, thanks to a ripple effect, at the forefront of televised reports and placing food security institutions as well as the UN's humanitarian officials in an awkward position. It reinforced, however, the perception of a population at the mercy of a natural disaster.

The "BBC effect" combined with other patterns. The French media flocked to Niger at the end of July, accompanying Bernard Kouchner and the Minister of Foreign Affairs, Philippe Douste-Blazy. Kouchner, heading the NGO Réunir, himself participated, not without some excesses,[18] in mobilizing the French media by speaking several times about the "Niger emergency" in the

[17] "300,000 People Could Die in Niger Famine," *Daily Mirror*, 1 July 2005 (http://www.mirror.co.uk).

[18] His public statement on 22 June that 30,000 children were dying every day in Niger had aroused the anger of the country's Minister of Health, who relied on the mortality figures of MSF in Maradi to make a formal denial and reckoned that such mortality would mean the complete disappearance of the population of Niger.

wake of MSF's press releases. Douste-Blazy, for his part, crafted Jacques Chirac's appeals for solidarity with Niger at the G8. MSF centres were the focus of these official visits, and both these figures sought to associate themselves with MSF's actions in the crisis: Kouchner, who recalled his role as one of the founders of MSF, and Douste-Blazy as a member of the French government in solidarity with the work of a French organization.

While the tone of reports from the field during this visit was often restricted to the emotional, the major editorial writers in France strove to produce a joint analysis of the causes of the crisis. This provided MSF with the opportunity, at the end of July, to define a position consistent with the goal of raising awareness of malnutrition beyond the 2005 crisis. In public speeches and interviews, MSF's spokespersons still insisted on the ongoing emergency, but were now describing it as taking place in a context of chronic malnutrition. In view of the generally high proportion of malnourished children, they pointed to the charging of fees for medical care as revealing a political and economic logic similar to that which opposed free food aid in an emergency.[19] Hence, to the denial of the emergency, MSF now added a new target: the "chronic" denial of infant malnutrition in Niger. In an interview in *Le Monde*, the President of MSF criticized the socio-cultural explanations for malnutrition, which justified considering acute malnutrition and its associated mortality as "normal".[20] While MSF's programme officer wondered at the end of June whether, in view of the "seriousness of the situation and the ineffectiveness of the response ... those providing funds had not decided to accept the unacceptable,"[21] the attitude at the end of July was much more positive and was already looking beyond the framework of the crisis. Reference was also made to acute malnutrition, including both severe and moderate forms of this pathology, at a time when MSF, in addition to its support for severe cases, undertook the distribution of special food to 50,000 moderately malnourished children. Finally, MSF's public message included active communication about the therapeutic response available, which was also to emphasize the possibility of a treatment protocol outside the emergency context. Plumpy'nut was thus making its appearance in the mainstream press, along with accounts of the crisis.[22]

---

[19] "Les choix économiques et politiques ont autant contribué à la catastrophe que les conditions climatiques", *Le Monde*, 30 July 2007.

[20] "Une inégalité criante, même dans l'humanitaire", *Le Monde*, 22 July 2005.

[21] *AFP*, 28 June 2005.

[22] "Plumpy'nut, la portion magique anti-famine", *Libération*, 27 July 2005.

The change in MSF's public position corresponded to a change in understanding of the nutritional situation in the field. The trends observed since June in terms of the number of children admitted to the various nutritional centres were confirmed in July. Whereas MSF had focused its communications and its search for epidemiological and contextual data on the agro-pastoral zone, admissions in that region fell. However, they continued to grow in the agricultural zone around the southern town of Maradi. Moreover, information from one NGO based in the south of neighbouring Zinder region indicated a large number of severely malnourished children. It seemed clear therefore that the nutritional emergency did not correspond to the maps of food insecurity drawn up by the early warning system. This realization led at first to MSF's operational decision to go ahead with free distribution of enriched flour for moderately malnourished children only in the area south of Maradi. Only later did it take a public position, leading to a direct confrontation with UN agencies, especially the WFP, which was responsible for the free food distribution operations decided upon at July.

At the time when MSF, belatedly in terms of a decision initially taken in June, was beginning its distributions to moderately malnourished children, the WFP asked for advice to help it determine the targeting of general distributions. MSF defended the targeting of zones where the number of admissions of malnourished children was highest, but the WFP refused to adopt this criterion, deciding that targeting based on the incidence of malnutrition would be too complicated. Faced with media pressure and the anger of Jan Egeland towards WFP officials, who had been late to act and had thus considerably increased the costs of emergency distribution, the UN agency had to act quickly and visibly. In this context, a number of reasons could explain the decision, contrary to MSF's recommendations, to begin distribution in the agro-pastoral zone. To some extent, this can be seen as a desire not to discredit the indicators that guided the official food security system during the preceding months. Even more clearly, WFP officials who arrived from Rome relied on the available data concentrated on the agricultural deficit zones, and were no doubt afraid to implement rapid free distribution in very densely populated areas where the risk of a logistical breakdown, riots and diversions existed. Moreover, the government of Niger and international donors were still stressing the risk of grain price destabilization in a producing area as the harvest approached.

The same fears, particularly logistical ones, partly explained MSF's own delay in launching distributions. When the WFP showed MSF field officers its distribution maps, the operational decisions they reflected were at odds with MSF's current reading of the situation. In the latter's view, they indicated ongoing confusion on the part of UN agencies about the factors accounting for the crisis and more generally for childhood malnutrition. At the same time, MSF was experiencing strong internal tensions about the reasons for the delay in implementing distribution and setting up a programme in Zinder. From the start of the nutritional programme led by MSF-Switzerland, the large number of admissions of children in a serious condition showed that a priority zone for emergency intervention had been ignored for too long. The WFP's operational choices therefore seemed to be prolonging this lack of understanding of the context and the issues in play.

This led to public confrontation between MSF and the WFP. MSF timed a press release criticizing the erroneous targeting of the distributions to coincide with the visit of the United Nations Secretary General Kofi Annan on 22 August. This accusation was coupled with another, that of the inadequacy of the food being distributed, which took no account of the specialized foods for malnourished children. Thus, in this polemic about the emergency, there was a ready-made place for the message about a response adapted over time to the problem of childhood malnutrition. From the media's point of view, the phase of discovery of the crisis was followed by a phase of questioning and polemics, marked by shifting responsibility from one actor to another and the denial of a famine by President Tandja on 9 August. The polemic launched by MSF was also taken up by the press, but would largely be omitted in the various evaluation reports written throughout 2006. In effect, the polemic between defenders of the long-term development approach and proponents of the emergency response had a more lasting echo than the one among emergency actors themselves over the most appropriate emergency actions. At the time, however, the latter caused outrage and embarrassment among the agencies involved, but also laid the groundwork for a new future partnership.

A few days after his visit and MSF's press release, Kofi Annan published a column in *Le Monde* intended to re-establish consensus that the admitted need for development efforts should not in the future justify ignoring emergency situations. MSF, for its part, now described the situation in 2005 as an "epidemic" of malnutrition in an endemic context. In internal discussions, the president of MSF's French section called for a critical review of the delays attributable to MSF, emphasizing the fact that malnutrition in its moderate form had long been neglected in the NGO's operations. Thus the issue of treating malnutrition before its most severe stages was raised. This approach was also taken up with UN agencies during a visit to New York in September 2005, but came up against the high tensions arising from the polemic. The path of consensus was soon regained, however. As early as 30 September, in fact, a news release by UNICEF announced a partnership with MSF-Switzerland and the WFP in Zinder for the distribution of supplementary food for malnourished children. The conclusion of the release was eloquent:

In Zinder, MSF, UNICEF and the WFP are working together to carry out the largest targeted supplementary feeding programme in Niger. "This initiative shows the strength of the partnerships and synergies between the actors in the field," said Dr. Aguayo [UNICEF's regional nutritional adviser]. "This joint effort will provide a protective shield for children against severe malnutrition and will reduce infant mortality in Niger."[23]

Conclusion

In the French Senate on 29 September 2005, the two senators entrusted with the mission to evaluate France's assistance for the food crisis prevention and management system in Niger concluded that "the activism of certain non-governmental organizations had the positive effect of putting the issue of infant malnutrition on the agenda" (Sénat, 2005). For MSF, this effect was not a fortunate consequence of the crisis, but the result of a policy. This policy was carried out by combining an emergency aid operation with a strategy whose objectives went beyond the "situational" crisis of 2005. The forms it took—operational decisions, public and polemical position-taking—were shaped by the complex dynamics of the crisis, just as the crisis was shaped by the "activism" of MSF. Clearly, this play of interactions and the multiple rationales of the actors involved cannot be reduced to the cleavage between the "emergency" and "development" approaches. Indeed, this cleavage does not explain why an emergency aid organization had, since 2001, chosen to engage in the treatment of malnutrition in an environment where it was identified as being chronic. Or why this chronic problem did not attract the attention of development decision-makers. Similarly, putting malnutrition on the agenda does not simply indicate reconciliation between the two approaches, which many have called for since 2005. Behind the institutional façades of the so-called "emergency" and "development" actors, what may have been hap-

---

[23] "UNICEF, MSF and the WFP launch a joint nutritional programme in Niger", UNICEF news release, 30 September 2005.

pening during the crisis in Niger was the reassertion of the medical doctor's voice in the field of development policies, which had been dominated for some time by economists and agronomists. To be sure, the role of a northern humanitarian organization in promoting a public health policy in a southern country inevitably raises questions of sovereignty and of such an actor's legitimacy. There are no ready-made answers to these questions, but only a legitimacy of intervention that must constantly be renegotiated.

Translated from French by Frank Bayerl.

BIBLIOGRAPHY

Fassin, D., 2005. *Faire de la santé publique*, Rennes, ENSP.
IRAM, February 2006. *Evaluation du dispositif de prévention et de gestion des crises alimentaires du Niger: Rapport principal.*
————, 2006. *Crises alimentaires au Niger: les politiques de développement dans l'impasse?*
Jaffré, Y., 1996. "Dissonances entre les representations sociales et médicales de la malnutrition dans un service de pédiatrie au Niger," *Sciences Sociales et Santé*, 14 (1): 41–72.
———— and Olivier de Sardan, J.-P., 2003. *Une médecine inhospitalière: Les difficiles relations entre soignants et soignés dans cinq capitales d'Afrique de l'Ouest*, Paris, Editions Karthala, APAD.
LASDEL, 2006. *La crise alimentaire de 2005 au Niger dans la région de Madarounfa et ses effets sur la malnutrition infantile: approche socio-anthropologique*, Rapport principal: Mariatou Kone; preface: Jean-Pierre Olivier de Sardan.
Le Pape, M. and P. Salignon (ed.), 2001. *Une guerre contre les civils: réflexions sur les pratiques humanitaires au Congo-Brazzaville 1998–2000*, Paris, Editions Karthala and Médecins Sans Frontières, (2nd ed. 2003).
Sénat [French Senate], 2005. *Rapport d'information sur la mission d'évaluation et de contrôle du soutien français au dispositif nigérien de gestion de la crise alimentaire*, Rapporteurs: M. Charasse and A. Gouteyron, 29 September.
WFP, *Evaluation de la réponse du PAM à la crise alimentaire au Niger en 2005–2006.*

Part II

CONTEXTS

4

We Aren't the World: The Institutional Production of Partial Success

Kent Glenzer

The humanitarian response in Niger in 2004–6 was not a failure but another in a long line of partial successes in response to slow onset food crises in Africa. Nearly identical warning and response patterns are seen in the Southern Africa food crisis, the 1983–85 crisis and the 1972–74 drought and famine. In West Africa, the similarities extend to the colonial period.

Not only are the patterns of warning and response similar over time, but so too are the fixes proposed after each partial success. These fixes tend to fall into three broad categories: more timely, different, and reliable data; speedier decision-making within the response bureaucracies; or greater focus on disaster risk reduction (prevention). Frequently, these critiques derive from technical, expert discourses (Mitchell, 2002) that view the world through narrow disciplinary lenses, tend to efface power and sociohistorical processes and relationships, and propose what their proponents consider empirical, objective, scientific solutions. The deployers of such expert discourses apparently assume that early warning/response systems are transparently about saving lives and protecting livelihoods: if we can just improve *this* or *that* aspect of early warning data quality and completeness, analysts frequently argue, decision-makers will be convinced to act. What underpins the technical weaknesses of these systems—why the data, no matter how good or accurate they might be, will not in any simple way translate into faster, better, more targeted and effective response—is rarely analyzed deeply. Indeed, few studies pursue the question of why such an early warning/response system, one that is predictably only partially successful, persists over time.

Instead of asking "what's wrong, why, and how can we fix it?" I pose a different set of questions. What are the historical and institutional conditions of where we are, in a situation where partial success is the norm? In what sense is partial success useful, to whom, and for what ends? How is it normal that in slow onset calamities in Africa, the early warning/response complex as a matter of course lets thousands, sometimes tens of thousands of Africans die...and we can be pretty sure that this will be true, too, of the next disaster to strike? And what does such an analysis tell us about power, politics, and postcoloniality in the relief and development enterprise itself?

By "partial success" I mean that many lives are saved by the early warning/response apparatus, but only after substantial numbers of people perish. My core argument is that partial success of the early warning/response complex in slow onset disasters in sub-Saharan Africa is structured into and reproduced by the institutional field of relief and development. Particularly in the case of Niger, I argue that underpinning questions of political will, trust, geopolitical interests, etc. are deep assumptions and beliefs about the Sahel, drought, desertification and the kinds of people who live there. In addition, I argue that dilution, displacement, and blurring of responsibility, authority and accountability for diagnosis and response—always problematic—are exacerbated rather than mitigated by discourses of democracy, good governance, and partnership. Linked to this is the fact—strangely often tacit—that early warning-response systems are not designed for those in need but for those who respond. In such a situation, I argue, incremental improvements to early warning systems alone—better or different indicators, more trust among organizational actors, quicker data provision—will result in but modest gains. Such technical incrementalism may, ironically, enable the comfortable perpetuation of a system in which significant numbers of people die as it achieves predictable partial success.

Drought, desertification, and the normalization of partial success

Discourses of drought, desertification, and precariousness in the West African Sahel have changed significantly in the course of the twentieth century.[1] From 1900 to 1920, despite the occurrence of a drought from about 1910 to 1915 as bad as that of 1968–74, colonial officials and scientists constructed the Niger River basin as a new Nile valley. In 1910, Governor Clozel said that the Niger River valley, "of all the countries of Africa that I know, is the one whose agricultural potential is the largest and most certain".[2] As late as 1920, the French promoted the basin as a "*Mésopotamie nigérienne*" (Vuillet, 1920). Interestingly, colonial agricultural science during this period was fixated on the notion of *acclimatisation*, which aimed to demonstrate that plants could be trained to grow in radically different conditions. The environment *per se* was benign; the challenge of agriculture was to adapt the alien to the local rather than problematize the indigenous. In contrast to later claims, African farmers were described in this early colonial period as hard working, rational, and market-oriented. Comparatively little time or effort was accorded to questions of under- or over-population. Interestingly, British scientists, at the same time, were promoting a much darker vision of desertification in the Sahel and the debate about an expanding Sahara desert was more than 50 years old. Why, given the ample evidence for a very different narrative of the Saharan environment, did such consensus emerge between French scientists and bureaucrats?

Both scientists and administrators were under consistent questioning from critics in Paris. The budget problems of the colonies of Afrique Occidentale Française (AOF) and their need to attract investment made it in the interests of neither scientists nor administrators to construct the Soudanese environment—or its people—as problematic. To do so would have undermined the colonial project. Early warning systems were not needed, for example, only *sociétés indigènes de prévention* (SIPs), village grain banks that would act as buffer to production problems.

Between 1921 and 1950 drought and desertification were more openly acknowledged, but constructed as manageable problems. This evolution

[1] This section has been adapted from Kent Glenzer, "*La Secheresse*: The Social and Institutional Construction of a Development Problem in the Malian (Soudanese) Sahel, c. 1900–1982" (2002).

[2] "*de tous les pays d'Afrique que je connaisse, celui dont l'avenir agricole me paraît le plus vaste et le plus certain*", quoted in Delafosse (1972: p. 11).

reflected a new context. French colonial science was professionalized and scientists rose to positions of power, criticizing bureaucrats for failing to develop the agricultural potential of the AOF colonies. The rise of scientists in the colonial hierarchy dovetailed with the rise of a new scientific discipline, one that would serve the interests of both scientists and bureaucrats: ecology, a discipline that would eventually represent the Earth as a threatened space. The problem, it was thought, was human beings who upset the "natural" ecological balance. Still, the problem of drought and desertification in the West African Sahel prior to independence was deemed by both scientists and bureaucrats as manageable, largely by changing how Africans acted: "This state of equilibrium is upset when man, through forest clearing, excessive farming, and use of fire to clear fields depletes the land."[3]

Prefiguring late 20th century critiques by early warning systems technical experts, French scientists also blamed weak response on politicians and bureaucrats:

Broadly speaking [...] it is regrettable that all decision-making power regarding planned enterprises sits with those who have an economic interest in short-term results [...] It is of utmost importance to establish an appropriate organization, with decision-making powers, that can balance competing interests in matters of planning.[4]

In this particular manner of constructing the problem, short-term economism, bureaucratic inertia and conservatism, and lack of attention to empirical data by politicians and administrators combine with the harmful behaviour of West Africans to block increases in agricultural production and encourage desertification. On the bureaucrats' side, these years were a period of frustration as development efforts in the West African interior failed, customary village leaders in the rural hinterland easily found ways to manipulate the colonial system, and France's global economic, political and moral authority weakened in the wake of World War II. The 1921–50 period also coincided

---

[3] "*Cet état d'équilibre est rompu lorsque l'homme par ses défrichements, la culture excessive, l'incendie et les feux de brousse, détruit la formation végétale*" (Aubréville, 1949: p. 15).

[4] "*D'une façon générale [...] il est regrettable que le seul pouvoir de décision en matière d'entreprises planifiées soit réservé à ceux qui sont intéressés économiquement aux résultats immédiats [...] Il est de la plus grande importance de charger, en matière de planning, un organisme approprié, de jouer un rôle d'arbitre doté de pouvoirs de décision*" (Chevalier, 1950: p. 368). The theoretical similarity here to Niger's *Dispositif* for responding to food crises is revealing. As I will suggest later, such a structure represents a technical fix to what is a political problem, a form of solution that will rarely stand up in times of pressure, conflict, or high stakes.

with a flourishing of commentaries on the problem of under-population as large-scale irrigation efforts around the Niger River consistently failed to attract enough workers to make them profitable. Yet while battling for power and supremacy in the colonial bureaucracy, both administrators and scientists in the AOF in the 1930s–1960s period found it expedient to identify Africans themselves and their behaviour as the central issue facing progress. It remained in nobody's interest to construct drought or desertification as overly determinative of political, economic, or scientific success.

This would change in the post-colonial era. And the change would be due not so much to better data, better science, or new insights about drought, desertification, or livelihoods, but to the institutional apparatus that had, by the mid-1970s, come to characterize development and relief programmes in Africa. Development and relief actors created drought and desertification as a Sahelian problem and were, in turn, created by it in profound if subtle ways.

The great Sahel drought began in 1968—both the FAO and USAID reported on it then and USAID even began responding in 1969—but it was only in October 1972 that African governments requested emergency assistance from the Council of Europe (Hodder, 1973: p. 25). By 1974 the *Wall Street Journal* was issuing the alarmist prediction of 14 million impending deaths and the aftermath of the famine became "the scene of one of the most intensive international development efforts yet to appear in the Third World" (Franke and Chasin, 1980: p. 4). A massive response followed, in which relief aid was used across much of the Sahel for political purposes by African states, targeting of aid provision was amateurish, local grain markets were harmed, tens of thousands of Africans and their livestock perished, aid entrepreneurs enriched themselves, corruption was rampant, and scores of international NGOs planted permanent roots in countries in which they had never worked.

Critics pointed out these shortcomings and in the aftermath began the construction of the early warning and response system that has evolved into what we have today. The critiques were both technical and political; both offered arguments that would surface again in the 1980s, 1990s, and 2000s with regard to the interplay of Northern donor interests and emergency response scope and rapidity. Almost all treated the causative factor—drought and desertification—as unproblematic. However, what a history of drought and desertification discourses reveals is that in many ways, in 1968–72 international donors, the UN, private voluntary organizations, and African governments themselves had not yet learned to see and bracket the Sahelian landscape in a way that permitted the conclusion that hundreds of thousands of people were at risk of starvation. And as the emergency faded, decades- and sometimes century-old questions arose: is the Sahel drying up? Is this irreversible? How much are humans contributing to the problem? But while the questions were similar, they were debated under new conditions and within new discursive frames.

First, the power to define problems and implement solutions had become international by the 1970s, and the locus of decision-making and financial power had shifted to sites external to the region. During the first 60 years of the twentieth century, those responsible for defining environmental problems and implementing solutions also had to live with the effects of their actions. The same was true for Sahelian governments in the 1960s. In the wake of the 1970s drought, however, these responsibilities fragmented. Problem definition, planning, and resource distribution became the domain of external technical agencies and experts (FAO, UNDP, USAID, the many specialized consultancy groups in North America and Europe, etc.). Implementation fell to country-specific actors. And accountability for success was distributed unevenly and somewhat randomly in the system, particularly as donors sought to circumvent autocratic and patrimonial governments through the "NGO decade" (Fowler, 1988) of the 1980s. Accountability for *failure*, however, was crystal clear to most international actors: it belonged to the African state.

Second, this fragmentation occurred within a larger trend of increasing professional specialization (exemplified in the burgeoning numbers of UN specialist agencies, development consulting firms in Europe and North America, and international NGOs) and the formation of a broad and complex organizational field of development and relief organizations that subsisted, grew, and gained influence by obtaining contracts from multilateral and bilateral donors. Third, the problem of population growth had come to the forefront, evolving from a problem of *lack* of adequate numbers of people during colonial times to a new formulation in which *over*population was at the heart of a variety of African problems, including but certainly not limited to environmental degradation. And fourth, guiding notions from the then young discipline of development economics were coming into prominence, acting as a frame for the definition of sector-specific interventions.

These four factors combined to forge the twentieth century's third dominant discourse of drought and desertification in the Sahel. To begin with, the zone was now seen as a permanently precarious place: "The fact is that life in the Sahel is seldom more than a few steps from disaster. Drought is ever present." (USAID, 1977). This new discourse of the environment and development was codified in 1982 when the World Bank linked together the problems of drought and desertification, macro-economic mismanagement, overpopulation, undereducated Africans, and harmful herding and farming practices, and subordinated all to economic growth (World Bank, 1982).

In 1973 the governments of Sahelian countries affected by the drought created the Comité Inter-État de Lutte Contre la Sécheresse au Sahel (CILSS). This intergovernmental body was tasked with developing, implementing, and monitoring a region-wide strategy to address desertification. The CILSS' strategy statements ratified the World Bank's characterization of the problem, giving formalistic African government sanction to the perspective that overpopulation, ecological disequilibrium, harmful farming and herding practices, and lack of indigenous skills and knowledge, were to blame for Sahelian vulnerability.

The problem of the precarious Sahel, as defined in the 1980s, came to be construed as reaching crisis proportions far beyond the ability of African states to address. In this formulation, farmers were seen as trapped in a vast ecological and demographic shift that they could not possibly comprehend, help was to be found only from the outside, and solutions were contextualized within the objectives of Western science and free market economic development as exemplified by the decade's structural adjustment programmes. Such a construction of the problem and solution conjured into existence many of the early warning organizations and systems that remain today. By the mid-1980s, along with the CILSS, the FAO had established its Global Information and Early Warning System (GIEWS), USAID had its Famine Early Warning Systems (FEWS) with representatives in Niamey and other African countries, and the European Union had its Système d'Alerte Précoce (SAP) in neighbouring Mali. In their early days, all of these systems were more or less explicitly focused on funnelling data to donors and northern decision-makers. At root, the role of the international early warning and response system was to inform African governments when they had a problem and to initiate the process through which officials back home in Washington, Ottawa, Brussels, or other Western capitals made the political decisions to respond.

As the 1980s ended, therefore, the international relief community had built a system founded on African incapacity, assuming African corruption, deeply tied to export markets in the North, and focused on accounting for goods moved, not good done. The system constructed the problem as much larger than Africans could possibly handle on their own; therefore it required external experts who collected, analyzed and interpreted data. This produced debilitating gaps between those who diagnosed, those who decided, those who acted, and those whose sovereignty and human rights were at stake. The system also produced rivalry, jealousy, competition, and infighting between donors, UN agencies, independent scientists and academics, and NGOs, although most could unite behind the idea—in the structural adjustment climate of the 1980s—that if only the African state would change then early warning and rapid response would be much better. But this argument was a double-edged sword: the more one looked at issues of sovereignty, the state, and emergency response, the clearer it became that the system required a more credible, trustworthy, reliable African state. The absence of such an entity raised questions about the existence of the entire apparatus: Africa's "third wave of democratization", as Samuel Huntington called it (Huntington, 1991), came just in time.

Democratization and partnership: making partial success even more likely

As the 1990s dawned, the international, regional, and national early warning/ response systems in and for Africa were improving their technical capacities to predict and monitor slow onset crisis while making very little progress on the politics of rapid response. Indeed, one way of understanding the proliferation of early warning and response actors in the 1980s-90s is as a kind of safety valve mechanism through which both Northern and African decision-makers had no need to confront the politics of aid and relief. Competition, jealousy, and ambition among bilateral, multilateral, and expert actors had left decision making about response disjointed and idiosyncratic, while deep distrust between international actors and many African states had created a response system fixated on accountability for commodity donations. The room for manoeuvre for African governments and political leaders was quite high within this loose and multi-polar field. The national—rather than international—politics of rapid response meant that such aid was used, distributed, or rejected for reasons that had nothing to do with early warning data. The value of this system to the early victims of slow onset disasters in Africa was dubious. In many ways, Africa's third wave of democratization and its attendant discourses of good governance and, particularly, partnership exacerbated rather than eased these systemic weaknesses.

As the wave of democratization swept across Africa in the 1990s, early warning and response experts continued to call for different, more and higher quality data to prevent both under- and over-response. Meanwhile, it became increasingly clear that both African and donor state politicians—actors who authorize responses and resources—could contest any data to justify not responding to impending crisis before people began dying. There were almost always discrepancies between GIEWS, FEWS, CILSS, and national EWS analyses. The scope and effectiveness of external responses to disasters often depended more on the economic and political interests of donors than on other factors, such as the objective severity of a crisis, media coverage, or local actor credibility (Olson *et al.*, 2003).

Ironically, the rise of discourses of democracy interlocked with early warning and rapid response systems in ways that were not entirely positive.[5] Democracy and governance discourses in and about Africa had arisen in the wake of a consensus among external actors that Africa's development problems were not historical, post-colonial, or due to structural aspects of the global political economy but, rather, personal, political, and local. Ferguson summarizes the shift in thinking that this entailed:

In place of a modernizing national state bravely struggling against pre-modern ethnic fragmentation, the image now is of a despotic and overbearing state which monopolizes political and economic space, stifling both democracy and economic growth [...] What are called "governance" reforms are needed to reduce the role of the state, and bring it into "balance" with "civil society" (Ferguson, 1998: p. 51).

A central theme of good governance discourses is that of "partnership". "Good governance" is defined as mechanisms and processes that ensure that public resources are correctly managed, and such management requires a "partnership" between the principal actors in the design and implementation of public policy, resolution of public problems, and the allocation and management of resources.

The discursive shifts are visible in the plans and strategies of African states, donors, and local and international NGOs from the mid-1990s. In contrast to such plans in the 1960s-1980s era, each of these actors begins constructing the others as partners in development. Donors describe their role as that of

---

[5] It is useful to remember that discourses of democracy and good governance have a much deeper history in all of Africa. Africans have been hearing about democracy from their leaders since at least World War II and often earlier (Conklin, 1997). Nearly all sub-Saharan African countries adopted some form of democracy upon gaining independence and all but a handful rejected it within a decade.

catalyst, facilitator, and broker of new ideas, not givers of grants and loans. NGOs frequently deploy the same language. States, donors, and NGOs began referring to the poor as "clients", "customers", "consumers" and "citizens" and, of course, as partners too. In contrast to earlier constructions, of the poor as at worst incompetent and at best under-educated, in the 1990s Africans became rational, intelligent, interest-seeking and organization-creating partners in national development strategies. The state and international donors describe their actions as applying a nearly invisible, guiding hand to the project of modernization, limiting themselves to the humble act of identification of the broad strategic lines within which rights-bearing citizens and the private sector further the national development process. Initially constructed as a counterweight to donors, states and global capital in the 1980s, international and local civil society organizations in the 1990s became partners too, judged on their spirit of collaboration and shared sense of mission with their former antagonists.

The discourse of democracy and its relationship to neoliberal economic development became, for an inglorious decade, so obvious and commonsensical that it was difficult to find substantive disagreement. How could one be against free and open markets, democracy, decentralized decision making, political and civil rights, or civic engagement by citizens? Another sign and symbol: country development strategies[6] in the mid-1990s were often co-authored by the UNDP, while World Bank Poverty Reduction Strategy Papers in the 2000s became balletic choreographies of authorship. It became nearly impossible to differentiate between state, donor, and NGO analyses of the development challenges facing a country, and documents and public statements from international development and relief actors repeated constantly the message that the African state was in charge of its own development and that the vast aid and expert bureaucracy developed over the last 30 years was but a modest partner ready to help but never to interfere.[7] The comments of

---

[6] While the utility of such strategies may vary, three clear benefits are that they make it much easier for donors to discipline, to create appearances of equal power between states, and to convince developing country citizens and civil society groups that they have "participated".

[7] Couched, of course, at least from the US government standpoint, within political decisions about whether a particular state deserved US assistance in the first place. Particularly after 9/11, such decisions openly linked US support to national security and anti-terrorism efforts. It is worth remembering that at the time of the Niger crisis, the Bush Administration was under continuous fire about its claims linking Niger to Osama Bin Laden.

Daniel Runde, of USAID's Office of Global Development Alliances, at the height of the Niger crisis exemplify this:

> Well, I think there are a number of things the United States Government does. We're very big supporters of these early warning systems. We also, of course, are large donors of food to the World Food Program. But ultimately, we need to support—we need to continue to support agriculture in developing countries and that we do that in partnership with others. [...P]art of it is working with local governments, part of it is an emergency response, part of it is prevention. So there are a number of parts to that puzzle.[8]

Good governance discourses therefore accomplished the rather impressive feat of making African governments, economic actors, and civil society sectors responsible and accountable for the development and relief efforts for which international technical expert organizations plan, conceptualize, and determine standards, and Northern politicians provide funds. The discourses of partnership, collaboration, and mutual support make it awkward for a state to speak out against the system as, to all appearances, states have been included as equals in the decision-making process. The discourse of good governance and partnership mystifies and obscures the power of donors and Northern/ Western governments to determine African state policy, practice, and what constitutes success. At the end of the day international actors increase their power to determine African state strategies while removing themselves even further from the hair shirt of responsibility and accountability. Meanwhile, in another corner of good governance and partnership discourses far from the arena of crisis response—debt relief—African states are constructed as foundlings or children in need of tough love from the parental international community. These discourses also, however, bring with them an increased insistence on state sovereignty, which, at a pinch, can be invoked by African politicians to confront, modify, and mitigate the power of international actors.

Such prejudices about African political leadership—and such forms of African state resistance—have long existed among donor government politicians. The good governance and partnership discourse of the 1990s-2000s period wraps those prejudices in language that gives the appearance of treating Africans as equals. When these discourses interweave with those of the imperilled Sahelian environment, of the inevitability of drought and desertification,

---

[8] United States State Department, "Global Development Alliance Initiative", Foreign Press Roundtable, 18 April 2006 (http://fpc.state.gov/fpc/64991.htm).

of Africans' harmful practices that contribute to this, it spells particular trouble for the success of early warning and response systems. This is because African states are formally responsible for calling in aid but political decision-makers, some aid officials, and UN bureaucrats actually do not believe they are competent to do so. The image of the Sahel perpetually at risk and the encroaching desert makes African herders and farmers seem recalcitrant to politicians in the North and so less worthy of repeated assistance. The image of recalcitrance—what in an earlier age was constructed as a mass of humanity trapped by irrational tradition, magic, and superstition—is heightened by the fact that democracy and partnership discourses reconstruct African citizens as modern, rational actors, careful calculators of their interests. And prejudices about whether Africans, in Niger and elsewhere, deserve help get entangled with seemingly technical arguments about whether our data are good enough, whether we know enough of the predictive science, and whether African technical staff and politicians are "trustworthy", and concerns about over-responses or responses that do harm. The Niger case from 2004 to 2006 helps us see how this plays out on the ground.

The Niger early warning and response process

The first hints of a potential food shortage came in the summer of 2004 when large swarms of locusts had already spread to parts of the Sahel. The Niger government requested assistance in August 2004, with some media coverage, including *The New York Times*,[9] and again in November, citing a grain deficit of 223,500 tonnes and a pasture shortage of 4.6 million tons (IRIN, 2006).[10] Response, however, was tepid.

The Niger government—with strong backing by international donors, and despite urging by Médecins Sans Frontières (MSF) and other NGOs—at first refused free food distribution, opting instead for a subsidy on grain sales. While MSF and others criticized the Niger state for this, it would have been very difficult for the government to do anything else at this stage and still

---

[9] "Africa: Niger and Chad Appeal for Locust Aid", *New York Times*, 11 August 2004. Another repeated myth about slow onset disasters in Africa is that major media do not cover story until it is a full blown crisis. This is rarely in fact the case, although the stories are not splashed across the front page and television crews are, indeed, late.

[10] IRIN, "West Africa: Year in Review 2005—Hunger in the Sahel." 10 January 2006 (http://www.irinnews.org/S_report.asp?ReportID=51025&SelectRegion=West_Africa).

maintain and reproduce discourses of partnership and consensus between the state and its international donors. Worries about destroying local grain markets are not unwarranted in cases such as Niger, too. But putting concern for possible market disruption as a priority consideration at the start of a response debate inherently puts a brake on the system and contributes to the pattern of partial success we see over the past few decades. And such a principle is reinforced by discourses of drought and desertification which suggest to distant decision-makers that denizens of the Sahel are both hardier and somehow less worth saving than others. Slow, in other words, is okay.

By April 2005, the WFP team in Niger was eventually calling the situation there critical, and in July the Niger emergency hit the international media. With support growing for the WFP's position that free food distribution was now essential, the Niger government relented. On 15 August 2005, the *Washington Times* published an editorial, claiming that the "rich countries are watching the crisis in Niger unfold with horror, as pictures of severely malnourished babies appear in newspapers everywhere" and that "[t]he problems were exacerbated by donor nations' refusal to act more quickly to provide humanitarian assistance" and "the Niger government's refusal to provide free food aid."[11] Niger's first lady, Laraba Tandja, organized a charity concert against hunger in early August. Yet, the following day, her husband President Mamadou Tandja was denying any famine:

There is no famine in Niger. Who said there's famine? Anyone who's seen what's going on here and says there's famine in Niger is saying so for either political or economic interests. If there were famine in Niger, we would all have disappeared, because most of the money in the food pledge has simply not been delivered.[12]

The statement reveals signs of frustration with the international emergency response system, on the part of a leader perhaps wondering himself how many times the system has to "fail" before it works as it is supposed to. Ironically, around that same time, USAID's Assistant Administrator Michael Hess was touring Niger and claimed that the international community's early warning systems were unable to predict all of the shocks to Niger's food market systems and that "to prevent future emergencies USAID is spearheading efforts to improve these vital warning systems."[13] It was a statement that could have

[11] *Washington Times*, 15 August 2005.
[12] Quoted on National Public Radio, "As Aid Arrives, Niger Crisis May Worsen", 16 August 2005 (http://www.npr.org/templates/story/story.php?storyId=4802485).
[13] USAID, "USAID Assistant Administrator Michael Hess Touring U.S. aid efforts in

been—and usually has been—made after any major slow onset disaster in Africa since the 1960s.

With the Niger emergency making television news in Europe and the United States, Western/Northern governments began to make large pledges of aid: by December 2005, around $113 million in pledges had been received, far surpassing initial requests. The discrepancy, the lack of firm connection with "objective" data, and the unpredictable way in which pledges translate into action are all products and evidence of an early warning and response apparatus designed for responders and not for the vulnerable themselves. It is also revealing that once a response was organized in the summer of 2005, it was achieved not through the carefully choreographed dances of partnership, consensus and cooperation but through their breakdown. With that breakdown, as so many times before in Africa, the response system lumbered towards partial success.

Yet the politics of famine relief grated on the Niger government. Once again, it had taken images of starving babies, well-rehearsed stories about the permanently precarious lives of those living in and on the fringes of the Sahara desert ("Why DO those people keep living there?"), and just a *soupçon* of incompetent and probably uncaring and avaricious African leaders to convince political decision-makers and aid officials in Europe and North America to respond. The manner in which the discourse of good governance and partnership can complicate rather than streamline famine response can be seen in the then Prime Minister Hama Amadou's frustration:

During talks on the overall response to Niger's food crisis, Prime Minister Amadou Hama said that some members of the aid sector had undermined the government's credibility and sovereignty by putting more trust in NGOs than in the authorities to save lives.

Hama also said the world must help countries like Niger tackle poverty in the long-term. "It is useless to continue to mobilise short-term aid through the media which relieves just momentarily a mother's angst but leaves her to live through her child's inevitable relapse, and the worry that her other children will be born into the same conditions, because of crippling poverty," he said.[14]

A particular structural feature of Niger's early warning and response apparatus is central to understanding this. In some sense, Niger's government had given up certain aspects of its national sovereignty regarding food security to

---

Niger and Mali", 24 August 2005 (http://www.usaid.gov/press/releases/2005/pr050824.html).

[14] Quoted in IRIN, "West Africa: Year in Review 2005", *op. cit.*

a donor-controlled organization, referred to commonly as the *Dispositif*. The *Dispositif* was intended to provide official early warning data, donors were to keep a grain bank fully stocked for rapid response, and the promise of the *Dispositif* was to remove aspects of trust, perceived government incompetence, corruption, and conflict over data quality and comparability from the calculus of crisis response. What became quickly clear, however, in the early and middle stages of the crisis in Niger was that the actual decision-makers—distant politicians—did not consider the *Dispositif* an authoritative source and, instead, placed greater trust on the data and admonitions of NGOs like MSF.

Hama Amadou was justified in feeling betrayed, particularly when a primary part of the emerging story for media markets in the North was that the government of Niger was to blame for much of the crisis. But most revealing about the structural weaknesses that plague the early warning-response apparatus were aid and Western government officials' explanations for why, once again, the system had only partially succeeded. The French Foreign Minister Philippe Douste-Blazy said the *international community* was guilty of indifference and avarice, while Emmanuel Insch of World Vision Canada said that *the world* all but ignored United Nations warnings of impending disaster.[15] In 2005 Stéphanie Savariaud, spokesperson for the WFP in Niamey, bemoaned the feebleness of prevention because "*the world* has to wait for images of dying children to react."[16] At the height of the Niger crisis in 2005, USAID Assistant Administrator Ed Fox gave a press conference in Washington on the US government's response:

Question: Just a little bit about what is the situation, as you view it, how many people are at risk of literally starving and, you know, there seems to—my impression was that there was some food kind of on its way, but you have like a very short amount of time to get it.

Administrator Fox: First, I'd like to answer that by recognizing the fact that the United States, to its credit and, particularly, the Embassy and our colleagues at the State Department were instrumental in helping *the world* identify this crisis.

It was back in October of last year, in 2004, that the first declaration, disaster declaration, was made by the embassy and called attention—our attention and *the world's* attention to this problem. We sent in some teams from our FEWS NET organization, which is, once again, a United States-founded and organized effort with other countries in the region to monitor, on an ongoing basis, famine indicators.

---

[15] *National Post*, 2 August 2005 (emphasis added).

[16] Quoted in *Associated Press*, "Region on the Brink," 31 July 2005 (http://www.msnbc.msn.com/id/8767038/), emphasis added.

And we made an assessment in November of last year that this problem existed and that extraordinary measures may be needed to address some of the problems. So this, while a crisis, has been something that has been ongoing for several months and that the United States has played a critical role into helping to analyze and *bring to the world's attention.*[17]

The use of "the world" in all these officials' statements is curious and revealing. It usefully displaces responsibility for acting on early warning data from aid officials and their political leaders to a faceless crowd. If "the world" is needed to sanction emergency response, no particular person or organization can be fully accountable or responsible. And so, only when "the world"—not USAID's Director, nor the head of the FAO in Rome—wakes up to the severity of the problem can aid flow. If the 1980s was the time of "We Are the World" around the Ethiopia famine, our highest aid and government officials seem now to prefer "We Aren't the World" and a shell game of accountability for disaster response and prevention.

Later in Fox's press conference, the thin façade of "partnership" and collaboration disintegrates completely:

Question: [T]he United Nations appealed for $81 million in humanitarian aid, up from $16 million. So in other words, they've increased by fivefold their appeal. Can you explain to us what this is for? Is this appropriate? Is this warranted? It seems to be a bit out of sync with some of the picture you're describing for us.

Administrator Fox: Yeah, I—no, you would have to ask the United Nations exactly what they're basing that on. All I can tell you is that the United States, based upon what we know and what we believe the needs are, have contributed generously to this process....But at the moment, we, as I say, feel comfortable that we are appropriately responding to the needs in the amount of about $14 million overall....

Question: Now is this part of the UN appeal or is it separate?....

Administrator Fox: Well, we began to do this in response to our own understanding of what the problem is. There is—this is a direct bilateral effort. We provide this assistance either to, I believe, in this particular case, we're doing it through a variety of nongovernmental organizations on the ground who are implementing partners of ours, such as Africare, CARE, Catholic Relief, Helen Keller, World Vision. [...] The United Nations in its appeal is looking for donations and contributions to either the World Food Program or to them directly....There's some question as to how they add those numbers up. You'd have to ask them exactly what the basis of that counting is...[18]

---

[17] United States State Department, "U.S. Humanitarian Efforts to Food Crisis in Niger", 5 August 2005 (http://www.state.gov/p/af/rls/rm/2005/50866.htm), emphasis added.
[18] *Ibid.*

As happened in Niger with the Prime Minister's complaints about international disregard for his government's figures and opinion, the façade of partnership quickly crumbles at the level of major actors themselves. Governments in both North and South, UN agencies, NGOs, media and experts alike all engaged in finger-pointing and voiced suspicion regarding each other's estimates of the situation.

This situation made clear that whenever it is convenient for those who hold the purse strings and define what constitutes a successful response, an argument can be launched that the data are insufficient, faulty, or just not the right numbers to instigate action. Science, data, and expert knowledge are used cynically by decision-makers to justify any course of action that is politically expedient and affordable.

Arguments that the problems with the early warning response apparatus are technical—there is need for better data, different data, more efficient forms of decision-making, better pre-positioning, etc.—are not wholly incorrect. Yet such technical observations and improvements have consistently failed to create anything but partial success. They are quite likely fated to accomplish more of the same.

Discourses of good governance and of drought, desertification, and the threatened Sahel contribute strongly to the normalization of this state of partial success. They do so by constructing Africans as atomized, individual, self-interested and rationally calculating actors—a cultural construction dear to neoliberals and neoconservatives alike—who clearly have a choice to move away from such vulnerable and fragile zones yet do not. Governance discourses have also reinvigorated the idea of the sovereign African state with rights-bearing citizens through and with whom all development and relief activities are channelled. This is for the most part a fiction: donors and their harems of experts still determine much of development in Africa, Western educated African political and technical elites are more like them than different, and national relief and development policies in Africa are subject to the scrutiny of only a small percentage of the citizenry. Better or different early warning data do not address this.

The fiction is perpetuated through the mantra of partnership, which constructs policymaking and programme development as a collaboration and act of consensus while simultaneously placing accountability for success on Africans themselves. Indeed, donors have profited from this state of affairs by increasing their demands for accountability and proof of "impact" while failing to allocate adequate funds to meet such demands. Meanwhile, macroeconomic policies, practices, and programmes have changed very little in the past decade. The language of partnership also permeates relations between external actors, so that even the most unilateral of actions—USAID's efforts in Niger—is described as collaborative, part of a greater response, and as supportive when in fact it might be just the opposite. Better or different early warning data, at least for an early warning response apparatus that would save all lives rather than just some, do not address this.

The productivity of partial success

In the face of such contradictions, slippages, and displacements of accountability and responsibility, and with a clear history of similar patterns of partial success despite three decades of technical tweaking, we would be wise to ask what such a system accomplishes, and for whom. What, we should ask, does the system do particularly well?

The system I describe in this chapter does five things very well. First, through delays, awkwardness, and resource allocation processes that make Africans beg for help with every major natural calamity, we constantly remind the continent's leaders that the power to save the lives of their citizens is in the hands and bank accounts of others. Second, the system allows Northern politicians and senior aid officials to joust with and send political signals to other Northern politicians and senior aid officials and to spend, build and occasionally lose political capital: Fox's jibes during his press conference at other actors are a small but concrete example. Third, the system provides an interface between technical actors and response decision-makers—politicians and senior aid officials—who would probably act even more cavalierly towards Africa's poor were the system not to exist in its present form. Fourth, the existing system ironically makes expert knowledge both essential *and* moot, in effect placing a premium on knowledge and technology of which most African states possess little, while retaining the right to ignore that knowledge unless it is produced by external actors. And fifth, the current system permits its participants to assuage consciences and at least save most lives while conveniently blaming partial failure on unspecified others ("the world", "the international community", "the media", etc.). All of this is diametrically opposed to the qualities of a system that needs to respond decisively, quickly, and boldly.

A crucial, yet mostly overlooked, aspect of the early warning and response system is that it is designed for responders and not for the vulnerable. Every check and balance is owned by actors other than those at risk of malnutrition, illness, displacement, and death. Numerous actors have the power to stop comprehensive and rapid responses to large-scale and widespread crises while no single actor has the unilateral power to start one. In this context, even well meaning actors are enmeshed in and reproduce discourses that normalize partial success.

The politics of aid is both openly acknowledged by actors with the power to respond—the Prime Minister of Niger, USAID's former Administrator[19]—and then said not to be an issue in the context of any particular response. Indeed, the principle of instrumentalization of aid as a reward for good behaviour and its denial as a punishment for bad behaviour has been adopted as a central guiding principle in USAID's strategic thinking. But the politics of disaster response is not simply a geopolitical technique, a policy option of neorealist strategists. The system's modest power to effect rapid, coherent, and early responses reveals disturbing calculations about the value of African lives. The instrumentalization of aid and the politicization of crisis response are made possible by such unspoken beliefs: instrumentalization is a symptom, not a cause, of what ails the crisis response profession.[20]

When one steps back from the pattern of partial success, the embarrassing fact that thousands of lost African lives *are acceptable* to those with the power to do things differently reveals itself as what it is: a root cause for the system itself. Technical fixations regarding, and fixes to, the early warning and response system obscure this. Response and early warning professionals may or may not believe this; at the very least, they work around actors who do.

For the past 30 or more years, we have fostered a system in which the most important measure of accountability is the least possible quantity of food, money, or other commodities gone missing. Not, for example, the loss of even a single African life to slow-onset crisis. For the past forty years, the tens of thousands of Africans who have died over the years because of system slowness and delays are a shame, an unfortunate side effect that we need to gradually work on and improve. It is possible to imagine a system, however, that

---

[19] "The system of foreign aid is very political", Andrew Natsios, former Administrator of USAID, told *Salon Magazine* in June 2006. "Does it make sense? No." Quoted in *Salon Magazine*, "Starving Season," 13 June 2006 (http://www.salon.com/news/feature/2006/06/13/famine/index_np.html).

[20] Of course, USAID justifies its thinking with a discourse of resource scarcity. Arguments of budget constraints only make sense if we do not question the full range of principles, values, and politics surrounding the way those budgets are constructed and agreed in the first place, however.

reverses these ideas, a system that prioritizes every African life as its starting point and that then repositions waste, corruption, and market disruptions as the unfortunate side effects that need to be worked on gradually. A very different system would arise. A new radicalism is needed if we wish to construct early warning and response systems that are anything but partially successful.

BIBLIOGRAPHY

Buchanan-Smith, M., 1997. "What is a Famine Early Warning System? Can it Prevent Famine?" *Internet Journal of African Studies*, 2, March (http://www.ccb.ucar.edu/ijas/ijasno2/ijasno2.html).

Charlick, R., 1992. "The Concept of Governance and its Implications for AID's Development Assistance Program in Africa", Prepared for the AID Africa Bureau under the Africa Bureau Democracy and Governance Programme, Washington: Associates in Rural Development, Inc.

Chevalier, A., 1950. "La décadence des sols et de la végétation en Afrique Occidentale Française et la protection de la nature", *Revue Internationale de Botanique Appliquée et d'Agriculture Tropicale*, nos. 333–4 (July-August): pp. 349–69.

Conklin, A., 1997. *A Mission to Civilize: The Republican Idea of Empire in France and West Africa, 1895–1930*, Stanford University Press.

Cooper, F. and R. Packard, 1997. "Introduction" in Frederick Cooper and Randall Packard (eds), *International Development and the Social Sciences: Essays on the History and Politics of Knowledge*, 1–41, Berkeley and Los Angeles: University of California Press.

Delafosse, M., 1972. *Haut-Sénégal Niger*, Book 1: *Le Pays, Les Peuples, Les Langues*, Paris: G. P. Maisonneuve et Larose [1912].

Ferguson, J., 1998. "Transnational Topographies of Power: Beyond 'the State' and 'Civil Society' in the Study of African Politics", in H. S. Marcussen and S. Arnfred (eds), *Concepts and Metaphors: Ideologies, Narratives and Myths in Development Discourse*, pp. 45–71, Occasional Paper No. 19, Denmark: International Development Studies, Roskilde University.

Foucault, M., 1980. *Power/Knowledge: Selected Interviews and Other Writings, 1972–1977*, ed. C. Gordon, New York: Pantheon Harvester Press.

Fowler, A., 1988. *Non-Governmental Organizations in Africa: Achieving Comparative Advantage in Micro-Development*, Discussion Paper 249, Institute of Development Studies, University of Sussex.

Franke, R. W. and B. Chasin, 1980. *Seeds of Famine: Ecological Destruction and the Development Dilemma in the West African Sahel*, Totowa, New Jersey: Rowman/ Allanheld.

Glenzer, K., 2002. "*La Sécheresse*: The Social and Institutional Construction of a Development Problem in the Malian (Soudanese) Sahel, *c.* 1900–1982", *Canadian Journal of African Studies* 36, 1: pp. 1–34.

Hodder, B.W., 1973. "Logistics of Transportation, Marketing, Storage and Aid", in R. Dalby and R.J. Harrison Church (eds), *Drought in Africa*, London: University of London.

Huntington, S. P., 1991. *The Third Wave: Democratization in the Late Twentieth Century*, Norman: University of Oklahoma Press.

Mitchell, T., 2002. *Rule of Experts: Egypt, Techno-Politics, Modernity*. Berkeley: University of California Press.

Olson, G. R., N. Carstensen and K. Høyen, 2003. "Humanitarian Crises: What Determines the Level of Emergency Assistance? Media Coverage, Donor Interests and the Aid Business", *Disasters* 27, 2: pp. 109–26.

Simmons, I. G., 1993. *Interpreting Nature: Cultural Constructions of the Environment*, London: Routledge.

USAID, 1977. *United States Response to the Sahel Drought: 3rd Special Report to the Congress on the Sahel Drought*, Washington, DC: Government Printing Office.

Vuillet, J., 1920 "L'Agriculture dans le pays de Ségou", *Renseignements Coloniaux*, 11 (November): pp. 169–86.

de Waal, A., 1997. "Democratizing the Aid Encounter in Africa", *International Affairs*, 73, 4: pp. 623–39.

Watts, M., 1984. *Silent Violence: Food, Famine, and Peasantry in Northern Nigeria*, Berkeley and London: University of California Press.

World Bank, 1982. *Accelerated Development in Sub-Saharan Africa*, Washington, DC: World Bank.

5

The Paradox of Chronic Aid

Benedetta Rossi[1]

Introduction

The 2005 Niger crisis was characterized by ongoing debate over the interpretation of child malnutrition. In Niger aid informs governance, setting criteria for monitoring, classifying, and acting upon the state of the country and its people. At the beginning of 2005, early warning systems focusing primarily on cereal production and price dynamics failed to notice a steep increase in cases of child malnutrition. By April 2005 MSF, echoed by other emergency NGOs, announced that the numbers of severely undernourished children admitted to their centres had increased beyond expected levels, and that available surveys showed levels of child malnutrition in Niger reflecting a situation "comparable to that of countries at war" even in years of normal production. Other commentators claimed that child malnutrition was structural, and should not be seen as indicative of famine. The debate between different interpretations of children's emaciated bodies was referred to as "the paradox of chronic emergency", and actors were divided between partisans of long-term "development" or short-term "emergency" solutions. This debate illustrates how aid institutions think (Douglas, 1987): the early warning systems' selective blindness with regard to health indicators and the selective deafness of

[1] Research for this paper was supported by a three-year Economic and Social Research Council Research Fellowship, including one year of Niger-based fieldwork in 2005.

105

"urgentistes" and "developers" to each other's arguments revealed the proclivity of institutions to treat fatless bodies as "signs" in their normative systems of reference. In the face of hardship, poor Nigériens relied primarily on endogenous strategies, which reflected their own (in the case considered here, Hausa) interpretations of child thinness and disease. These strategies were coupled to efforts directed at understanding how aid institutions "think", and thereby taking advantage of whatever aid was available.

As aid workers toured the country examining "signs" of crisis, poor mothers visited rehabilitation centres trying to understand on what basis their thin children would be admitted, so that they could benefit from free treatment and stocks of food for the entire family at a time when cereal prices were 92% higher than the previous year (IRAM, 2006: p. 14). Faced with aggravation of the poverty of Nigérien households, aid agencies exhibited great dynamism. They were able, after considerable debate, to agree on a course of action and to meet the objectives they had set for themselves (WFP, 2006: p. 30). More important, many human lives were saved. But despite the good intentions and technical competence of individual aid workers, aid to Niger may turn out to contribute to the recurrence of such crises. It has already been noted that, by depoliticizing its effects, aid induces its self-perpetuation (Ferguson, 1990: p. 256; Escobar, 1995: p. 9). This paper argues that the abolition of famine in Niger requires the (self) transformation of famine victims into rights-holding political actors, and that international strategies to grant destitute people access to food may be entrenching, rather than reducing, their political voicelessness.

"Crisis" in policy and in practice

While in a democracy governors are answerable to the governed for their actions, and may lose the support of their voters should their governance be perceived as misguided, "little democratic accountability has operated in respect of contemporary global governance arrangements" (Scholte, 2004: p. 211). This is due to the *de facto* capacity of international institutions to impose their rules and perspectives upon weaker states and subjects, even though they are assumed to derive their legitimacy from the consent of all participating governments (Held and Koenig-Archibugi, 2004: p. 125; Soederberg, 2004: p. 2). Different groups enrol into policy programmes for different reasons. Ministers in poor countries may enrol in a particular policy as a condition for obtaining loans and development assistance. Destitute people support policies that increase their chances to avoid hunger or obtain jobs. Yet, choosing whether or not to participate in one or the other aid programme is often not an option for them. Scholars have argued that politically marginal actors, enrolled willingly or unwillingly in different policy models, attempt to turn to their own ends policies that are not of their own design. The greater the disparity in power between dominant and subordinate, the more the subordinate will appear to accept the hegemony of dominant discourses. Those Nigériens who are most exposed to hardship cannot negotiate the terms in which development is framed. Yet they maintain some control over interventions that concern them by reinterpreting and manipulating aid in surreptitious ways. On the other hand, policy is produced by individuals and groups able to represent the "crisis" in policy.

In the case discussed in this paper, international institutions were struggling to reduce the increased mortality of children, in the context of Nigériens' lowered ability to access food. Humanitarian efforts enrolled in their vision a number of originally dissenting actors, including Niger's government, and thereby were able to prevent the death of many children. But the corollary of their success should give us pause. First, it was as victims of "famine", rather than as rights-holding citizens, that the right to food of poor Nigériens was recognized. Second, aid intervention makes up for the failure of national governments to guarantee citizens' access to food, and thereby shifts the axes of accountability away from where they should lie. Thus, unwillingly, humanitarian organizations inhibit the transformation of famine victims into political actors able to use political instruments to avoid the onset of famine. Instead, they encourage them to use their dispossession instrumentally to obtain food or support from international organizations that are not politically accountable to them.

The majority of Niger villagers are cut off from the "network society" (Castells, 1996) where global activism is possible. They cannot join global civil society networks mobilizing, for example, on the internet and through demonstrations at G8 meetings. They are aware of their slight chances of influencing the workings of policy, and have found ways to reap some benefits from their inevitable integration in the field of aid. Interacting in their everyday life with aid's more concrete facets, they relate to aid as one more potential source of income (along with labour migration, farming, herding, and other ways to make a living). Their tactics are different from political representation through voting and delegation. They rely upon forms of brokerage that fit policy rationales (Bierschenk et al., 1999; Lewis and Mosse, 2006). Inducing one's children's weight loss may prove a more effective way to gain access to free food than voicing political demands. But if political participation is not to be foregone in favour of economic need, or even health need (Sen, 1999: pp. 146–59), aid institutions should reflect carefully on the structural effects of their intervention.

Counting fatless bodies

The Niger crisis became a matter of international concern in April 2005, when MSF announced that the numbers of undernourished children admitted to their centres signalled the onset of a major nutritional crisis (IRAM, 2006: p. 11). This announcement sidestepped what was considered one of the best performing early warning systems in the region, which, focusing on food production, had interpreted the country's situation as being somewhat worse than usual, but not critical. The debate became polarized in two positions, one giving prominence to cereal production and the other to headcounts of undernourished children as primary indicators of crisis. While the national cereal deficit had been estimated at 12% of global production for that year, localized nutritional surveys carried out by some NGOs found levels of malnutrition comparable to those of countries at war (Delsol and Prevel, 2005: p. 3; IRAM, 2006: p. 66). A discussion ensued on whether high levels of child malnutrition should be seen as indicative of a country-level emergency or a famine. Emergency NGOs decried the paucity of reliable information on the nutritional status of the population in the early warning systems (Jézéquel, 2005: pp. 8, 29). While most commentators agreed on this point, some suggested that child malnutrition is chronic in countries like Niger, and should not be considered as equivalent to famine (AFD, 2006: p. 4; LASDEL, 2006: p. 7). Other authors argued that Western audiences misread the situation on the basis of their tendency to associate widespread child malnutrition with famine: "For the public opinion in the West, the equation 'child malnutrition = famine' has become self-evident. But this equivalence is false." (Olivier de Sardan in LASDEL, 2007: p. 7; my translation). Irrespective of what the true or false signs of "famine" may be, here I am concerned with what Foucault calls discursive "truth-effects", which influence how a specific problem (in this case, child health) is addressed.

In a highly informative and carefully researched study, Mariatou Kone pointed out that "malnutrition" is not a relevant nosological category in Hausa folk medicine, where children's extreme thinness is attributed to other conditions, none of which finds an appropriate translation in "malnutrition" (LASDEL, 2006: pp. 37–9). The report suggested that the 2005 crisis, and particularly the forms of care introduced by MSF and other NGOs, had induced both the appearance of malnutrition as a medical condition amongst villagers and a heightened concern with child malnutrition in national public health institutions (LASDEL, 2006: p. 10). But I would rather suggest that what was observed in the 2005 crisis was not so much the "discovery" of malnutrition in rural Niger but a confrontation between the different nosopolitics of local, national and international actors (Foucault, 1980: p. 166). That is to say, following Foucault, that health policy reflects historically rooted understandings of health and disease. These understandings do not overlap across Niger villages and international health organizations. The 2005 crisis may have contributed to bringing forth such an alignment, or it may have merely made both parties aware of their differences. In any case, it is worth pointing out that child health has been a contested discourse in European history also, undergoing profound changes in its conceptualization and in the definition of practices of child care and medicine (Rollet-Echalier, 1991).

We do not have consistent and comparable time-series data on child malnutrition in Niger. Yet, when nutritional assessments were carried out in various regions, the results were consistently described as "alarming". This was the case with the 1992 and 1998 CARE administered Demographic and Health Surveys, and the 2000 national multiple indicators survey conducted by UNICEF in cooperation with Niger's government. In the first months of 2005, however, MSF was still alone in Niger in treating severe malnutrition in its therapeutic units, located in the south of the Maradi region. By July 2005 the media had raised international awareness on Niger's situation. Other indicators, primarily a steep growth of cereal prices, led to the adoption of an emergency plan, while no consensus was reached on how to interpret the increase in the numbers of malnourished children. Between July and December 2005, the number of nutritional rehabilitation centres in the country grew from 144 to 861. In the same period, at least four nutritional surveys were conducted by several institutions in Maradi, Zinder and Tahoua and at national level, while the cases of severely undernourished children accepted in inpatient and outpatient nutritional centers grew from 15,800 to 69,300 and those of moderately undernourished children admitted to nutrition programmes went from 38,000 to about 180,000; 75,650 children were targeted by preventive operations (WFP, 2006: p. 25). These changes reflect the onset of a different way to address child health on the part of governance institutions. As the stimulus for such change was exogenous, it is difficult to predict whether new rationales of child nutrition and care were actually appropriated by Niger's state and Nigérien people and, if so, whether the change will be long-lasting.

In 2005, the debate hinged upon identifying the appropriate label for the "crisis". In an interview with the BBC on 9 August 2005, President Tandja denied that Niger was experiencing famine and suggested that the idea of a famine was being exploited for political and economic gain by opposition parties and aid organizations. In a follow-up comment a WFP spokesman, Greg Barrow, told the BBC "we have not spoken about famine but about pockets of severe malnutrition."[2] The Niger President's statement and the debate that followed it constitute negotiations over how Niger's problems should be interpreted. The famine label is not neutral. How a "crisis" is interpreted determines how it should be acted upon. Whether a situation is or is not characterized as "famine" influences how much money can be spent, where and how it should be spent, and who should administer relief funds and operations. The plight of poor people of Niger hardly makes it to the news, unless, as in 2005, it can get there under the "famine" label. This raises the question of whether Niger's problems could receive international attention in the absence of high media-shock potential and strategic relevance for donor countries.

Famines lend themselves to political manipulation. Because they appeal to important humanitarian values, they can be used instrumentally by politicians and the media. In Niger's history, famines have worked as a destabilizing factor in presidential careers, and the recurrence of presidential elections in November 2004 prevented the disclosure of early crisis indicators by Nigérien sources (Jézéquel, 2005: p. 33). When, by the spring of 2005, the international media publicized the situation, the diffusion of pictures of undernourished children set off reactions that escaped the control of the institutions directly involved. Images of famine precipitate a chain of associations in international public opinion that have consequences of their own. Reports on the 2005 crisis recognized the media as new powerful actors in shaping public representations of Sahelian crises, adding a new level of complexity to their management (IRAM, 2006: p. 62; WFP, 2006: p. 15; AFD, 2006: p. 5).

While the media tended to characterize the situation as a "famine", the word "crisis" was retained in expert reports and policy documents, pointing to the disorientation of aid institutions confronted with problems that did not

[2] Quoted in BBC News, 9 August 2005 (http://news.bbc.co.uk/2/hi/africa/4133374. stm).

conform easily with existing policy discourses. Expost assessments explained this confusion, reflected in prolonged debate and hesitation to identify a course of action, as due to the exceptional nature of the 2005 crisis:

> The 2005 food crisis differed, in its nature and evolution, from the other crises that have affected Niger heretofore, which were essentially "supply crises". [...] The [2005] crisis did not follow the "typical" structure [*le schéma "habituel"*] of falling cereal production due to external shocks, which is the scenario monitored by the SAP; thus, the proportions it would assume were not "announced" in advance. (IRAM, 2006: p. 1, my translation)

But the 2005 "crisis" only appears exceptional and unusual from the perspective of aid organizations preoccupied with fitting it into existing rationales and their own institutional mandates. Even though Niger has, in the past, experienced famines largely due to discrepancies between food supply and demand, it has been widely acknowledged, at least since the publication of Amartya Sen's *Poverty and Famines* in 1981, that a decline in food availability is not the only indicator of a crisis.[3] Even shifting the focus from "food supply" to "food availability" is not sufficient, on its own, to understand the 2005 crisis and work to prevent its recurrence. The focus on food should be replaced with a focus on livelihoods, health, and the political accountability of various (national and international) aid structures to those Nigériens who experience the crisis in practice. To be sure, this view informed the understanding of most consultants, who produced rich and insightful reports on every aspect of the crisis. But it was overshadowed by the debate between partisans of "development" or "emergency" solutions.

"The paradox of chronic emergency"

The "paradox of chronic emergency" is not an appropriate characterization of Niger's situation, which is not paradoxical, but can be explained by an analysis of the multiple problems confronting different sectors of Nigérien society. Olivier de Sardan suggests rightly that the "paradox of chronic emergency" and the ensuing debate between the humanitarian and development approaches shed light on the functioning of the aid apparatus more than on the phenomena they purport to explain: "We know very well that many international organizations (and MSF in particular) built their identity in this

---

[3] "Starvation is the characteristic of some people not *having* enough food to eat. It is not the characteristic of there not *being* enough food to eat." (Sen, 1981: p. 1).

debate (it is their history and their right). But we are dealing here primarily with a contradiction internal to the North, with typically North-North politics, that sometimes appears puzzling seen from Niamey" (LASDEL, 2006: p. 11, my translation).

The few available nutritional surveys suggest that child malnutrition levels in Niger are consistently and chronically beyond levels characterized as "critical" by international conventions on these matters. Such levels, usually found in countries at war or amongst displaced groups, call for "emergency" operations managed by humanitarian actors. Emergency aid is usually short term, and relies vastly on its own structures and logistics, which are discontinued once a famine is declared ended. But in Niger, judging by nutritional and health statistics, the fluctuation of cereal prices, and other indicators of social development, "emergency" conditions are recurrent and/or chronic, and therefore should fall into the agenda of institutions focused on addressing long-term "development" issues. Niger's situation is seen as paradoxical because it contradicts the institutionalized division of labour between humanitarian and aid organizations. The "paradox", as perceived and debated by aid actors, is clearly summarized in the IRAM report:

Schematically, positions were divided between two perspectives bearing upon different referents: (1) humanitarian actors considered that the observed levels of severe malnutrition attested to the gravity of the crisis and justified, alone, the distribution of free emergency aid; (2) development and prevention actors evaluated the crisis on the basis of less alarming information provided by the food security apparatus. They were troubled by the situation and the critiques, but lacked the means to assess the nutritional dimension of the crisis. In the course of this debate, at the end of June, MSF attacked head-on the government, donors, and the food secuity system. On a visit to Niger (20–25 July), the CILSS Executive Secretary criticized an exaggeration of the crisis' gravity by the media, international agencies and NGOs. And on 9 August the President declared that in Niger there was no famine, but only a serious food crisis. (IRAM, 2006: p. 22, my translation).

The terms "emergency" and "development" are a function of institutional criteria of classification. In Niger the persistence of severe poverty violates the internal boundaries of the aid apparatus. "Chronic emergency" is perceived as an oxymoron by institutions whose approaches are predicated, alternatively, upon "emergency" or "chronic poverty" rationales. In 2005, conflating these two discourses amounted to blurring an operational distinction between two distinct intervention schemes. This type of problem is not restricted either to the world of aid or to "North-North" reasoning. Thus, for example, similar conundrums characterize debates on how to cure people affected by "chronically terminal" conditions, with participants asking whether patients should receive curative care provided by standard medical treatment, or should be referred to institutions that deal with terminal patients (cf. Ward, 2006).[4] Such apparent paradoxes illustrate the institutional reasoning behind situations that do not fit clearly in any one particular institutional mandate.

Activists engage in interpretive struggles to support lines of action that they believe, at any one time, to provide more effective solutions to human suffering. Mary Douglas reminds us that individuals making life and death decisions do so from within the workings of institutional thinking: "Who shall be saved and who shall die is settled by institutions. Putting it even more strongly, ratiocination cannot solve such problems. An answer is only seen to be the right one when it sustains the institutional thinking that is already in the minds of individuals as they try to decide" (Douglas, 1987: p. 4).

The separation between the logics of "development" and "emergency" intervention models becomes more problematic when it is projected onto Nigérien society, mistaking divisions that belong to policy discourses for real boundaries between "normal poverty" and "critical poverty": "In Sahelian countries, where the border between 'normal poverty' and 'crisis periods' is so thin, the future challenge lies in identifying and carrying out rural poverty reduction strategies able to simultaneously target short-term necessities with long-term development objectives" (WFP, 2006: p. 34, my translation). Clearly, the multiple dimensions of the crisis are not compartmentalized. But they appear to be so to institutions forced to modify the boundaries of their institutional mandates. As we have seen, this way of reasoning underpinned representations of the 2005 "crisis" as unusual and paradoxical. It only makes sense to talk of a "paradox of chronic emergency" from within the confines of institutional thinking. Aid institutions, mostly functioning through Northern funding, depend on "intervention" and their thinking conforms to their interventionist nature. Their models for intervention are projected onto the world, and their strategies are thereby justified (Douglas, 1985: p. 92).

Media reporting of this debate reproduced the dichotomy between "chronic poverty" and "emergency". The US-funded crop forecasting website FEWS stated that: "Although the willingness of much of the world to address these 'famine' conditions in Niger is appropriate and welcome, without a similar commitment and prolonged attention to addressing the chronic issues

---

[4] K. Ward, "OpEd—Hospice moves to redefine chronic illness as terminal", North Country Gazette, 26 September 2006 (www.northcountrygazette.org/articles/092606ChronicTo Terminal.html).

that are at the heart of the current localized crises, the same problems will re-occur again soon".[5] The WFP Niger Country Director, Gian Carlo Cirri, also emphasized the long-term dimension of the crisis: "Niger has sadly slipped down the international agenda, which could have disastrous consequences for those who are still suffering from this year's crisis. But Niger needs more than a quick fix—it needs sustained and targeted support to help it out of its crushing poverty once and for all".[6] Along similar lines, Professor William Easterly of New York University argued that Niger had not experienced a sudden catastrophe in 2005, but chronic malnutrition making people vulnerable to rises in food prices.[7] Other commentators reiterated the emergency nature of the crisis. Referring to the above-mentioned FEWS position, an ODI Briefing Note claimed that "the fact remains that current levels of malnutrition are above crisis levels, and therefore warrant an emergency response. To argue that such levels are 'normal', even if true, is dangerously beside the point."[8]

The debate illustrated above did not result in deadlock. After initial disagreements on the nature of the crisis, in July 2005 the WFP opted for the adoption of an emergency strategy aimed primarily at "saving human lives", which led to the implementation of emergency measures, including free food distribution (IRAM, 2005: p. 15; WFP, 2006: p. 19). This decision was initially perceived by the representative of Niger's government as a unilateral choice that bypassed the Niger authorities, and contradicted the "spirit" of existing food-security structures in which responsibility is split between the government (the food security structure being coordinated by the Prime Minister) and international donors represented by the WFP (IRAM, 2006: p. 16; Jézéquel, 2005: p. 22). But eventually all actors aligned themselves with the WFP, and most ex-post evaluations of the operation considered its action successful. A number of recommendations indicated how the system could learn from the 2005 crisis. These called for improved monitoring of the health and nutritional state of the population; better coordination of the strategies of different development actors; and strengthening of the food-security apparatus and strategies of response to crises.

---

[5] Cf. article by David Loyn, "How many dying babies make a famine?", BBC News, 10 August 2005 (http://news.bbc.co.uk/2/hi/africa/4139174.stm).

[6] Quoted in WFP press release, "Niger faces prolonged suffering: more aid urged," 23 November 2005 (http://www.wfp.org/english/?ModuleID=137&Key=1932).

[7] BBC News, 1 February 2006 (http://news.bbc.co.uk/2/hi/africa/4185550.stm).

[8] HPG Briefing Note, "Humanitarian Issues in Niger", Overseas Development Institute (http://www.odi.org.uk/hpg/papers/HPGBriefingNote4.pdf).

The debate continued after the crisis ended, with some suggestion that the divide between development and emergency views may be overcome by an integrated, if not unified, position (WFP, 2006). These changes may signal a turn towards the consolidation of new nosopolitics in developing countries, but they do not indicate a change in how the aid apparatus works. In this process, Niger's problems are reduced to a question of discursive alignment behind the arguments of "*urgentistes*", "developers", or more conciliatory integrated positions. The rules and stakes of the game remain structurally unchanged. For all its internal merits, this debate deflects attention away from the dependence on aid and political voicelessness of rural Nigériens.

Nigérien dimensions of the crisis

If one shifts from institutional thinking to a more comprehensive approach to Niger's socio-economic situation, the 2005 crisis appears far less paradoxical. While in Niger agricultural production has been growing at a rate of 2.2% per year, over the 1990s Niger's population has been growing at a rate of about 3.45%, doubling every 20 years (Jézéquel, 2005: pp. 6–7). At a national level, the growing cereal deficit has been compensated by imports, primarily through informal channels from Nigeria, encouraged by a devalued naira (which made Nigerian goods cheaper for Nigériens), and by Nigerian demand for CFA francs, pegged to the euro and guaranteed international convertibility. In the mid-1990s, the 50% devaluation of the CFA franc and changes in Nigerian cereal supply led to a rearrangement of regional trade dynamics, and to Niger's increased dependence for cereal imports on other West African countries, including countries of the Franc Zone (IRAM, 2006: p. 38). For Niger, this enlarged regional integration of cereal markets signifies, *inter alia*, greater competition with its richer neighbours over access to cereals and increased volatility of the determinants of cereal prices.

Even though overall production has increased, the progressive cultivation of marginal lands and the shrinking size of farm units are resulting in chronic production deficits for a growing number of rural households. Indicators of social inequality and the percentage of "poor" households have been rising over the last ten years. As inherited plots of land shrink, a class of landless peasants grows. The farming potential of lands in the region at the interface between the savanna and the desert is not similar everywhere, and depends on geomorphology and soil type. In regions characterized by poor quality soils, the annual amount of rainfall is less important than rain distribution. A dry interval longer than ten days, depending on when it occurs in a plant's growth, may retard or kill the growth of grains (Faulkinghan and Thorbahn, 1975: p. 464). Rains are highly localized, and pockets of drought affect certain regions even in years marked by overall higher than average rainfall (cf. Raynaut, 1975: p. 30; Swift, 1975: p. 90). During multi-year droughts, reserves are consumed early by family members and relatives in need, and this leads to the collapse of traditional safety nets. When their own stocks are depleted and wealthier relatives' willingness and capacity to help has been eroded, poorer households fall into debt.

The state has food security reserves, which it releases to stabilize cereal supply and prices during shocks. However, the quantities made available are insufficient to cover the needs of areas affected by food shortage, and distribution is often marred by poor logistics and corruption (Keenan, 2005: p. 408). Wealthy merchants purchase grain in quantity at the harvest, operating through close trade networks (Gregoire, 1992; Najman, 2006: p. 17). They resell it in rural areas at high margins of profit, often stocking millet until its price has risen. Speculators tend to release stocked cereals through trade networks reaching myriad small rural markets, which are not included in surveys. This trading system conceals increased cereal supply by breaking it up into small, widely scattered quantities. This explains in part why commentators still disagree on the role played by Nigérien traders in the crisis. My own research confirms that speculative strategies are constitutive of marketing practices in Niger. The supply side is usually able to impose prices because demand is based on structural deficit.

The trade system works like a rhizomic structure (Gregoire, 1992). At its top, the biggest traders have ties to politicians at the highest national and international levels (Jézéquel, 2005: p. 33). Often, these merchants are also large producers and creditors to poorer farmers who pay back in kind at high interest rates. While they are able to take advantage of the system, they also invest in it by employing and supporting cohorts of clients, giving alms, and meeting the continuous demands of kin and associates. They are often involved in endogenous development, and may finance privately the maintenance of roads and other important infrastructure. The most important of these businessmen can employ hundreds of people as farming labour on their fields and as drivers, intermediaries, mechanics, and manual labour to load their trucks, build and guard store-houses, and fill cereal bags. They have assistants who monitor specific trade networks and who, in turn, rely on collaborators. A large part of the stocks are siphoned off away from the main markets through a network of retailers (often buying on credit) who resell them in geographically marginal villages. Here cereals are sold in small quantities, at the highest prices, to the least mobile people (mostly elderly and wives of migrants), who rely primarily on the help of relatives (local and far) and secondarily on bought food.

Poor infrastructure and high costs of transport increase the vulnerability of people settled in scarcely productive hinterland regions. Only about 8% of Niger's road network is paved. Dirt roads are the main avenues connecting rural areas to urban centres, where consumer goods (including food) and services are available. The state lacks resources to maintain the rural road network, and communications may be interrupted for days during the rainy season, when dependency on bought food is highest. The rising price of oil functions like a tax on food and services, which weighs disproportionately on the population living in the rural hinterland. Lack of access to credit at reasonable rates undermines the capacity of subsistence farmers to buy food, seeds, and agricultural inputs. Small-scale farmers who have literally "eaten up" all of their stocks may fall into debt to buy seeds and agricultural inputs at the beginning of the farming season. The decision to take a loan, sometimes at high interest rates, is related to expected returns from farming. The owners of marginal lands who have consumed all of their stocks, including seed, may give up farming for one or more consecutive seasons and instead work as agricultural labourers in neighbouring villages, earning cash to cover immediate family subsistence needs. Travelling in the rainy season, it is possible to see farms left uncultivated because immediate food needs require the poorest farmers to sell their labour on wealthier people's farms and neglect their own fields, or leave them in the care of their wives and children. In regions where land is more valuable, pledging is common (LASDEL, 2006: p. 27).

The migration of one or more family members after the harvest is a way to decrease pressure on household stocks and, when possible, to save cash to cover the following agricultural season's household food needs. In small rural centres, locally available employment opportunities are very few. In these circumstances, "migration is the strategy by which villagers avoid starvation" (Painter, 1987: p. 6; Rain 1999: p. 202). Usually the members of extended families alternate different migratory/productive strategies amongst them across years: one brother may be an international migrant, while another farms in the village and a third relative works for wages in a nearby town. Migration is possibly the most important way to supplement local production. In the dry season (from September to May), the inhabitants of hundreds of small villages and hamlets settled on marginal lands cannot find employment opportunities locally. This accounts for a high dependency ratio on migrants' remittances in sending areas (Faulkingham and Thorbahn, 1975: p. 472), and for the vulnerability of Nigérien households to economic retrenchment in the countries of destination (Main, 1989). Thus, product and labour market integration of coastal and Sahelian countries reflects the subordination of the latter to the former, which constitute poles of labour attraction and have a superior buying power.

As shown in other contributions to this book, women whose husbands practise long distance labour migration are *de facto* heads of household for a varying number of months every year, or for a number of consecutive years. Migrant husbands may be unable to support their families, and multi-year droughts put a strain on local support networks. Gender ideologies limit the range of opportunities available to women responsible for their own and their dependents' subsistence. Control over family labour is another important factor in the politics of household subsistence. Male migration induces heavy reliance on child labour by mothers, accounting, *inter alia*, for Niger's very high fertility rates (Lesthaeghe, 1986).

There is regional variation in the dynamics that characterize recurrent Niger crises, which could be explained more accurately as the interaction of localized crises than as a uniform drought-induced threat of starvation. Structural unemployment and production deficit characterize the livelihoods of the poorest Nigériens, who reduce the risk of livelihood failure by diversifying productive activities and relying on networks of mutual support. A large proportion of Niger's population is vulnerable to recurrent crises: life expectancy at birth is 46 years; with an average of eight births per woman, Niger has one of the highest fertility rates in the world; it has the second highest mortality rate of children below five; 25.1% of men and 9.3% of women are literate; and more than 60% of the population lives below the $1/day threshold. "Chronic emergency", or more simply structural poverty, is what one would expect. As described in previous sections of this chapter, institutional thinking casts these complex socio-economic processes into one or the other intervention scheme. This induces institutional self-preservation. It ties the release of aid to the identification of variously characterized "signs" of (chronic or urgent) poverty, thereby encouraging brokerage tactics to display poverty instrumentally in order to obtain support. The following section suggests that aid agencies should resist being caught in this dynamic, and instead should strive to identify strategies that will gradually enable poor Nigériens to translate their demands into political action.

Conclusion: The paradox of chronic aid?

During the 2005 crisis the separation between humanitarian assistance and development actions functioned as a *modus operandi* of the system, and debates around "the paradox of chronic emergency" recurred in policy documents and in the press releases of aid institutions. These debates were well meaning. They constituted attempts to enrol supporters for strategies perceived as most effective in action against hunger and poverty. Neither of these positions was inherently "wrong". Free food distribution, arranged and financed by donors and international organizations, does not address the structural causes of widespread malnutrition. But indeed, as the supporters of humanitarian assistance remind us, they save lives that would otherwise be lost while we wait for the results of development actions, which have often proven misconceived or even counter-productive. The "chronic poverty" or "famine" labels that were used to define the 2005 crisis imply different intervention approaches, means and solutions. Aid workers and potential beneficiaries are engaged in a political struggle over meaning (Carney and Watts, 1990; Cooper, 1995), which consists in framing the "crisis" along one or the other model, while trying to enrol various audiences in their respective interpretations. Poor Nigériens cannot frame the terms of the debate, but they understand the rules of the game. They have become rhetorical specialists, proffering ad hoc answers to visiting aid workers, in the hope of gaining access to income generated by aid, taking various forms—sometimes free food, other times recruitment on projects. Development brokerage can be seen as a fallback position of voiceless citizens, silenced by their own political and economic dispossession. This is not to portray aid recipients as passive. Indeed, brokerage is one more way by which poor people, making a virtue of necessity, effectively manage to add aid income to ingeniously diversified livelihood portfolios. At the same time, it exposes the workings of a system in which the axes of accountability are not where democratic principles of government would expect them to be.

Amartya Sen has argued that India's success against famine was due fundamentally to respect for political and civil liberties and functioning democratic institutions (Dreze and Sen, 1989; Sen, 1990). Alex de Waal has criticized international humanitarianism which, through reference to universal rights and technical solutions, weakens the forms of political accountability that underlie the prevention of famine, while itself benefiting from the deficit of accountability that characterizes all forms of international governance (de

Waal, 1997). Rural Nigériens, like the citizens of many African states, are doubly removed from democratic mechanisms of political accountability. First, national governance institutions are characterized by factionalism, clientelism and, sometimes, outright corruption. Second, international organizations are able to impose their policies on African states. In the 2005 crisis, this situation was bitterly commented upon by Niger's Prime Minister, who regretted that donors "believe that, in order to save Nigérien lives, they should trust NGOs and international charitable institutions better than the government" (quoted in IRAM, 2006: p. 21, my translation).

De Waal has suggested that "generalised, internationalised responsibility for fighting famine is far less valuable than specific, local political accountability" (1997: p. 5). Recognizing this does not deny the important role that international humanitarian institutions can play, but it forces us to put their role and long-term objectives in perspective. More importantly, it reminds us that the aid system should strive towards the achievement of an anti-famine political contract between Niger citizens and their chosen representatives: "an anti-famine political contract involves several things, including a political commitment by government, recognition of famine as a political scandal by the people, and lines of accountability from government to people that enable this commitment to be enforced" (1997: p. 2).

Rural Nigériens today do not recognize their vulnerability to famine as a political scandal. And the aid system does not encourage them to do so. Development discourses, at several levels, lead Nigériens towards accepting their poverty, and possibly using it instrumentally. The paradox of chronic aid is that the greater the efforts of aid workers to reach the poor, count them, identify them and assist them, the greater the premium on exhibiting characteristics of poverty in a context where there are few income alternatives to aid. The way in which the aid apparatus transforms individual biography into policy discourse collectively creates a sense of community characterized by dispossession and need of assistance. It is as "poor" and "undernourished" that destitute Nigériens are entitled to access to aid revenue, rather than being encouraged to think of access to food as a fundamental right they can claim through political action as healthy people, and before becoming victims of hunger. Thus, amongst several practices identified as ways to access food in 2005, some mothers were reported as trying to induce thinness in their children in order to have access to free food distribution at MSF centres. According to an anonymous MSF agent quoted in Mariatou Kone's report, "the mothers of fat babies explain to us that even if their children are not undernourished yet, they are at risk of becoming so because they have nothing to eat. Some mothers return to see us several times; we weigh the baby and s/he has no symptoms. After their fourth or fifth visit we realise that the baby is moderately malnourished. [...] If we don't do something for this child, who has now become moderately undernourished, soon s/he will reach us in a state of severe malnutrition." (LASDEL, 2006: p. 61, my translation)

Free food distribution may serve not so much to raise awareness of malnutrition as a "true" nosological condition in Nigérien villages, as to improve local understandings of how to manipulate aid nosopolitics. Careful consideration must be given to the unwanted consequences of humanitarian assistance for people faced with extreme need and lacking alternative sources of support, as well as political representation. This situation favours the development of brokerage tactics through which actors who cannot influence aid design attempt to manipulate policy to their advantage. In Niger, accountability lies not in liberal democracy, but in a network of personal ties of allegiance and reciprocal obligation that characterize patron-client relations spreading broadly from rural villages to urban centres, and from the country's hinterland to government positions in the capital (Blundo and Olivier de Sardan, 2006). This logic of patronage is based on personal, sometimes kinship, alliance, rather than impersonal and/or anonymous voting and delegation. Often characterized as "corruption" in Western literature, it is an alternative form of political contract that is not, of course, exclusive to Africa, but operates in Euro-American and Asian contexts as well. But acknowledging the workings of clientelism and local politics does not mean that they should be expected to substitute or compensate for the shortcomings of national and international policies. Malnutrition and structural poverty are deeply rooted in Niger's problems, and crises like the one experienced in 2005 will recur. One can only hope that the sufferings of undernourished children and their families will be relieved by the activities of humanitarian institutions. Meanwhile, the aid system should focus on enabling poor Nigériens to acquire the political and economic means to choose how to leave poverty—and aid—behind.

BIBLIOGRAPHY

Abdulmaliq, S., 2001. "Straddling the Divides: Remaking Associational Life in the Informal African City", *International Journal of Urban and Regional Research* 25 (1): pp. 102–17.

ACF, November 2005. *Etude de l'état nutritionnel et du taux brut de mortalité chez les enfants âgés de 6 a 59 mois des zones agricole, agropastorale et pastorale des régions de Maradi et de Tahoua, Niger.*

AFD, 2006. *L'intégration des programmes d'aide alimentaire aux politiques de développement du Niger: le cas de la crise alimentaire 2004–2005*, Working paper by D. Chen and N. Meisel.

Baier, S., 1976. "Economic History and Development: Drought and the Sahelian Economics of Niger", *African Economic History* 1: pp. 1–17.

—— and P. Lovejoy 1977. "The Tuareg of the Central Sudan: Gradations in Servility at the Desert's Edge (Niger and Nigeria)", in I. Kopytoff and S. Myers (eds) *Slavery in Africa: Historical and Anthropological Perspectives*, Madison: University of Wisconsin Press.

Bayat, A., 1997. "Un-civil Society: The Politics of the 'Informal People'", *Third World Quarterly* 18 (1): pp. 53–72.

Bernus, E., 1974. "L'Evolution récente des relations entre éleveurs et agriculteurs en Afrique tropicale: L'Exemple du Sahel Nigérien", *Cahiers ORSTOM* XI (2): pp. 137–43.

Bierschenk, T., J.P. Chauveau and J.P. Olivier de Sardan (eds), 2001. *Courtiers en développement: Les villages africaines en quête de projets*, Paris: Karthala.

Blundo, G. and J.P. Olivier de Sardan (eds), 2006. *Everyday Corruption and the State: Citizens and Public Officials in Africa*, London: ZED.

Bonte, P., 1976. "Structure de classe et structures sociales chez les Kel Gress", *Revue de l'Occident Musulman et de la Méditerranée* 21: pp. 141–62.

Bourdieu, P., 1984. *Distinction: A Social Critique of the Judgement of Taste*, London: Routledge and Kegan Paul.

—— 1990. *The Logic of Practice*, Cambridge: Polity.

Bourgeot, A. 1975. "Analyse des rapports de production chez les pasteurs et les agriculteurs de l'Ahaggar", in T. Monod (ed.) *Pastoralism in Tropical Africa*, Oxford University Press.

Carney, J. and M. Watts, 1990. "Manufacturing Dissent: Work, Gender and the Politics of Meaning in a Peasant Society", *Africa* 60 (2): pp. 207–42.

Castells, M., 1996. *The Rise of the Network Society*, Oxford: Blackwell.

Certeau, M. de, 1984. *The Practice of Everyday Life*, Berkeley: University of California Press.

Colburn, F. (ed.), 1989. *Everyday Forms of Peasant Resistance*, Armonk: M.E. Sharpe.

Comaroff, J. and S. Roberts, 1981. *Rules and Processes: The Cultural Logic of Dispute in an African Context*, University of Chicago Press.

Cooper, B., 1995. "The Politics of Difference and Women's Associations in Niger: of 'Prostitutes', the Public, and Politics", *Signs* 20 (4): pp. 851–82

Delsol, H. and Y. Martin-Prevel, 2005. *Aide-mémoire de mission: L'information nutritionnelle dans un contexte de surveillance de l'alerte précoce, éléments de réflexion*, Niamey.

Douglas, M., 1987. *How Institutions Think*, London: Routledge and Cregan Paul.

Dreze, J. and A. Sen, 1989. *Hunger and Public Action*, Oxford: Clarendon Press.

Epicentre, June 2005. *Statut nutritionnel et mortalité rétrospective: deux enquêtes réalisées en zone rurale des régions de Maradi et de Tahoua au Niger (28 avril-3 mai 2005)*.

Escobar, A., 1995. *Encountering Development: the Making and Unmaking of the Third World*, Princeton University Press.

Faulkingham, R. and P. Thorban, 1975. "Population Dynamics and Drought: A Village in Niger", *Population Studies* 29 (3): pp. 463–77.

Ferguson, J., 1990. *The Anti-Politics Machine. "Development Depoliticization, and Bureaucratic Power in Lesotho"*, Minneapolis: University of Minnesota Press.

Findlay, S., 1992. "Circulation as a Drought Coping Strategy in Rural Mali" in C. Glodscheider (ed.) *Migration, Population Structure, and Redistribution Policies*, Oxford: Westview Press.

Foucault, M., 1980. "The Politics of Health in the Eighteenth Century" in Gordon, C. (ed.) *Power/Knowledge: Selected Interviews and Other Writings 1972–1977*, Brighton: Harvester Press.

Gregoire, E., 1992. *The Alhazai of Maradi: Traditional Hausa Merchants in a Changing Sahelian City*, London: Lynne Rienner.

Held, D. and M. Koenig-Archibugi, 2004. "Introduction", *Government and Opposition* 39 (2): pp. 125–31.

IRAM, 2006. *Crises alimentaires au Niger: les politiques de développement dans l'impasse?* Dossier préparatoire 15 Sept. 2006, ed. J. Egg.

Jézéquel, J.H. 2005. *"Ici, l'enfant n'a pas de valeur." Sécurité alimentaire, malnutrition et développement au Niger*, Report for MSF-France.

Keenan, J., 2005. "Famine in Niger is Not All that it Appears." *Review of African Political Economy* 32: pp. 405–8.

Koechlin, J., 1997. "Ecological Conditions and Degradation Factors in the Sahel", in C. Raynaut (ed.) *Societies and Nature in the Sahel*, London: Routledge.

LASDEL, 2006. *La crise alimentaire de 2005 au Niger dans la région de Madarounfa et ses effets sur la malnutrition infantile: approche socio-anthropologique*, Rapport principal: Mariatou Koné; preface by J.P. Olivier de Sardan.

Lesthaeghe, R., 1986. "On the Adaptation of Sub-Saharan Systems of Reproduction", in D. Coleman and R. Schofield (eds) *The State of Population Theory*, Oxford: Blackwell.

Lewis, D. and D. Mosse (eds), 2006. *Brokers and Translators: The Ethnography of Aid and Agencies*, Bloomfield: Kumarian.

Main, H., 1989. "Workers, Retrenchment and Urban-Rural Linkages in Kano, Nigeria", in K. Swindell, J. Baba, and M. Mortimore (eds) *Inequality and Development: Case Studies from the Third World*, London: Macmillan.

Mitchell, T., 2002. *Rule of Experts: Egypt, Techno-politics, Modernity*, Berkeley: University of California Press.

Mosse, D., 2004. "Is Good Policy Unimplementable? Reflections on the Ethnography of Aid Policy and Practice." *Development and Change* 35 (4): pp. 639–71.

———— 2005. *Cultivating Development: An Ethnography of Aid Policy and Practice*, London: Pluto.

Najman, V., 2006. *Les facteurs économiques de la production de la malnutrition dans la région nigérienne de Maradi*, Report for MSF-France.

OXFAM International, 2006. *Causing Hunger. An Overview of the Food Crisis in Africa*.

Painter, T., 1987. *Migrations, Social Reproduction, and Development in Africa: Critical Notes from a Case Study in the West African Sahel*, Working Paper No. 7. London: The Open University.

Poster, M., 1994. *Foucault, Marxism, and History*, Cambridge: Polity Press.

Rain, D., 1999. *Eaters of the Dry Season: Circular Labour Migration in the West African Sahel*, Boulder: Westview.

Raynaut, C., 1975. "Le Cas de la région de Maradi (Niger)" in J. Copans (ed.), *Sécheresses et famines au Sahel II*, Paris: Maspero.

Rollet-Echalier, C., 1991. "La Politique à l'égard de la petite enfance sous la 3e République", *Population* (French edition), 46th year, no. 2: pp. 349–58.

Rossi, B., 2006. "Aid Policies and Recipient Strategies in Niger", in D. Lewis and D. Mosse (eds) *Development Brokers and Translators. The Ethnography of Aid and Agencies*, Bloomfield: Kumarian.

Scott, J., 1985. *Weapons of the Weak: Everyday Forms of Peasant Resistance*, New Haven: Yale University Press.

Sen, A., 1981. *Poverty and Famines: An Essay on Entitlement and Deprivation*, Oxford: Clarendon Press.

———— 1990. "Individual Freedom as a Social Committment", *New York Review of Books*, 14 June.

———— 1999. *Development as Freedom*, Oxford University Press.

Scholte, J. 2004. "Civil Society and Democratically Accountable Global Governance", *Government and Opposition* 39 (2): pp. 211–33.

Soederberg, S., 2004. *The Politics of the New International Financial Architecture. Reimposing Neoliberal Domination in the Global South*, London: Zed.

Swift, J., 1975. "Une économie nomade sahélienne face à la catastrophe: Les Touareg de l'Adrar des Iforas (Mali)" in J. Copans (ed.) *Sécheresses et famines au Sahel II*. Paris: Maspéro.

Turner, M., 2000. "Drought, Domestic Budgeting, and Wealth Distribution in Sahelian Households", *Development and Change* 31: pp. 1009–35.

de Waal, A., 1997. *Famine Crimes: Politics and the Disaster Relief Industry in Africa*, Oxford: James Currey.

WFP, 2006. *Evaluation de la réponse du PAM à la crise alimentaire au Niger en 2005*.

WFP, 2006. *Ending Child Hunger and Undernutrition Intitiative. Global Framework for Action* (Revised Draft December 2006).

WFP and HKI, 2005, *Évaluation de l'état nutritionnel des enfants de 6 à 59 mois dans les régions rurales de Maradi et de Zinder. Rapport de deux enquêtes*, Niamey.

6

De-Feminization of Agriculture in Southern Niger: A Link with the Crisis?

Marthe Diarra and Marie Monimart

This chapter is based on a study conducted for IIED[1] in June 2006. The goal of the study was to examine how women in the Niger countryside deal with land pressure and the increasing difficulty of accessing natural resources within changing agricultural production systems. What does this have to do with the food crisis of 2005? Generally overlooked, a focus on rural women's access to natural resources and land helps shed a different light on the root causes of this crisis. In particular, it allows research into possible links between, on the one hand, existing exclusion mechanisms and changes in livelihood and social status, and on the other, household food sovereignty and childhood malnutrition.

The research was based on case studies conducted at seven sites (see map facing): Dan Kullu, Sherkin Hausa, Jiratawa and Gazori in the Maradi region; Tigar, Eliki and Dungu in the Zinder region. These sites are representative of

[1] International Institute for Environment and Development, Summary of the study that appeared in the Drylands issue paper No. 143: Marthe Diarra and Marie Monimart, "Landless Women, Hopeless Women? Gender, Land and Decentralisation in Niger," October 2006 (http://www.iied.org/pubs/pdf/full/12535FIIED.pdf).

Republic of Niger, Climate and Livelihood zones and sites of the Gender Land Decentralisation Study (IIED, London)

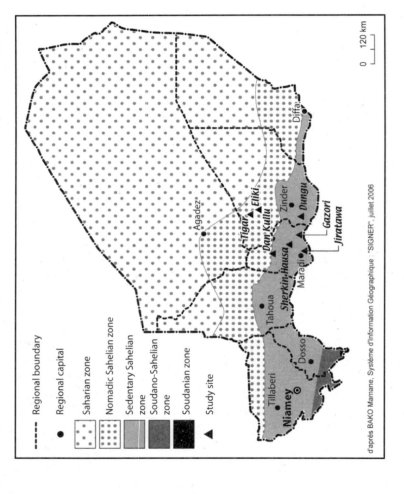

d'après BAKO Mamane, Système d'information Géographique : "SIGNER", juillet 2006

diversity criteria focusing on agroecological zones, population pressure (from 2 to 150 inhabitants per sq. km), dominant agricultural production systems, presence or absence of irrigated crops, and social role valorization practices. The four southern sites may be considered part of Niger's most productive farming area. In 2005, this millet "breadbasket" also "produced" the most malnourished children.

The study shows that a de-feminization of agriculture is under way, leading to increased poverty for women in the broad sense of the term: economic poverty, of course, but also decisional, legal, cultural, and nutritional poverty. This impoverishment has repercussions in both the private (household) and public spheres. These observations were noted during the report-back conducted at each site in March 2007. The men and women whose input we sought are not optimistic. In their view, the 2005 food crisis reflects a chronic crisis. For more than 20 years, the rare good years have been insufficient to allow people to recover from the frequent and increasingly closely-spaced shocks of the bad years.

We strongly believe that among the varied structural causes of food insecurity in rural Niger households, the de-feminization of agriculture and the feminization of poverty aggravate childhood malnutrition. The growing gap between men's and women's decision-making power in terms of production, access to shared natural resources, recourse to emergency aid and the household use of that aid has been underestimated or neglected. Thirty-seven years after Ester Boserup published her famous work on the crucial role of women in economic development (Boserup, 1970), stereotypes of men and women's roles in household food security persist. There is reason to fear that most decision-makers still believe that "men bring home the food and women prepare it" (Mead, 1949). Once again, gender issues have been typically marginalized in both analysis and management of the food crisis in the Sahel. We seek to restore that specific insight in this chapter.

Agricultural production systems in flux

The economic geography of Niger has been shaped by its traditional agricultural and pastoral production systems, which have complementary but divergent relationships to land. As a result, the country is divided into two distinct areas: an agricultural zone and a pastoral zone. Both activities are permitted within these zones, with greater prerogatives given to one or other production system according to the zone.[2] Through exchanges between the sedentary population and pastoral herders, the systems' complementary nature has long favoured optimization of production and nutritional balance. Traditionally, land was developed as families cleared it and created water points under the direction of the head of the clan or family. Land had to be left fallow, so more distant fields were cultivated and farming hamlets established, which in turn led to the development of new villages that recognized the authority of the original head of family or clan. This system of agricultural production continued for a long time thanks to the availability of vacant lands (bush).

Among the Hausa, collective farm units known as *gandu* are controlled by the *mai gandu*, who organizes the agricultural work. The *gandu* is a collective asset, which is overseen by the *mai gida* (patriarch), who manages production so that everyone's needs are met. In addition to collective fields, which all active farmers work, individual fields (*gamana*) are assigned to married women and dependents (such as young men). These fields are farmed simultaneously, on the basis of a schedule that allocates two or three days a week for working in individual fields. The *gandu* (the farming unit) is controlled by the members of the *gida*, the basic social unit in Hausa communities. The *gida* is an enclosure in which one or several married men live, each with his own household. In the latter case, the *gida* is home to an extended family headed by the *mai gida*, who is usually the oldest man in the unit. The death of the family head (or an internal challenge to his authority) may splinter the group into smaller family units. Sutter (1982) reported that the extended family also tended to fragment into smaller family groups when non-farm income increased significantly, if the *mai gida* could not meet the financial needs of the family, or if he only had a small holding. However, until the 1980s, the extended family constituted the ideal and dominant model of familial groupings (Diarra-Doka, 2000). The major drought of 1984 dealt a decisive blow to this model, yet transitions were already underway.

Indeed, the colonization of land for agriculture began in the early twentieth century in response to demographic growth and escalating financial needs and obligations, accelerating rapidly from the 1950s onwards until village lands became completely saturated. In 1975, Raynaut spoke of "an overloaded agrarian system" where the most favourable areas for farming (such as southern Maradi) were reaching population densities of 35 to 100 persons per sq. km

[2] Law 61–5 of 26 May 1961, which establishes a northern boundary for farming activities, prohibits agriculture beyond the 350 mm isohyet, considered a pastoral region, but permits those raising livestock to carry out subsistence farming.

(Raynaut *et al.*, 1988). One of the consequences of this was the loss and even the disappearance of pasture. The only remaining pastures are the livestock corridors, and these have been encroached upon by fields used to produce annual or permanent crops. This saturation also affects the practice of fallowing, which was essential for the balance of the traditional system, but is now declining or disappearing altogether. The absence of fallow is a decisive indicator of land saturation at the household and village levels, and raises the fundamental question of how soil fertility can be renewed. Two common responses to this are to apply organic manure or wait for the most useful species of trees and shrubs to regenerate naturally (*Faiherbia albida* or gao, *Adansonia digitata* or baobab, etc.). However, these practices fail to prevent the loss of field productivity. Combined with population growth and increased demand for grain, this drop in yield is a powerful incentive to pledge or sell fields to make up for grain shortfalls or to raise enough money to migrate, in the hope that this will prove more profitable. As we were told in Sherkin Hausa in March 2007, "you sell your field because you can't stand seeing your family and your children hungry; as long as you have land, you keep selling it bit by bit. When everything is sold, you leave. There are no more reserves. Here, no one can be fed from his field."

The process of farm fragmentation has brought about a gradual but fundamental change in the traditional management of *gandu*s: the individualization of land ownership. This first phase of individual appropriation marginalized women, although they generally retained their use rights to the *gamana*. When these use rights were guaranteed, young dependent males and women never needed to have their own personal land, but the situation has changed as the individualization of inheritance and increasing demographic pressure have dramatically reduced the size of plots and holdings. Issaka (2000) refers to average field size of 0.73 ha in Jiratawa, while sizes range from 2.5 ha to over 10 ha in Sherkin Hausa, and 4 ha to 20 ha in Dan Kullu. Along with individual inheritance, land has acquired a market value and is now pledged, leased, sold, and purchased.

Because they have more available land and financial assets, it is only the least vulnerable households that are able to acquire land through inheritance, and, of course, purchases and pledges. Initially only family members and, later, other villagers could buy land. Now this option is open to everyone. Maradi traders and civil servants buy land for market gardening in Jiratawa and those in Zinder do so in Dungu. Other, more precarious means exist to gain access to land: vulnerable households access land via renting; extremely vulnerable households that cannot rent a field are reduced to borrowing. Registered land transactions show a constant rise in the price of fields, with costs reaching or exceeding $200–300 per hectare, which is more than Niger's average per capita GDP (estimated at $184 in 2004).

Trees have also taken on an increasing value and are often priced based on the income they generate. A gao sells for between 3,000 and 5,000 CFA francs and a baobab for between 15,000 and 50,000 CFA francs. The enhanced value of trees also extends to their sub-products. Women *gamana* owners retain rights to the trees' fruits but not to high value-added produce like leaves (a bag of baobab leaves, used in particular to prepare sauces, sells for 1,000 CFA francs). Trees now have as much economic potential as the fields in which they grow and are dealt with separately from them: they may be loaned, rented or pledged, cut by the owner, or sold separately to the person who acquires the field or to a third party. The growing power of landowners over the natural resources in their field means that the poorest groups, and women in particular, are doubly excluded—from both the land and its resources—and are thus made even more vulnerable.

The most obvious consequence of these changes in access to land and its resources is greater and accelerated social differentiation between "the rich" and "the poor", between "rights holders" and "the disenfranchised". The exclusion of women and young men is an ongoing process, reaching various stages depending on the degree of land pressure—heightened in the south compared to the north—but also on the extent of social vulnerability.

De-feminization of agriculture: local and social disparities

The practice of sharing out farmland following the death of the head of the family began in the 1970s as a response to the growing number of households within the extended family, the impossibility of colonizing new land, falling yields, and the growing monetarization of transactions. Land on small farms was shared out between rights holders, which meant that women were excluded owing to the principle of virilocal residence, whereby married women no longer stay with their original family group, but go and live with the husband's group.

Other forms of land distribution include donation, when the head of the farm gives fields to his children during his lifetime. When the *mai gandu* dies, the remaining land should be shared out between male children who have not benefited from donation. The *mai gandu*'s wives retain their *gamana* as part of their inheritance. His daughters, who have already left to go and live with their husbands, or who are expected to do so, must exercise their use rights in their new family through access to the *gamana*, which they may then appropriate (inherit) when their husbands die.

In areas where the pressure on land is greatest, such as Sherkin Hausa or Gazori, a growing number of women have succeeded in claiming their part of the inheritance. By contesting the way that land was distributed some thirty years before, women, or rather their children, have been able to obtain their share of the holding. Family disputes over land have taken on such importance that the current trend is to distribute land in accordance with Koranic law, which grants a half-share to girls. This practice is systematic in the south of the country (Jiratawa and Dungu), where there is so little land to be shared out between the heirs that it is usually sold and the proceeds divided between rights holders according to Koranic law. As a result, we are now seeing a generation of young people who have little or no land.

While customary law certainly prevented women from owning land and denied them the freedom to transfer it to their heirs (male or female), it was relatively equitable insofar as it guaranteed women access to the resource according to their needs and their capacity to put it to productive use. This practice is still alive in northern Niger, where there is less pressure on land. Its limitations are already visible, however. Women in Dan Kullu use what they grow to cover their own needs, and also for household consumption if food is in short supply—as is often the case now after successive poor harvests. Further south, in Gazori and Sherkin Hausa, women who still have access to *gamana* grow a combination of millet, sorghum, cowpea and sorrel in association with each other. Some *gamana* cover about a hectare of land. The trees growing in the *gamana* belong to their husbands, but women can use their produce (trimmings, pods, fruit). In Sherkin Hausa, young married women no longer have access to *gamana* because the *gandus* have become too small. In March 2007, the trend towards young women's eviction from land was confirmed, even in Dan Kullu.

Dungu and Sherkin Hausa are witnessing the emergence of the first generation of women not to work on the land. This process begins when a woman's *gamana* is cultivated by her husband because it is so small that her labour is only required for certain types of harvest, as for groundnuts, which are winnowed in the field. This lack of control over agricultural production marks the beginning of their exclusion from access to land. Further south, in Jiratawa, we found a second generation of landless women, who have never farmed because they never had the opportunity to help their mothers in their *gamana*s as the mothers were landless too. They don't even know how to sow seeds! These women are often very vulnerable, and are effectively excluded from all agricultural work: here, the de-feminization of agriculture is a reality. In March 2007, this observation was unanimously confirmed. People reported that "farming is no longer an activity for women here. They no longer know how to work." As a result, they are hidden away, "to save face".

De-feminization is thus under way throughout Hausa areas, although not to the same degree everywhere. This process is directly proportional to the population density of the study sites: the greater the population density, the greater is women's exclusion—and the earlier it began. This has consequences for childhood nutrition and helps explain why the incidence of malnutrition appears much higher south of Maradi and Zinder. Indeed, women have successively lost the decision-making power that individual farming conferred and the income (frequently in kind, including grain or groundnuts) that they received from their participation in family agricultural work. This exclusion from the fields thus has a direct impact on their ability to feed their children. The simultaneous loss of access to baobab leaves and other high value-added resources contributes to the declining quantity and quality of family food intake. "All the produce gathered that the children eat has disappeared here," the women of Jiratawa confirm.

Nonetheless, the de-feminization of agriculture can be seen in terms of both poverty and wealth. In the predominantly pastoral north, it does not affect women from less vulnerable households as they do not farm and have no wish to control what is seen as a rather secondary or even degrading activity. In the south, it does not affect women from less vulnerable households, who maintain a good level of control over production and are thus in a stronger position. For the latter, the growth in numbers of landless farmers (a phenomenon bolstered by the acute 2005 crisis that precipitated loss of capital among the most vulnerable) has created new opportunities to obtain access to land, notably purchasing and pledging. Yet, these practices do not always ensure land ownership for women. The development of statutory law could offer women a new way to reclaim their agricultural lands. It does not seem to be operating as yet, however.

Decentralization and the role of the state

What is the role of the state in regulating access to land, with regard to the de-feminization of agriculture? Can it play a protective role? The example of the Communal Lands Commission (COFOCOM),[3] established in 2006 under the decentralization framework, illustrates the ambiguities of state intervention in the area of land rights.

Local actors, notably male and female communal councillors, are particularly uninformed regarding land tenure security and the composition and role of COFOCOM. In addition, they have little awareness about women's land rights. Female councillors do not appear to feel any particular responsibility to defend the rights of their women constituents, who in turn do not seem to recognize these councillors as their legitimate representatives. Women either are completely unaware that there are women on the municipal council or know nothing about their role, firmly believing that such women are selected by their political allies or other people, but certainly not by them. To be sure, female councillors are not mandated to represent only women, prioritize women's issues or specifically defend their rights, but this in turn raises questions as to the role of quotas (at least 10% of councillors must be women) and their impact in terms of representing women. It is interesting to note that the few women mentioned in the land transaction certificates we saw were all categorized as "housewives", whether they were farmers, herders, traders or even teachers. This denial—often unconscious—of rural women's socio-professional status has profound consequences in terms of equitable access to natural resources, farming responsibilities, and household food sovereignty.

All these observations regarding women's formal access to land are very unevenly reflected in the registrations of land transactions carried out with local commissions. Purchasing and pledging (in which money is exchanged and disputes may arise) are the best documented; inheritance and customary holdings are somewhat less well documented; and borrowing, the main mode of access to land for women (notably through the *gamana*), is not documented at all. Renting is never mentioned. The under-representation of women in land transactions is blatant everywhere. Only 5.9% of registered sales beneficiaries are women; that percentage exceeds 10% only when pledging is the mode of access, as in Sherkin Hausa.

Registering transactions with the land commission may also turn out to be a double-edged sword, precipitating the formalization of women's exclusion from land ownership. We have thus observed that in some cases land purchase conducted by a woman was registered in the name of the husband, who was

---

[3] The land commissions (COFO) are responsible for implementing the Rural Code at three levels: departmental (COFODEP), communal (COFOCOM, since 2006) and village or nomadic group (COFOB). Women make up at least 10% of those bodies.

physically present when the transaction was witnessed (always by men) and personally carried out the registration procedures. While in 2006 such cases could be ascertained at only one site, their occurrence was confirmed at all sites during the March 2007 report-backs. This is creating considerable concern among local officials, who fear that this may disrupt harmonious relationships within households and in communities. The objective of the Rural Code—to achieve equitable land tenure security—is threatened not only by general ignorance of one's rights (particularly among women), but also by possible manipulation from all sides and bad faith on the part of the registrant or witnesses. In the long term, the superposition or coexistence of three legal systems that seems to persist within the land commissions could pose problems. Women still appear to be largely bound by customary or Koranic laws, which hold for instance that if they are to serve as witnesses (which they are not always permitted to do), two are required to "equal" one male witness. However, land commissions are supposed to be subject to statutory law, where the rule of equality between male and female citizens should apply.

Ultimately, the decentralization policies implemented by the state incorporate not a few principles that on paper should be favourable to women. Yet, women appear to have limited access to them.

Inheritance issues: negotiating legal standards

Inheritance is a central issue, on which the conditions for transferring and providing access to land depend. Multiple standards, however, govern inheritance in the Hausa environment (including "traditional" law, Muslim religious law and the state-promoted new land law). Local actors exploit these multiple rules to restructure the terms of access to land. Like the state's role and that of the decentralization policy, inheritance laws have an ambiguous impact on redefining women's access to land.

Although inheritance under Koranic law is inequitable in absolute terms (women get half the men's share), it does give women a formal and fairly secure means of access to land since it is done in the name of religion. There seems to be a fairly strong social consensus in Hausa communities that women have the right to inherit land, and this right is increasingly being claimed. Yet, while women's right to dispose of their share of land and transfer it to whomever they choose is acknowledged, their access to land or control over production is not necessarily guaranteed, as they often have to redistribute the land among their male heirs first because of social pressures and pressure on land.

Nevertheless, with the gradual disappearance of land loaned for *gamana*, this is becoming the only way that women can obtain recognition of their land rights.

While religious law protects women in the transfer of land, it may also serve as a cover for their total exclusion from land, justifying this through *kubli* (forbidding women to leave their home), also known as *hutun gandu*, or "rest from the fields", or *kublin gona* (denial of access by forbidding women to go out to the fields), which are all decreed by the husband. These practices, which affect growing numbers of young women in areas where pressure on land is most intense (Jiratawa, Dungu), are beginning to affect very young women in Sherkin Hausa. The women of Sherkin Hausa are not fooled: "It's a trick! They tell us to rest, but it means that destitution is starting for us. It's the 'rest' of poverty! Husbands are making us 'rest' because they've got nothing to give us!"

Public land law, introduced in the countryside via the land commissions, places men and women on equal footing, particularly with respect to selling and pledging, the new modes of formal land acquisition (on condition, as we have observed, that ownership declarations are scrutinized carefully). In practice, however, the diverse local structures responsible for regulating and negotiating access to natural resources are actually used more than the land commissions. The family remains the first locus of arbitration in the redistribution of land or its assignment to an outsider. In this context, women are in a poor negotiating position and have scant recourse if land is taken away, all the more so as religion may be used to support eviction (through "rest") and loans are not secured via a formal land commission process (registration).

Is the Rural Code accomplishing its mission of advancing human progress by securing the livelihoods of rural actors? There is a tendency towards excluding the most vulnerable—sometimes entire communities—who are losing their status as small landholders to become "proletarians"[4] serving affluent landowners, either resident or absentee, as is the case with city dwellers.

Thus, women may rely on certain legal standards to try and protect access to land compromised by the dynamics affecting Hausa societies. However, the large number of legal registries is also frequently relied upon to legitimize or strengthen their exclusion.

---

[4] The term "agricultural worker" does not seem to us to capture the considerably precarious situation of these landless peasants, who receive a poverty wage on a piece-work basis and are completely dependent on the law of supply and demand for seasonal agricultural labour, with no opportunity to negotiate.

Local access to alternative resources

Increasingly excluded from working and owning land, women try to respond by pursuing alternative revenue-generating activities that could compensate for their loss of power and resources. However, not all women enjoy the same access to these economic activities either. For the most vulnerable segments of the female population, ongoing dynamics make it impossible to halt the feminization of poverty.

Women's primary income-generating activities were initially developed on the basis of agricultural produce. Their agricultural production has long served as a means of saving and also provided gifts for ceremonies (*bikis*).[5] The surplus of so-called cash crops (cowpeas, sorrel, okra and sesame) were sold at market to raise cash to meet basic needs (including food), buy animals and assemble their daughters' wedding trousseaus. Families have also needed cash to pay taxes. The monetarization of the economy gradually eroded the barter system, which has, nonetheless, survived for a long time through exchanges between sedentary and pastoral communities, such as milk-cereal exchanges carried out by women (which allowed both communities to have a more balanced diet), and manure agreements for fertilizing fields. Now that everything is bought and sold, including the food that is lacking, where will the money come from?

Sedentary women also used to raise livestock, specializing in fattening cattle, sheep and goats. However, environmental and, subsequently, economic constraints have now mainly restricted them to raising a few small ruminants. Some women have no more livestock, "not even a chicken!" Livestock rearing plays an important role in women's economic activities. It represents capital that can be easily mobilized in an emergency and provides savings "on the hoof" in times of plenty (offering interest, since the animals reproduce). Its social significance influences the status of women in sedentary and pastoral societies and it contributes significantly to reducing household vulnerability. In pastoral communities, women own livestock (large and small ruminants) that are kept within the family herd. However, repeated crises have drastically reduced, and sometimes even wiped out, the family herds, forcing women and men to seek other resources or even change their way of living, as in Eliki.

[5] *Bikis*: gifts of money or goods exchanged among women during birth and marriage ceremonies. The rule governing this practice holds that the value must be doubled at each turn until one person ends the cycle. More closely-spaced births have accentuated the phenomenon, which is, ultimately, financially devastating. Not being able to participate in the *biki* represents a major social exclusion.

Women (particularly older women) quickly made a niche for themselves selling processed goods, especially doughnuts but also homemade groundnut oil, groundnut meal and porridge (*fura*). The sale of processed goods and cooked food has gradually diversified (including millet dough, rice, pasta known as *tallia*, pancakes, vegetables, leaves and meats in sauce, etc.), accompanying changing dietary habits and in response to the rising cost of millet.

While the informal sector is developing, particularly in the field of repairs and crafts, it involves primarily men. For various reasons, very few women are involved in this new technical sector. They have a lower rate of education, their mobility is restricted (owing to confinement and early marriage) and they are disadvantaged by the discriminatory apprenticeship system. The large diversification of new trades illustrates the capacity of the informal learning systems to respond to new needs. Pending equal access to them, however, they could intensify further the exclusion of women and young girls.

At the same time, the income generated by traditional female crafts is declining sharply as a result of competition from manufactured products like plastic mats and factory-produced condiments. Sewing, a trade previously limited to men, is becoming a woman's occupation, like knitting and selling cold drinks in electrified areas. The range of alternative economic activities open to women varies with age, which determines their mobility. Older women may travel to rural markets, where they sell manufactured goods purchased in neighbouring Nigeria, or deliver orders to people's homes. Young girls are small-time travelling traders too, selling their wares in the streets or markets. They work for their mothers so that they can assemble their wedding trousseaus more quickly. Young married women are the most severely restricted in terms of mobility (being forbidden from going to the market or confined, for example) and are thus more constrained in pursuing and diversifying their economic activities.

Women from less vulnerable households run their businesses from home, getting their husbands or relatives to buy goods for them. However, using intermediaries affects profitability and it is difficult to acquire start-up capital if one cannot pursue agricultural activities. Married women who are confined to their homes must conduct all their activities within the domestic sphere. Here, too, they lack control over the activity and the cost of intermediaries reduces already tight profit margins. In addition, they must now compete with village shops (run by men) that sell staple goods almost everywhere.

This apparently broad diversification of activities does not offer opportunity to all women. Women from poor households are involved in economic activities based primarily on the direct extraction of natural resources. They sell firewood, leaves and wild harvest produce, water, straw and stalks gleaned from fields. They also sell their labour, performing physically difficult tasks like pounding, and poorly-paid agricultural work (300 francs per half-day for women, compared with 600 francs for men). Agriculture provides the most vulnerable population groups with food for only three to five months per year, and sometimes less, as in 2004–5. These groups have developed strategies to ensure that there is food on the table during the farming season. For example, women process cereals often bought on credit from dealers in their village. They know that the profits will be minimal, so they pursue several other activities at the same time, not only to diversify their income, but also to reduce the risks associated with a single activity.

In such an economic context, the loss of access to land appears to be closely correlated with the practice of alternative economic activities. Mature or elderly women with the social capacity to undertake viable alternative activities are also those who still have access to land (the *gamana*) and are in a position to buy land or obtain it through pledge agreements. Younger married women without land try to make money through activities, such as processing a few measures of peppers given to them by their husbands. However, as the women themselves say, these are "poverty jobs", poorly paid and closely controlled by their husbands. Furthermore, having responsibility for many young children does not promote young women's ability to emerge as economic actors. Mother-daughter support often becomes critical. Elderly women thus continue their agricultural activities (in the Jiratawa case) to help their daughters and grandchildren. This produces a doubly counterproductive social drama: worn-out older women who legitimately seek to withdraw from strenuous activity but cannot and idle young women who would like to work but are prevented from doing so.

Migration: a changing alternative strategy

The evolution of migratory practices, in relation to heightened household vulnerability, may also play a part in the feminization of poverty. Women themselves are beginning to migrate, although for now this remains a very risky strategy.

Migration by young men is a well-established strategy, but it has now become a vital one for rural households, practiced by expanding age groups in both good and bad years. From the time the harvest ends to the resumption of work in the fields—that is, over six to eight months—most men from 15 to 40 leave their villages to find work elsewhere. The head of the family closes the family storehouse after the harvest has been distributed. Women are left "to manage on their own" (a key phrase) to feed the family with the harvest they have received, the *gamana* production (kept in a separate storehouse, managed by the woman) and their ancillary economic activities. Depending on the amount set aside, the family storehouse will not reopen until the rainy season, to ensure that everyone is strong enough to cultivate the fields. Sometimes it does not open until the second hoeing, in July or August. No woman would dare ask that it be opened, even if she and the children have no grain left to eat. That would be "the millet of shame", a significant social stigma among co-wives and in the community. Managing food shortages thus falls first to women and becomes an impossible task, especially if they no longer have *gamana* stocks. Migration is not easy for the men, but even if it produces little or nothing, at least, they say, they will not have "eaten from the storehouse" during their absence. This lean period, between the time when stocks run out and the new harvest, is lengthening. It is thus no surprise that half the children suffer from chronic malnutrition.

The structure of young men's migration is changing profoundly, as has been confirmed widely. While seasonal migration to Nigeria continues, it has become less viable and more risky. This is a "food" migration—seasonal and stopgap—and does not allow for accumulation. It is the migration of the poor, undertaken by the heads of the most vulnerable families.

Today, households are organizing a new strategy that involves sending young men further for longer periods to more profitable destinations, including Libya and Mecca. This requires considerable advance financing and family investment and cannot be an individual undertaking. It involves a complex, smoothly-running mechanism that can nonetheless place the household land capital at risk. When the young man migrating is married (a situation to be avoided), it has a negative impact on the young women left behind to care for the children. If remittances are insufficient to buy back the pledged fields, the household lands may be lost forever and the family will join the landless population. The very difficult journey between Algeria and Libya, made on foot (entry is often clandestine), also entails many risks, sometimes mortal. The men refer to a "lottery" and "forced labour". In spite of the difficulty and exile, this strategy is taking root among all with the resources to finance the investment, which does not include the most disadvantaged. It demonstrates the speed with which village residents adapt to change. They are using new technologies to bolster these strategies, like cell phones, which play an unexpected role in providing security to rural households. This was expressed during a meeting in Dan Kullu in March 2007:

Every family here has a son who migrated to Libya for two or three years. They pledge their fields to finance the trip. Everyone pledges to send their son there and you get the money back when the boy sends his first remittance. If you lose the lottery (if the trip fails and the son is turned back), you start over again. You need 300,000–350,000 francs, but in three years you can earn three million. The young men open a bank account in Maradi and send their money transfers via Western Union so that they aren't robbed. If there's an emergency in the village, you call them on the *cellula* (cell phone) up there, in the dunes, and they'll help you out. The *cellula* is better than any development project. You can call your parents in Niamey and they'll send you a bag of rice on the market truck.

The migration of young woman to expensive destinations far from home, like Mecca and Libya, for prolonged periods (up to several years) is a more recent phenomenon that seems to be developing primarily in the Zinder region. It has yet to be seen whether this strategy is profitable and sustainable: the young women we met in Dungu may have assembled their marriage trousseaus, but have not been able to accumulate enough capital to embark on a meaningful business venture or buy fields. Besides, the community does not always approve of young women's mobility. Even the large-scale international trips made by the famously mobile and independent WoDaabe[6] women, such as those from Eliki, do not appear to have compensated for the loss of their livestock. They have been unable to reconstitute the reproductive core of herds decimated by successive crises and are now turning to sedentarization as a last resort, selling their labour for a pittance to perform the most menial tasks and waiting for free food aid at cereal banks.

A "gender crisis"

The diverse strategies of local actors and, specifically, women are not sufficient to remedy the processes of impoverishment. Those forces are so strong that the tensions they generate within Hausa society result in a genuine "gender crisis".

Most women, especially young women, affected by exclusion from the dominant production system (farming and herding) do not seem to have the opportunity or capacity to launch reliable economic activities that can com-

---

[6] A nomadic herding people in Niger and neighbouring countries.

pensate for that loss. When we reported back on the study findings, we were struck by the clarity of the analyses offered, notably in southern Maradi, with brutal frankness, regarding the loss of bearings and the values crisis underway within social systems. The disruption of long-standing behaviour, specifically regarding population growth and strategies responding to impoverishment, reveals a profound social crisis seen first within male-female relationships.

Population growth, and the pressures it generates on both land and natural resources, is widely acknowledged as a factor aggravating an already difficult situation. Here, too, women—particularly young women—are singled out for criticism, both by men and older women. We heard very painful public comments that spoke to this distress. "Our girls give birth like goats here. Abstinence lasts just for the 40 days and even so, the 40 day period isn't always observed. It's their fault—they should refuse, but it's the men's fault, too!" Speakers referred repeatedly to the lack of respect for tradition, age and values. Early marriage and polygamy are also acknowledged as aggravating factors. "Here, 17-year-old boys are fathers, married with very young girls. Because of polygamy, there are lots of children. But it's better to marry the girls early. They'll have babies, anyway." But what recourse and what decision-making space are available to these very young married women, who are confined to "save face", condemned to idleness and lacking resources? Some already have several children by the age of 20. Has the situation of these adolescent parents, deprived and dependent, been studied in the context of childhood malnutrition?

Poverty, and the idleness it generates among those excluded from the production system and who have not found alternative livelihoods, is analyzed as a factor in the erosion of behavioural standards generally and in male-female relationships specifically. Bringing food back to the home, which justifies the title of *mai gida* and the respect that accompanies it, also becomes an impossible task and a source of shame for some men. Not all men are indifferent to the food shortages affecting their households. The men will manage, "even dishonestly". In addition, men think that "there are too many women" and that they die earlier than women because of the worries they bear and because women do not get so tired. On their part, women enter a devastating cycle of indebtedness to cover the costs of the *bikis* (gift ceremonies) that they can no longer afford from their own income or agricultural production—again, to save face and protect their social capital.

Polygamy exacerbates rivalries, including rivalry over the number of children a woman bears. Children become stakes in the power struggle even if,

---

Models of social role valorization in crisis

Where agriculture is the predominant form of livelihood, women unanimously report that wealth and reputation are built on farming. However, the merit-based valorization mechanism that provides access to the status of *tambara*[7] endures only in areas where land pressure has not yet generated wide-reaching exclusionary dynamics. The alternative spaces for female leadership are still small and the new models struggle to take shape. While the *tambara* model is in decline, that of the *Hadja*, the pious woman who has made a pilgrimage to Mecca, is expanding. The female group president and communal councillor do not enjoy the same level of social recognition. The women of Sherkin Hausa analyze with disenchanted lucidity this loss of status, the absence of female voices in the public sphere and women's social impoverishment: "The *Hadja* stays at home. She accepts everything. The president holds her position for three years and if you're not re-elected, you're nothing. There are no more female leaders in the community like the *tambaras*. There won't be permanent women leaders any more." A *tambara* in Gazori confirmed those comments. "Today, the *tambarci* is over. Women have gone backwards. The great *tambaras* could speak everywhere, even among men!" As impoverishment advances, social success is measured increasingly through money and individual ownership of material goods, in keeping with the model of the wealthy trader. However, in the absence of their own agricultural production, the majority of rural women—particularly young women—have very limited opportunities for accumulation.

---

after the fact, there is no guarantee that they can be fed. The woman who gives birth is "queen for a day" when the ceremony marking the birth is held. The *bikis*, and the related extravagant expenses, contribute to impoverishment rather than building social capital and social solidarity. This constitutes a competition among women, rather than redistribution, that ultimately proves suicidal. It is a means of existence based on appearances when one no longer has anything—still "saving face." It may also be a way to humiliate a poor husband who cannot fulfil his obligations as the head of the family.

The social crisis is profound, the loss of bearings is deplored everywhere and older generations seem to have lost their standing. Confining young women without providing them the resources necessary to ensure a decent life for themselves and their children is a sign of powerlessness. It is certainly not

---

[7] "A woman whose economic success has won her social recognition and renown." See pp. 27–33 in our IIED report "Landless Women, Hopeless Women?" for a detailed presentation of the *tambarci* and the Hausa social role valorization system.

a sustainable strategy. Behind the veil and the lowered gazes exist the despair, boredom and likely revolt of young women without dreams. Sexual relations no longer observe well-established practices of spacing births because young women must hold a husband jealously coveted by other current or potential co-wives. Marriage appears as the only bastion against poverty in the absence of dependable economic activity, and maternity as the only guarantee of social respectability.

Conclusion

This sombre view comes from the women, and many men, with whom we had long conversations. We would have liked to encounter more optimism, positive visions based on real alternatives and innovations, in the formal or informal system, in response to new constraints and opportunities: the demands of the urban market, new occupations, rising rates of education and local development. However, no one expressed those perspectives and we respected what they had to say. But how can we move beyond this depressing conclusion?

The mechanisms that produce exclusion from agricultural production have triggered a merciless backlash: social exclusion. The impoverishment of most rural households, especially of women and young dependents, is at the heart of the food crisis, while a well-off minority profits from this poverty. However, exclusion develops resistance and that force is not necessarily negative. Perhaps this is the path to follow.

The choices regarding agricultural development will have major consequences. The illusion of agribusiness could promote exclusion and worsen the social gap between rich and poor, between landowners and landless. Increased agricultural production alone will not eradicate food crises unless equitable access and redistribution mechanisms are put in place. There are options available to promote a family-based agriculture that is "sustainable, modern and competitive, relying primarily on a system of tenured family agricultural operations."[8] The socio-professional status of farm operator (both male and female) must be defined and recognized. Women play a specific, determinant role in agricultural production (including raising livestock). They are not simply "housewives" who work in the fields from time to time. This creates directions for development policies: a family-based agriculture that also seeks to establish food sovereignty for producers' households, in which the diversity

[8] Quoted from Mali: *Loi d'Orientation Agricole*, 5 September 2006.

of women's crops (sorrel, *woandzu*, etc.) and their post-harvest use in feeding the family are taken seriously and properly supported, in both research and agricultural training. The first task is to avoid strengthening mechanisms that promote exclusion, like those dealing with access to land.

Another direction to take is to reduce the vulnerability of rural households and help them strengthen promising strategies. During a workshop with local actors in Dakoro in the autumn of 2005, we reviewed the last six years of assistance.[9] In response to the question, "What was most helpful to you during the crisis?" the leading answer was emergency food aid, followed by cereal banks and, last, training. In response to the question, "What made you less vulnerable over the past six years?" actions targeting capacity building and assistance to local organizations came as the first answer and food aid as the last. Polemics between "humanitarian aid" and "development" are sterile. We must learn to work together on the deep-seated causes of a crisis that is structural, so that critical emergency responses, which save lives, can be integrated into a consistent, long-term approach. Finally, we must not fool ourselves by thinking that we can help only the poorest or the most malnourished, while ignoring those who are less at risk. Food aid and development aid are seen as gifts that must be redistributed and shared to preserve social capital, which is the only reliable recourse remaining after the "foreigners" (whether humanitarian or development workers) leave.

A new model offers a glimmer of hope, as both women and men noted: the educated professional who achieves social success by combining personal merit, lasting status (education) and a certain well-being. This model is not achievable in the village or local community, however, and is still seen as the privilege of a minority. Furthermore, we must believe in the young people. Some are starting to use contraception "quietly", hiding the practice from parents or refusing to marry before accumulating resources. Not everyone wants 12 children and three wives. Even older people are beginning to practice family planning, sometimes with the tenth child, and talk about it in public. Better late than never: this strikes a blow against taboos. The key areas of training and education represent a major challenge and one of the rare ways out. Last, but not least: there is a question for all actors to answer—the state, technical and financial partners, humanitarian and development aid workers, civil society organizations. When will we understand that greater gender

---

[9] Projects for Securing the Livelihoods of Rural Households in Dakoro, carried out by CARE International with funding from the European Commission (NGO/Food Security line, 1999–2005).

equity is a priority in the struggle against poverty and that strengthening women's capacity is key to the fight against malnutrition?

Translated from French by Lou Leask (for IIED) and Leah Brumer.

BIBLIOGRAPHY

Boserup, E., 2007. *Woman's Role in Economic Development* [1970] London: Earthscan.

Diarra Doka, M., 2000. "Evolutions à long terme de l'organisation sociale et économique dans la région de Maradi", Drylands Research Working Paper 26, Crewkerne: IIED. 2000.

———— and M. Monimart, 2004, "Women's Access to Land: The De-feminisation of Agriculture in Southern Niger?" Drylands Issue Paper 128, London: IIED.

Diarra, M. and M. Monimart, 2006. "Landless Women, Hopeless Women? Gender, Land and Decentralisation in Niger", Drylands Issue Paper 143, IIED, London, October.

Issaka, M., 2000. "Evolution à long terme de la fertilité de sol dans la région de Maradi", Drylands Research Working Paper 30. Crewkerne, IIED, 2000.

Mead, M., 1949. *Male and Female, A Study of the Sexes in a Changing World*, New York: William Morrow & Co.

Raynaut, C. *et al.*, 1988. "Le développement rural de la région au village—Analyser et comprendre la diversité. Projet de développement rural de Maradi", G.R.I.D. Université de Bordeaux, 1988.

Sutter, J. W., 1982. "Peasants, Merchant Capital and Rural Differentiation: a Nigerian Hausa Case", PhD thesis, Cornell University.

7

Chronic Malnutrition and the Trope of the Bad Mother

Barbara M. Cooper

One often hears among embassies and UN agencies' officials that the cause of malnutrition is cultural: in Niger, children do not count, they are neglected, hence malnutrition runs high. (MSF, "Niger: les sacrifiés du développement", June 2005; translated from French)

We are now witnessing abandonment... Some mothers leave their weakest child with us so that they can save the other ones. Sometimes, I feel that what I'm doing has little more weight than a drop in the ocean. (MSF doctor quoted in Patrick Forestier, "Halte à la mort lente des enfants du Niger'" *Paris Match*, 28 July 2005; translated from French)

In this multifaceted crisis, everyone tries to understand what is going on. Why are children below 26 months of age most affected? Humanitarian agencies even call on anthropologists to document what they prudently refer to as "the cultural aspects of malnutrition", such as premature weaning or inadequate food practices. (Caroline Dumay, "Niger: les multiples facettes de la 'crise alimentaire'", *Le Figaro*, 23 August 2005; translated from French)

As argued in other contributions to this book, perceptions of the crisis of 2005 in Niger have frequently shifted since 2005. As the causes and responses to the crisis have been evaluated in the wake of the disaster, more and more attention has been given, at long last, to the problem of malnutrition in Niger. Yet Niger's Prime Minister Hama Amadou's rejection in June 2006 of UNICEF's figures on child malnutrition in the country, and his claim that "in some regions of Niger, we face a problem of malnutrition that has more to do with cultural behaviour than with a lack of food",[1] point to an enduring debate as to where responsibility lies for this problem. Indeed, one of the repeated claims of studies of malnutrition in the Maradi region is that because childhood malnutrition is to be found among households of all income levels and social statuses, its causes must be "socio-cultural" rather than economic.

During the 2005 crisis attention was focused upon the populations of Maradi and Zinder in particular, but it is worth pointing out that an argument suggesting a wide spread of malnutrition in Niger across all but the wealthiest households has certainly been made in the past and holds true across the entire country, not simply for the Maradi region. In an analysis of the 1995 DHS surveys for Niger, researchers associated with the World Bank noted that "a high degree of malnutrition exists, even in the richest quintile of the population. This finding suggests that, overall, the nutritional status of the children in Niger is very poor and is not entirely related to only the income levels of the families [...] more than 50% of children under the age of three are moderately or severely underweight among the [first] four quintiles (80% of the population), suggesting a very high degree of malnutrition" (Oomman *et al.*, 2003: pp. 11, 13). Since 1992 research has consistently shown that Niger has appallingly high infant and child mortality rates, and that those rates have been most distressing for the region of Niger which ought to have the best nutritional status as it is so central to food production, namely the Maradi region.

If childhood malnutrition is a general problem across a society as diverse as that of Niger, then it is not entirely clear which "socio-cultural" practices are being referred to in attributing malnutrition to culture rather than to economics or underdevelopment. Such widespread malnutrition cannot be readily associated with any one ethnic group; so, in debates about Niger's malnutrition, the "socio-cultural" practices are often left under-specified and extremely vague. We are told, for example, that infants are weaned too early, or that they are fed inappropriate food. However, such observations tell us little about why the problems are so pervasive and so resistant to change. Fortunately we do have rich and detailed studies of perceptions of health and healing in Zarma speaking regions of western Niger by Yannick Jaffré, which shed light on some of the reasons why treatment of child malnutrition in Niger has often been so unsuccessful and why high rates of child malnutrition have therefore been stubbornly persistent.

[1] Interview on *Radio France Internationale*, 21 June 2006.

Jaffré points out that among Zarma speakers, malnutrition in itself is not understood to be a source of ill health; rather children become ill as a result of fright. The fright may be caused by genies, witches, magicians, or even involuntarily by the powerful eye of a jealous or admiring neighbour. Hence the "cause" of a child's diarrhoea, vomiting, trembling, and loss of weight has nothing directly to do with food. Given that Western style medical treatment centres are sources of fright in themselves, and expose those who enter them to the gaze and potential malevolence of others, they are not the immediate sites of treatment for children with such symptoms; instead, loving parents take their small children to a healer first. Rather than simply seeing "ignorant" Zarma parents as culpable, Jaffré emphasizes the lack of consonance between the interpretive frame and treatments offered in bio-medical settings and parents' understandings. Parents who do not bring their children to the hospital are not "neglecting" their children so much as acting upon their own assessments of how best to protect and heal them. The burden, in his work, falls upon a medical system that must take the time to learn more about the settings in which it works and to adapt itself to the needs of its clientele. In this case, the key problem for biomedicine is to bring malnutrition into visibility as an illness (*faire exister socialement la maladie*) and to improve interaction between medical staff and patients so that treatment can be effective (Jaffré, 1996).

Unfortunately, although we have a few studies of health issues in the Hausa speaking zones, they are much less richly drawn than Jaffré's work closer to the capital. Souley's study of Hausa understandings of "*tamowa*" nevertheless does suggest that some of the symptoms associated with malnutrition are not seen by Hausa speakers as constituting a specific condition, but rather as resulting from a variety of causes ranging from illness to magic to the breaching of a taboo by the mother or a failure to grow (Souley, 2003). Similarly, Mariatou Kone found in a fascinating post-mortem of the 2005 crisis that most mothers in Madarounfa did not know that their children were "malnourished", but rather came to clinics because they saw a variety of signs (diarrhoea, vomiting, weight loss) that seemed to them to indicate an indigenous category of illness, particularly *ciwon filani* (a contagious illness children are understood to get from the dust of a passing herd of cattle), or *tamowa* (the range of conditions described by Souley, linked to weaning, bad milk, or inappropriate actions on the part of the mother during pregnancy). Only in the wake of the crisis has a new term come into usage, "*kwamisu*", which was invented by workers at the therapeutic centres to designate "malnutrition" and has come to be one of the terms popularly used to describe the 2005 crisis as a whole (LASDEL, 2006). Here again the issue facing the medical system becomes finding ways of bringing malnutrition into visibility as a specific health problem in ways that local populations can grasp and for which treatments are understandable and available.

Doris Bonnet points out that work on childhood malnutrition has tended to fall into two camps in the past several decades. One very visible strand has tended to take on an implicitly accusatory approach focusing largely on the failings of the mother, an approach that Bonnet terms the "social negligence" strand in the literature. Bonnet observes that "the death of a child attributed to the selective negligence of the mother takes the responsibility off the health services, which tend to blame mothers. This notion of the 'bad mother' can only have negative effects and lead women not to have anything to do with the health services." (Bonnet, 1996: p. 10). A very common thread in the literature on the treatment of childhood illnesses related to malnutrition is women's quest for exculpation in the face of this pervasive discourse (see for instance Desjeux, 1993). Another strand, less influential of late, takes a critical approach to the health delivery system itself, focusing largely on the failings of the state or on the health implications of class differentiation (Bonnet, 1996).

Jaffré's and Souley's approach offers a new way forward, for both eschew the social negligence approach in favour of a richer anthropological analysis that can then serve to improve the workings of the health delivery system. Yet in placing all the burden of moving forward on the formal medical system one runs the risk of neglecting the importance of choices made by parents, both women and men. Interestingly one of the strengths of the social negligence strand is that it insists upon the agency, sometimes apparently passive, of mothers, whereas the critique of the medical system tends to leave parents as actors under-explored. Incidentally, very few studies give much, if any, attention to the role of fathers, a subject to which I will return. In arguing that some children do not survive because their parents neglect them these social negligence theorists sometimes see women not merely as ignorant, but as using what they know to favour the survival of some children over others. However, the analytical weakness of social negligence as an approach is that it often takes as its point of departure the apparent lack of emotion of parents upon the death of a child, when Bonnet points out that parental diffidence is extremely difficult to interpret.

There is one further site where one could locate agency or responsibility for the illness and death of small children, and that is with the children themselves.

This notion of agency is entirely alien to most parents in the West, for whom an infant is, by definition, a powerless creature with no will of its own. Their innocence renders "negligent" parents all the more culpable on the occasion of their death. Yet it is important to emphasize, however strange it may seem to outsiders, that many African parents are extremely attentive to what they understand to be the will and desire of the child. Small children, as Alma Gottlieb explores in her refreshing and thought-provoking book *The Afterlife is Where We Come From*, are quite commonly understood to have desires and a will of their own (Gottlieb, 2004). Babies emerge from the "other world" and they may choose to stay or to return. Parents in effect see themselves as wooing children by making this world a pleasant and desirable place with no tears, nothing frightful, and no one forcing things upon them.

This might explain in part the pattern of puzzling passivity African mothers sometimes exhibit when their malnourished babies cease to show a desire to eat or drink. As Bonnet observes, "a good mother doesn't get ahead of the desires of her child, she knows simply how to discern them and to respond to them, whereas for health personnel a 'bad mother' is one who doesn't know how to anticipate the needs of the child" (Bonnet, 1996: p. 9). Nancy Keith notes that there is a real lack of fit between the nutritional advice proffered to Hausa mothers who are urged to "feed" children certain nutritious foods, and the imperative mothers feel to submit to the will of the child: "Contrast this [nutritional advice] with the Hausa view that the child has the right to decide whether or not to eat, and that it is not the mother's place to interfere by poking food into the child's mouth or otherwise coercing the child to eat" (Keith, 1991a). One important psychological implication of this may be that as malnourished children lose appetite, their apathy is experienced by their mothers as a kind of rejection, setting in train a particularly unhealthy dynamic (Bonnet, 1996: p. 14).

Beyond "culture": women's educational and economic marginality

In the debates about the purported "socio-cultural" origins of Niger's 2005 malnutrition crisis one rarely finds the kind of subtle and ethnographically informed cultural analysis offered by Bonnet, Jaffré and Souley, which I have sketched above. Rather, invoking cultural causes seems to be primarily a way of deflecting responsibility away from the state and other established institutions and onto "those cultures out there". Despite the reality that malnutrition in Niger is a nation-wide phenomenon, the shape of the discussion has tended to locate the cultural problem as far from the capital as possible.

One begins by noting, as President Tandja did, that unlike the general famines of the early 1970s and 1984, the 2005 food crisis did not result in massive influxes of rural people into the capital Niamey; this crisis did not "belong" to the whole country, it was the problem of isolated areas: "The people of Niger look well fed, as you can see [...] If these problems were serious there would be shanty towns forming around the big towns and people will flee [...]".[2] Then, one notes that malnutrition is not class-related (glossing over the significant differences between the households of educated functionaries and other relatively well-off families). As one Swiss development worker opined, "sometimes the youngest or the second child doesn't receive food [...] We have to recognize the fact that some families don't concern themselves with their children. The fact is that children die, but it isn't necessarily because the family is poor or lacking in food."[3] This enables one to suggest that the problems are "cultural" rather than "economic". Finally one implies (at this stage one is never explicit) that it is backward Hausa speakers who are to blame for their own problems. If one can simply show that culture explains the malnutrition of Hausa children, then one does not need to look too closely at the broader problems that contribute to a chronic if less acute pattern countrywide, or explore too deeply the relative underdevelopment of the Maradi region relative to other regions of the country closer to the reins of power among the elite of Niamey.

Key to making this argument work is an emphasis upon the poor child rearing practices of Hausa mothers. As is so often the case, women can then be seen to be the authors of their own problems and the solution would appear to be a vague attention to "*sensibilisation*" of such women to their poor practices. This was a tried and true strategy for evading issues of inequality and underdevelopment during the colonial era, as Anne Hugon observes for the colonial Gold Coast, where a "purely culturalist approach" relieved doctors and administrators of the need to reflect upon the social and material obstacles to women successfully providing their children with rich and varied food (Hugon, 2004: p. 153). One sees something of this kind of slippage, from regarding women as the victims of certain structural disadvantages to regarding them as the source of the problem themselves, in media references to "customs and beliefs" that contributed to the food crisis, including food

[2] President Mamadou Tandja quoted in "President Tandja: The People of Niger Look Well Fed, As You Can See", *RedOrbit News*, 10 August 2005.

[3] Peter Bieler of the Direction Suisse du Développement et de la Collaboration, quoted in "Désaccord autour de l'aide alimentaire au Niger," *Swissinfo*, 19 September, 2005.

taboos that disadvantage small children and the withholding of colostrum. While the sources for one such article emphasize women's legal constraints and their lack of access to education, the article itself concluded by stating that the crisis is structural, "not to say cultural", leaving one with the clear impression that the traditions in question are largely due to women's "traditional" practices.[4]

Certainly it is true that studies show childhood malnutrition in the Maradi region to be chronic and not limited to the most poverty stricken households. Yet the wealth and status of the "households" in question in these studies are understood to be determined largely as a function of the wealth and capital of the male household head. A man with many fields, a market garden and a truck is deemed to render his entire household "rich", even if his wives' children are malnourished.[5] Claire Robertson long ago argued that class is gendered in Africa, meaning that given the flows and distribution of wealth, labour, property, and productive assets between married couples, the class positions of husbands and wives in a single household can differ radically. In general, she argues on the basis of work in Ghana, women as a group have gradually become disadvantaged relative to men over the course of the twentieth century (Robertson, 1984). This argument has prompted the spilling of much ink both for and against the notion of the gendering of class in Africa, and argument over the causes and timing of any such difference. Nevertheless, given all that we now know about intrahousehold dynamics and the separation of male and female budgets in Africa it seems peculiar in the extreme to assume in advance that husbands and wives occupy the same economic stratum.

In Maradi, as Marthe Diarra and Marie Monimart show in their contribution to this volume, women have gradually lost access to land, the single most important resource in this agro-pastoral economy.[6] Furthermore, women are often left to fend for themselves and their smallest children for much of the year as their husbands, brothers and sons increasingly migrate elsewhere to get through the dry season. Men's dry season migration can mean the difference between the viability and the collapse of a village community if they send income back, but women have little or no control over whether male out-migration will produce food and income to keep the family afloat. This occurs

---

[4] Axel Gyldén "Traditions fatales," *L'Express*, 15 September, 2005.
[5] Mariatou Koné points out the contradictions within such "rich" households using precisely such an example (LASDEL, 2006: pp. 54–5).
[6] See their chapter in this book.

in an environment of "cost recovery" which guarantees that access to the most basic of health-care is prohibitively expensive for most women. Niger has the flimsiest of primary health-care systems at the moment because almost no one can afford to pay the extortionate fees so "inhospitably" imposed there (Jaffré and Olivier de Sardan, 2003).

Some women excluded from land themselves are constrained to sell their labour very cheaply on other people's farms, making it hard for them to see to their small children's needs back home during the peak of the malaria season, which coincides of course with the farming season. More desperate women, particularly those whose husbands disappear indefinitely, migrate to urban centres to get access to cash employment, food aid and emergency medical services. They may find that they have to rely upon exchanging sexual favours for food, cash, and access to such necessities as medicines and clothing. Moralistic religious leaders then attribute the general downturn in the well-being of the community to the immorality of such women, who are scapegoated and can be extremely vulnerable to physical and verbal abuse.[7] The dysfunctional economy is regularly projected upon the most vulnerable of women. Women who are married young to prevent "immorality" and who have had little opportunity to go to school are excluded from the exchange of information that provides an understanding of biology, knowledge of the potential of contraception to help them space and control their births, and most significantly a grasp of nutrition and hygiene. However much one might fault the "domestic" education that has so consistently been provided to African women in lieu of the kind of technical and professional training they would need to take positions of leadership and earn salaried employment, at least such education does potentially have the virtue of providing a foundation in basic understanding of health, which is traditionally the responsibility of women as mothers. Women's extraordinarily low literacy levels in Niger are very much a part of the story of the 2005 crisis; women's exclusion from schooling is bound up with their relegation to a second-class status as a group. While malnutrition is often said to cross income groups, there is a very clear connection between childhood malnutrition and the low educational levels of women in Niger (Harouna, 1998: p. 74). Informal conversations with unemployed educated women suggest to me that such women may be cynical about the benefits of Western education in a deteriorating job market that in any case

---

[7] See my book *Evangelical Christians in the Muslim Sahel* (Cooper, 2006) for an analysis of the assault upon single women in times of crisis and its relationship to development discourses.

privileges men, but they do deeply value the access it has given them to a better understanding of health issues.

Seclusion of married women aggravates this problem of women's lack of access to information, for such women have little access to the kinds of gatherings in which nutrition and health information is conveyed. Tellingly, one study by CARE found that struggling but mobile single women often have healthier infants than secluded women in "rich" households for precisely this reason—single women who benefit from an institutional support network are more likely to seek out and obtain information that can contribute to the health of their children, and they engage in a range of economic activities that can improve their children's nutrition, such as cooking nutritionally rich snack foods for sale (such as *kosai* bean cakes). In normal times such women's children sometimes fare better than the children of their "wealthier" sisters. But in times of crisis it is the children of isolated single women who are most vulnerable to severe malnutrition (CARE, 2000). Under the circumstances it is nonsensical to de-emphasize "economic" factors in favour of "socio-cultural" practices to account for childhood malnutrition in Niger. Women's exclusion from the means of production and from education is an economic issue.

Nonetheless, Maradi's "bad mothers" are regularly credited with a range of ignorant and perhaps even infanticidal behaviour that imperils the lives of their children. It includes withholding colostrum from their newborn babies, feeding infants water and other suspect fluids when they should be limited to breast milk, "violent" and "premature" weaning of their children, poor birth spacing that contributes to poor weaning practices, feeding weaned children inappropriate food, and a reluctance to seek medical help for children, particularly later born children. And of course it is women who are said to prevent their daughters from going to school by keeping them home to assist in housework and small-scale trade. Beneath the oblique reference to "cultural factors" there seems to be a notion that if only women in the region were better mothers, Niger would not suffer from the embarrassing appearance of having trouble feeding its population.[8]

---

[8] That humiliation is a key issue in the reaction to this crisis in Niger's capital is shown in President Tandja's remark to the Voice of America that while Niger was grateful for food aid, he begged donors not to "*aller exposer dans le monde entier ce qu'ils font pour les petits enfants malnourris*" [go and expose to the whole world what they are doing for young malnourished children]. Quoted in Philippe Bernard, "Niger: les leçons d'une 'famine' annoncée", *Le Monde*, 5 August 2005.

Let me be clear here. I am not arguing that certain child-rearing practices common in Niger (and not necessarily limited to Hausa communities) are not detrimental to the health of Niger's children. All of the above mentioned practices can, indeed, lead to weakened immune systems, greater vulnerability to disease, and increased childhood mortality. My point is rather that such practices persist for a reason. Niger's health and educational resources are not evenly distributed, and those women who benefit from education and from proximity to medical services will have rather different experiences of pregnancy, childbirth, and childrearing than those who do not. The problem is simultaneously one of access to information (which is related to education in part) and access to services. If one compares a map showing the distribution of health services in Niger relative to density of population with a map of relatively high infant mortality, it becomes immediately clear that children die in areas that are underserved by medical services, schools, and wells.[9] The elite of Niamey can congratulate itself that it is more enlightened and that therefore its children survive well, but the rest of Niger suffers from the reality that quite sizeable populations lack the critical density of services necessary to have a significant impact on infant and child mortality.

Do women in Niamey give their newborn infants water to drink (contrary to the ideal feeding practices recommended by Western practitioners) with a few adverse consequences? Probably. It is not simply a matter of "culture" that some Nigériens have clean water, so that their infants do not suffer any ill consequences from being fed water in addition to breast milk, while others have no access to clean water. Because so many small children die quietly far from the capital their deaths are not considered to qualify as a "crisis".

To offer another very concrete example of the complex dynamic between infrastructure and parenting practices, we know that women whose births are assisted by trained personnel are far more likely to nurse their newborns immediately (République du Niger, 1997: p. 147). If one does not have access to medical facilities it follows that one does not have access to encouragement to provide the infant with colostrum. Do women withhold colostrum because of "culture", because they are deficient in maternal affection, or because they are not well served by the existing health system? Soumana Harouna found that among the most important variables affecting the likelihood of women seeking care was whether they lived more than five kilometres from a suitable

---

[9] The office of the Prime Minister is acutely aware of what I am arguing, for my evidence comes in part from the government's own planning document (République du Niger, 2002). See maps 114, 115, 116, 118, 120. See also Balk *et al.*, 2003.

health centre (Harouna, 1998: p. 62). While the intention of the study seems to have been to place the responsibility for infant mortality on mothers, the details that emerged also revealed profound problems of infrastructure. Certainly some parenting practices should be discouraged, but correcting them is a matter of economics and political will, not simply culture.

One of the most common interventions to "sensitize" women who are seen to be inadequate mothers is to encourage them to diversify their children's diets. As I mentioned above, the notion of "feeding" children is somewhat problematic in this setting. Nevertheless women in Maradi are generally aware that providing their children with more protein, oil, fruit and vegetables would benefit them, and in my experience mothers are quite open to offering quite small children bits of foods from mango to cooked spinach to taste and to play with. Nevertheless decades of intervention to teach women the benefits of better nutrition have not had stunning results. Why? To begin with, such intervention is often rather sporadic, subject to shifting fashions and political winds (Parlato and Seidel, 1998). Above all, however, women who cannot afford millet when the price peaks cannot, *a fortiori*, afford expensive meat, snacks, fruits and vegetables. However much they might like to offer their children nutritious foods, the imperative to raise cash to buy the staple food is so pressing that it pre-empts all other needs. Similarly, farmers make decisions on what to plant on the basis of their estimation of their best bet in terms of raising the cash they will need to meet the food and other expenses of the year. The absurdity of the notion that women would feed their children better "if they only knew better" is reflected, I think, in the laughter of women in one of MSF's feeding centres in Maradi when asked when they had last served meat.[10]

Final in the list of Hausa mothers' failings, improper weaning practices seem to have become a favourite whipping boy, with emphasis being consistently placed on both "premature" and "sudden" weaning. Nancy Keith's 1991 dissertation is one of the few studies to offer close ethnographic data on these practices; she found that contrary to the common assumptions within the development literature, Hausa women in her village study seemed more inclined to provide their babies with colostrum than in the past. Most women breastfed on demand until the child reached the age of two, unless they became pregnant. While the final weaning of a child was decisive, taking place in one day, the process of weaning could take up to 18 months and many babies were introduced to supplementary foods by seven months. Keith's

[10] Matthew Green, "Too poor to live: poverty kills Niger's hungry", *Reuters*, 2 July 2005.

research does not seem to confirm the image of "sudden" and "abrupt" weaning as typical of ideal Hausa parenting practice (Keith, 1991b).

The fixation with "*sevrage correct*" is quite striking in debates about how to respond to the malnutrition crisis in Niger, but rarely is it accompanied by any discussion of the relationship between weaning, birth spacing, sexuality in marriage, and access to medical services.[11] Birth spacing norms in this region seem to have changed over time, with intervals declining as the twentieth century progressed. In the nineteenth century Hausa women could count upon sexual taboos during a lengthy lactation period to assist them in spacing their children.[12] Hence the end of the period of nursing ideally marked the resumption of sexual relations between husband and wife. One can readily imagine that some parents were eager for the signs that a child was ready to be weaned—the beginnings of being able to walk might be a critical marker. One aspect of that taboo was that should a woman become pregnant while nursing—something of a scandal—the nursing baby had to be weaned immediately. It continues to be true today, even as the sexual taboo seems to have fallen by the wayside, that when a woman becomes pregnant she weans her nursing child as quickly as she can, as pregnancy is widely seen as spoiling the mother's milk.

But when condemning Hausa weaning practices, development practitioners seem to forget that intervention by Western institutions in African nursing and birth spacing practices has a long history. Like interventions to teach women better nutrition, this intervention has not historically been particularly consistent. Nancy Rose Hunt has provided a fascinating study of the ways in which Belgian colonialism intruded into the intimate spheres of nursing, weaning, and marital sexual relations in an effort to discourage lengthy nursing, reduce birth spacing, and encourage the resumption of marital sexual relations relatively soon after childbirth—all in an effort to increase the population of the Belgian Congo (Hunt, 1988). While the kinds of institutions upon which the Belgian colonial administration depended, including secular voluntary associations such as Goutte de Lait and Catholic missions, were never as fully embraced by the French colonial administration and certainly

---

[11] See for example Communiqué de presse du Coordonateur humanitaire Niamey, Niger. United Nations Office for the Coordination of Humanitarian Affairs (OCHA), 20 September 2005.

[12] For a sense of how older women as a group imposed their ideal spacing expectations upon men and younger women in the late nineteenth and early twentieth century see Mary F. Smith, *Baba of Karo: A Woman of the Muslim Hausa*, 1981: pp. 149–50.

did not have any real purchase in Niger, it is nevertheless clear that until the post-colonial period French and Western institutions more broadly did not *discourage* women in Niger from reducing the lengthy lactation period and the prolonged sexual taboos that ensured a healthy birth spacing and facilitated a more gradual weaning. France's preoccupation during the entire colonial period, like that of Belgium, was with increasing the population in order to effect the *mise en valeur* of the territory under its control. For their part, Anglophone missionaries in Niger encouraged good Christian wives to resume sexual relations with their husbands early, in an effort to combat the presumed evils of polygamy and to compete demographically with the dominant Muslims (Cooper, 2006). Perhaps most important, as Islam came to have greater and greater judicial and social significance in Niger as the colonial period progressed, and indigenous practices (as argued by Kent Glenzer elsewhere in this volume) were increasingly seen as "ignorant", the traditional taboo on marital sex while nursing gradually gave way to the generally accepted practice in Muslim societies whereby sexual relations could be resumed 40 days after the birth of the baby.[13]

Given this complex and inconsistent history, when women's pregnancies today are not spaced optimally, should this be seen as women's superstitious adherence to age-old "socio-cultural practices", or as an indication of women's declining bargaining position in marriage as a result of changes during the colonial and post-colonial periods? Women I interviewed in the late 1980s emphatically regarded birth spacing at less than two years and nine months (meaning pregnancy before a nursing child has benefited from mother's milk for 24 months) as a problem related to a lack of "shame" or "respect" (*kunya*) on the part of men. From these women's vantage point, it was men's unwillingness to wait for the customary two years before insisting upon sexual relations with their wives that led to the early weaning of babies. One can argue that it is ignorance and superstition about the qualities of mothers' milk that lead women to wean their infants rather abruptly as soon as they become pregnant, or one can see the proscription of pregnancy before a timely weaning as part of a cultural complex that enabled women to enforce optimal birth spacing in the past. If husbands no longer respect the taboos that made such spacing possible, one cannot fault wives alone for following the residual requirement of "precipitous" weaning upon pregnancy. How a woman whose body is already

---

[13] Etienne and Francine van de Walle note that postpartum abstinence for a period of 40 days is typical throughout Islamic Africa, while much longer periods are typical in non-Muslim regions (van de Walle and van de Walle, 1988: pp. 25–6).

taxed by limited caloric intake and nutritional variety is to be expected to feed both an unborn child and a nursing infant while maintaining her own health and very likely engaging in strenuous farm work is a question that those who criticize pregnant women's abrupt weaning of infants don't tend to address. Obviously contraception would help. Abrupt weaning in the region, then, is surely as much a "problem" of men's education and will as it is of women's culture.

Population size and birth control

Beneath the critique of Hausa women as bad mothers, then, lies a deeper malaise over their fecundity that recalls President Kountché's famous pronouncement to Niger's women: "*Excusez-moi, mes soeurs, mais vous pondez trop.*"[14] Niger is now seen by the outside world as overpopulated, and when there are too many babies, it is implicitly seen as the fault of women who, like mindless animals, breed too much. Little consideration is given to local perceptions that in fact growing villages are more successful than declining or stagnating villages and that diversified income through male migration can be critical to sustaining such villages (Rain, 1999: 188–189). Media images of food crises in Niger are ambivalent. On the surface in the narrative there is sympathy for the predicament of neglected populations of women and children. Yet one reads such double-edged comments as, "[f]or some women, who often have eight children, there is faint hope of keeping all their infants alive."[15] The visual images, in particular, convey a story of rampant and unrestrained reproduction. If only African women had fewer babies there would be no food shortages, so goes the unspoken logic.

Two Niger intellectuals—Alpha Boureima Gado, a historian of famine in the Sahel, and the economist Chako Cherif—argue that at least in part the problem at the national level must be addressed through a coherent and proactive population policy. Both have been much solicited by the media for thoughts on the drought, food shortage, and food distribution. Although Gado is interested in the demographic implications of food crises, he does not argue that famines prior to the 1984 famine were related to overpopulation.

[14] "Pardon me, sisters, but you lay too many eggs." The comment, made in a speech in 1986, is much quoted in literature on family planning and population in Africa. See Thérèse Locoh and Yara Makdessi, 1996: 15.

[15] Matthew Green, "Too poor to live," *op. cit.*

Nor does he argue for a strong gender dimension to them, despite interesting evidence of women's vulnerability during crises (Gado, 1993). Renewed study on the food crises of the post-war period would be most welcome. I certainly agree that a strong population policy and in particular a frank and open discussion not simply of birth spacing, but of the need for population control, would be a very welcome development in Niger. Such a discussion would require a great deal of political self confidence on the part of Niger's leadership given the resistance of some of Niger's more activist and outspoken religious groups to the very notion of contraception. But here it is the question of where responsibility lies that interests me. As Kountché's *bon mot* reveals, only rarely are the men who produce numerous children faulted for failing to match their ability to provide for them with their production of offspring. The burden is so often (and so improbably) laid at the door of women. In debates about revising the legal code to make more protection for women and children, men in Niger regularly make the argument that because under Islam they are responsible for their wives and children, they should continue to benefit from the unequal inheritance patterns and marital provisions that disadvantage women. Yet when it comes to making good on their obligation to care for all their dependants they suddenly find it convenient to argue that it is Allah who will provide for them.

Niger's women do have, on average, eight children, but the harsh reality is that many of those children will die before they reach the age of five. One faces the classic conundrum: do women have many babies because so many of them will die, or do their children die because women have so many? Studies of fertility objectives of women in West Africa have consistently shown that women tend to want to have as many children as God will give them, a formulation that is pious but less revealing than it might at first appear to be, for it does not necessarily imply that women don't wish to control their reproduction. Women tend to see an optimal childbearing outcome as being contingent upon their own health, upon good birth spacing, and upon the health of the children they already have.[16] Simply getting pregnant immediately after childbirth to maximize one's offspring is not, in fact, what most women regard as ideal. Relatively few women have access to the contraception that would enable them to optimize their childbearing potential in the absence of postpartum abstinence, not simply because of the scarcity of services, but because

[16] For a paradigm-altering exploration of the realities of childbirth and reproduction for African women see Caroline H. Bledsoe, *Contingent Lives: Fertility, Time, and Aging in West Africa*, 2002.

the ideological resistance to contraception among women's husbands is profound. There are issues of sexuality here that go consistently unaddressed—if sexual intercourse is to occur only in the context of childbearing, then there is no room for regular sex in a marriage where spacing is desired. But such attitudes leave couples unsatisfied for unrealistic periods of time and reduce women's sexuality to procreation.[17] Not surprisingly women find themselves bearing children too close together, and then having to watch those children die.

Does the high infant and child mortality rate provide an indirect index of more or less conscious and wilful neglect? There is now a rich and contentious literature debating whether poor women are not sometimes driven by a callous international system and unfeeling religious dogma to "permit" some of their weaker offspring to die. In her rich and provocative book, *Death Without Weeping: The Violence of Everyday Life in Brazil*, Nancy Scheper-Hughes struggles to do justice to the unspeakable subject of childhood mortality and how Catholic mothers without contraception in Brazil respond to it:

I have stumbled on a situation in which shantytown mothers appear to have "suspended the ethical"—compassion, empathic love, and care—toward some of their weak and sickly infants. The "reasonableness" and the "inner logic" of their actions are patently obvious and are not up for question. But the moral and ethical dimensions of the practices disturb, give reason to pause... and to doubt (Scheper-Hughes, 1993).

Scheper-Hughes' work is deeply textured and complex and it would be a disservice to dismiss it as inapplicable to African realities without very close study. However, other recent work suggests that West African women may suffer the deaths of their children very differently for a host of historical, spiritual, and economic reasons. Alma Gottlieb's study of the culture of infancy in West Africa offers a vision of an extraordinarily loving relationship to infants among the Beng community in Côte d'Ivoire. We see Beng parents anxious to persuade their babies to remain in the world of humans through whatever means they can devise (Gottlieb, 2004). That those means are very different from what a middle-class Western mother or father would employ (and may at times appear positively detrimental from a Western vantage point) does not mean that Beng parents do not love their children deeply and do not mourn their deaths as fully as their Western counterparts with fewer births. Jónina Einarsdóttir argues explicitly against the universality of Scheper-Hughes' findings using evidence from Guinea-Bissau, giving particular

---

[17] For a thought provoking study of the psychology of fertility and infertility see Dominique Lutz-Fuchs, *Psychothérapies de femmes africaines*, 1994.

attention to the painful pervasiveness of grief in women's lives when their children die seemingly inexplicable deaths (Einarsdóttir, 2004). Without knowing a great deal more about the emotional, spiritual and moral world of rural Niger it would be callous in the extreme to assume that the children of Niger die because their parents choose to permit them to.[18]

Beyond the blame game: learning from the Plumpy'nut revolution

I hope that I have conveyed some of the reasons for my deep malaise at the emphasis on "socio-cultural factors" in accounting for the malnutrition crisis. It is urgent that solutions to the food security and nutrition crisis in Niger take gender issues into account as an absolute priority, and my fear is that attributing malnutrition to "culture" tends to obscure more than it reveals.

Even those commentators who have focused more on economic solutions than on "culture" have, it seems to me, neglected the importance of a real analysis of gender. For example, solutions to the current food security crisis in Niger that would rely upon a sort of African Green Revolution (such as the Alliance for a Green Revolution in Africa recently launched by the Bill and Melinda Gates Foundation together with the Rockefeller Foundation) will be unlikely to address the malnutrition problems I have discussed, inasmuch as the key issue for women is exclusion from productive resources and social capital, particularly land and education. The likelihood that women will suddenly gain access to *improved* land and high yielding varieties of seed is not at all high given Niger's dismal history with *périmètres irrigués*. The prospect of modern irrigated agriculture in Niger may be a pipe dream in any case, given the gradual drying up of Lake Chad and the depth of the ever-evasive water table. But unless the gender imbalances in access to land and education are addressed this optimistic vision of Niger's future development will be very distant from the realities of women's lives.

Is there a positive lesson to be learned from all this mutual recrimination and the depressing images of 2005? Niger's chronic crisis of malnutrition came into visibility, so to speak, as a result of thousands of women seizing upon a new development in the treatment of malnutrition at the MSF feeding

---

[18] Neither Gottlieb nor Einarsdóttir deny that practices that amount to infanticide of certain babies who are regarded as exceptionally dangerous or non-human exist, but both authors are careful to distinguish those practices from the general course of childrearing. Neither shows any evidence of parents losing children merely through a kind of culture of neglect.

centres. Before 2003 malnourished children were hospitalized with their mothers for the length of their treatment, which could last a month or more. Aside from interfering with women's duties at home in ways that could be detrimental to the other children and potentially endanger women's pursuit of food and income, the fearsome context of the hospital with its association with death and sorcery was seen by many women as presenting yet a further risk to themselves and their children (LASDEL, 2006). Not long before the 2005 crisis MSF had begun to design a new ambulatory approach associated with a new product to treat children with malnutrition, known as Plumpy'nut. As André Briend and Isabelle Defourny's chapters in this book explain, this product's properties enabled a mother to take responsibility for feeding her suffering child while at the same time attending to the needs of other children safely at home. She no longer had to remain for weeks with a debilitated child at a fixed centre, but could instead return much more quickly with a supply of food she could effectively, and extremely successfully, administer herself.[19]

But it is also intriguing and probably important to note that women appreciated Plumpy'nut because their babies visibly responded to it. One reason women have often been reluctant to seek treatment for dehydrated and malnourished babies is that they have not perceived the treatments offered as addressing either their babies' desires or their symptoms. Acceptance of oral rehydration solution globally, for example, is notoriously low, an observation that prompted an entire cross-cultural study of how different societies understand the "ordinary illness" of diarrhoea (Desjeux et al., 1993). In a close study of acceptance of treatment for diarrhoea in Egypt, for example, the researchers found that women felt that a "good" medicine was one that "the child accepts and that heals it"; in other words, a treatment that the baby was willing to take without force and that appeared to redress the disturbing outward symptoms of diarrhoea (Desjeux et al., 1993: pp. 200, 210). Babies, those actors without a speaking part, do indeed seem as a general rule to "accept" Plumpy'nut with a certain enthusiasm, and so, it seems, their mothers generally see it as a "good" medicine.

To me this, more than anything else, proves that Maradi's mothers are not deliberately neglectful, nor are they merely victims. They are eager to be active participants in improving the well-being of their children and other members of their broader communities, but not if seeking treatment entails increased

---

[19] Christophe Ayad and David Revault D'Allonnes, "'Noix dodue' la bonne recette humanitaire", *Libération*, 28 September 2005.

risk. Plumpy'nut gave them a means of agency they seized upon because they could afford it and because it did not imperil their ability to meet other obligations in the home. The startling increase in demand for MSF's services dramatized the need for better, cheaper, and more appropriate health services in Niger; it also threw harsh light upon the degree to which Niger's government, international donors, and a number of male heads of household had for far too long conspired to accept the unacceptable, namely that women should suffer the deaths of many children as a regular and commonplace feature of their lives in Niger. Malnutrition had traditionally been treated as a problem for mothers, not as a public health problem, and not as an *illness* fathers and husbands needed to address. Now, in part as a result of women's alertness to their own babies' response to treatment, the malnutrition crisis is fully visible, and for the first time the cluster of symptoms associated with malnutrition is increasingly seen as a nameable and treatable condition. In Hausa that condition, and the babies who suffer from it, are now known by the term invented by treatment centres, *kwamisu*. Whether that term as popularly deployed corresponds precisely to what medical practitioners mean by "malnutrition" probably remains to be seen, but it is clear that there is the beginning of a ground upon which to build a mutual strategy involving parents and the medical services for improving infant health in Niger.

Given the clear role of women in bringing the crisis to visibility, what is the appeal of this tendency to blame mothers for the 2005 crisis? There is plenty of blame to go around: the procrastination of the Tandja government, the sluggish response of the international community, the ravages of structural adjustment, the confrontational style of MSF, the self-interested practices of American agro-industry, the speculation of grain traders...the list of contributors to the particular shape the crisis took is long and discouraging (see Mousseau and Mittal, 2006). Much heated debate has been spent on what I see as a false dichotomy between "development aid" and "emergency relief". With such high blown rhetoric and such major international dynamics in play, why must mothers be added to this list?

In part because women do have some responsibility in the malnutrition crisis. Women's agency is complex and contradictory—it would be foolish to simply applaud female agency as if it were either consistent or uniformly positive. Women have contributed to the malnutrition crisis in Niger in a host of ways. Older women propagate understandings about milk that are harmful to babies, and younger women submit to orders to withhold their milk. Some mothers do feed their children last, so that their food is just what happens to be left after all the adults have eaten. Some women accuse one another of sorcery when a child dies, rather than seeking causes that might implicate their own practices; co-wives abuse one another's children. In some villages women found that if they administered laxatives to their babies they could persuade emergency workers that they were sufficiently malnourished to merit treatment and the food aid so deeply appreciated back in the women's villages. Women also shared the bracelets that indicate which children are in treatment.[20] Women even reproduce the very conceptions that prevent them from having access to land and income by pursuing secluded marriage for themselves, their daughters, or their daughters-in-law.

For the relatively disempowered and humiliated Niger government the appeal of focusing on "culture" and women is clear—women cannot hit back and they provide as always a convenient scapegoat for the failings of those with greater power. Development institutions with their backs against the wall for the clear failure of decades of development intervention may find it expedient to suggest that culture is the weak link in failed development strategies. Let us hope that all the hand wringing yields approaches that genuinely address women's limited access to productive resources, education, and the cash so necessary to survival. And let us also hope that the Plumpy'nut revolution inspires all parties to cease seeing women as merely the problem and to begin instead working to find ways to provide women with other equally spectacular opportunities to have a constructive hand in shaping a better future for Niger.

---

[20] Mariatou Koné's study reveals the inventiveness of women in "capturing" the goods provided by the infant treatment centres (LASDEL, 2006). Women in Maradi, like those studied by Gottlieb (2004), use herbs and enemas to teach children very young how to regulate their bowels; their use in this context may simply be an extension of an existing practice.

BIBLIOGRAPHY

Balk, D., T. Pullum, A. Storeygard, F. Greenwell and M. Neuman, 2003. *Spatial Analysis of Childhood Mortality in West Africa*. Calverton, Maryland, ORC Macro and Centre for International Earth Science Information Network (CIESIN), Columbia University.

Bledsoe, H.C., 2002. *Contingent Lives: Fertility, Time, and Aging in West Africa*, University of Chicago Press.

Bonnet, D., 1996. "La notion de négligence sociale à propos de la malnutrition de l'enfant", *Sciences Sociales et Santé*, 14 (1), pp. 5–16.

CARE, 2000. "Rapport de l'étude de base", Projet Equité entre les Genres et Sécurité des Conditions de Vie des Ménages, "Tatalin Arzikin Gida" PN 51, September.

Cooper, B., 2006. *Evangelical Christians in the Muslim Sahel*, Bloomington, Indiana University Press.

Desjeux, D. *et al.*, 1993. *Anthropologie d'une maladie ordinaire, Étude de la diarrhée de l'enfant en Algérie, Thaïlande, Chine et Égypte*, Paris, L'Harmattan, 1993.

Einarsdóttir, J., 2004. *Tired of Weeping: Mother Love, Child Death, and Poverty in Guinea-Bissau*, Madison, University of Wisconsin Press.

Gottlieb, A., 2004. *The Afterlife is Where We Come From: The Culture of Infancy in West Africa*, University of Chicago Press.

Harouna, S., 1998. *Incidence du comportement des mères en matière de soins préventifs sur la mortalité des enfants au Niger*, Les Cahiers de L'IFORD, No. 22, July.

Hugon, A., 2004. "La redéfinition de la maternité en Gold Coast, des années 1920 aux années 1950: projet colonial et réalités locales" in A. Hugon (ed.), *Histoire des femmes en situation coloniale*, Paris, Karthala.

Hunt, N.R., 1988. "'Le Bébé en Brousse': European Women, African Birth Spacing and Colonial Intervention in Breast Feeding in the Belgian Congo", *The International Journal of African Historical Studies*, Vol. 21, No. 3, pp. 401–32.

Jaffré, Y., 1996. "Dissonances entre les représentations sociales et médicales de la malnutrition dans un service de pédiatrie au Niger", *Sciences Sociales et Santé*, 14 (1), pp. 41–72.

———— and J.-P. Olivier de Sardan, 2003. *Une médecine inhospitalière: Les difficiles relations entre soignants et soignés dans cinq capitales d'Afrique de l'Ouest*, Paris, Editions Karthala, APAD.

Keith, N., 1991a. *Alimentation, sevrage et maladie diarrhéique des enfants, pratique en vigueur chez les Hausa et implications en matière de sensibilisation*, MSP, Niamey.

———— 1991b. "Feeding, Weaning, and Diarrhoea Illness in Young Hausa Children in Niger", Doctoral dissertation, Lansing, Michigan State University.

LASDEL, 2006. *La crise alimentaire de 2005 au Niger dans la région de Madarounfa et ses effets sur la malnutrition infantile: approche socio-anthropologique*. Rapport principal: Mariatou Kone; preface by Jean-Pierre Olivier de Sardan.

Locoh, T. and Y. Makdessi, 1996. *Politique de population et baisse de la fécondité en Afrique sub-saharienne*, Les dossiers du CEPED, No. 44, Paris, November.

Lutz-Fuchs, D., 1994. *Psychothérapies de femmes africaines*, Paris, L'Harmattan.

Mousseau, F. and A. Mittal, 2006. *Sahel: A Prisoner of Starvation? A Case Study of the 2005 Food Crisis in Niger*, The Oakland Institute, October.

Oomman, N., E. Lule, D. Vazirani and R. Chhabra, 2003, *Niger: Inequalities in Health, Nutrition and Population*, Health, Nutrition and Population Discussion Paper, World Bank, June.

Parlato, M. and R. Seidel (eds), 1998. *Large-Scale Application of Nutrition Behaviour Change Approaches: Lessons from West Africa*, BASICS, Arlington.

Rain, D., 1999. *Eaters of the Dry Season: Circular Labour Migration in the West African Sahel*, Boulder: Westview Press.

République du Niger, 1997. *Niger: Rapport Démographique et de Santé.*

République du Niger, Office of the Prime Minister, 2002. *Full Poverty Reduction Strategy.*

Robertson, C., 1984. *Sharing the Same Bowl: a Socioeconomic History of Women and Class in Accra, Ghana*, Ann Arbor, University of Michigan Press.

Scheper-Hughes, N., 1993. *Death Without Weeping: The Violence of Everyday Life in Brazil*, Berkeley, University of California Press.

Smith, F.M., 1981. *Baba of Karo: A Woman of the Muslim Hausa*, New Haven, Yale University Press [1954].

Souley, A., 2003. "Représentations populaires hausa et songhay-zarma de quelques maladies (entités nosologiques populaires)" in Y. Jaffré and J. P. Olivier de Sardan, *op. cit.*

Van de Walle, E. and F. Van de Walle, 1988. "Birthspacing and Abstinence in Sub-Saharan Africa", *International Family Planning Perspectives*, 14 (1), March.

Part III

MAKING CHILDREN LIVE

8

Operational Innovation in Practice: MSF's Programme Against Malnutrition in Maradi (2001–2007)

Isabelle Defourny

The issue of childhood malnutrition in Niger has sparked many debates within Médecins Sans Frontières (MSF). Depending on the year and individual, the nutritional situation in Niger has been described as either an exceptional state of affairs or the normal state of affairs for the Sahel region. The situation has also been characterized alternatively as a nutritional emergency, an acute crisis, a chronic crisis, and a malnutrition epidemic. The role of a humanitarian aid organization such as MSF in a peaceful nation where malnutrition is a recurrent problem has also been frequently debated. The chronic nature of this malnutrition and its presumed causes translate into a problem that is usually seen as being under the auspices of the Niger state and organizations specializing in development.

This programme was originally started to address an emergency situation in the summer of 2001, which took place during a measles epidemic and a period of food shortages. From the very beginning, it was clearly specified that MSF's objective was not to prevent or reduce malnutrition, but rather to decrease its associated mortality. This was accomplished by developing a system of outpatient nutritional rehabilitation, which was presumed to be more efficient than the traditional system. In 2004, this project resulted in the treatment of some 10,000 children, with a recovery rate of more than 80%. In 2005, the very high number of admissions confirmed the large-scale effectiveness of ready-to-use therapeutic food (RUTF) and also enabled a better understanding of the nutritional situation in Niger's farming region. The excellent results achieved in 2005 suggested great promise, particularly in terms of the treatment of malnutrition at an earlier stage. In 2006, more than 70,000 children were admitted to feeding centres as soon as they reached a state of moderate malnutrition. The recovery rate was more than 90%. Furthermore, and for the first time since 2001, we did not observe an increase in severe acute malnutrition during the lean period.

The use of these RUTFs, combined with the outpatient system, has resulted in a tenfold increase in treatment capacities for children with acute malnutrition, while at the same time markedly improving recovery rates. Malnutrition could no longer be said to be a matter of fate. Nigérien mothers understood this change. Today, RUTFs hold great promise for advances in the field of preventative and curative medicine in precarious situations.

Setting and initial challenges

The Maradi feeding programme began in July 2001 in accordance with traditional intervention criteria: during a significant measles epidemic, rapid assessments revealed that 6- to 59-month-old children of the region were in a worrying nutritional situation. At the time, this malnutrition could be explained by the measles epidemic, but also by food scarcity, since Niger was confronting its third year of poor harvests. On the basis of these arguments, the decision was made to implement a feeding programme to last until the end of the lean period.

During the five months of the intervention, more than 3,700 children suffering from severe acute malnutrition were admitted into the programme in Maradi, and 738 in Dakoro. Many years had passed since so many malnourished children were treated in Niger's health facilities. As priority in health and nutrition had shifted towards preventative measures, former feeding centres had been transformed into educational centres. Because of this situation, the main strategies for fighting malnutrition at the time included dietary advice, assistance in the preparation of porridge (with mothers providing the food), and education on the appropriate way of weaning. UNICEF, Ministry of Health personnel, and several NGOs were disseminating these messages to mothers. Hospitals were only admitting a few malnourished patients, since they had no real ability to treat them.

For MSF, the number of malnourished children admitted in Maradi begged the question: why were there so many malnourished children in a region considered to be privileged in terms of access to food and nicknamed "the bread-basket of Niger"? At the time, the explanations were always confusing. Some at MSF described the malnutrition in Niger as a "complex problem, of a multifactorial nature, requiring an interdisciplinary approach to understand its unique dynamics".[1] The unusual situation in Maradi was explained by "a lack of social and cultural cohesion typical of a large city of traders, stagnant economic growth, and rising Islamic fundamentalism".[2] Also mentioned was the very high population density in this region of Niger. Whatever the cause, malnutrition was perceived as a development problem. Hence the project was recommended for termination at the end of the lean period.

In December 2001, however, the number of children in the programme remained very high. Even though it was obvious that the children with severe acute malnutrition would not be treated without MSF's involvement, the decision to remain in Niger was not an easy one to make. MSF had not long previously withdrawn from Zinder, where it had conducted a feeding programme in 1997 and 1998. Essentially, the reasons for ending this programme were its mediocre results and the lack of any promise to improve this outcome. Treating severe malnutrition was complicated and required several weeks of hospital treatment. In 2001 Plumpy'nut, a vitamin- and mineral-enriched paste, with a milk and groundnut base and composition similar to that of therapeutic milk, was given to several children suffering from severe acute malnutrition. This product had the advantage of allowing home-based treatment of malnutrition and thus held out the promise of increasing the number of children being treated without the need to strengthen hospital capacities. The principle is simple: those children who retain good appetites and show no signs of any severe associated disease are not admitted to hospital, but rather

[1] MSF Administrative Council report, 21 December 2001.
[2] MSF, report from a field visit to Niger, from 1 to 8 October 2001.

return to their families along with the amount of Plumpy'nut necessary for their treatment. Since 1998, MSF had been aware of this product, which was created to treat severe acute malnutrition and manufactured by Nutriset. It was used in Sudan, Congo-Brazzaville, and Afghanistan, but never for the outpatient treatment of severe malnutrition.

The results of 2001 were not immediately conclusive: of the 3,737 children admitted to the Maradi programme, only 57.7% left the programme cured. The dropout rate remained extremely high (almost 36%). The outpatient use of this product was implemented late and with difficulty. Physicians and nurses were not convinced. They thought it inconceivable to send such seriously sick children home with no medical surveillance. In Europe these children would have been admitted to a paediatric intensive care unit. But the Niger children's mothers had no choice. They could not stay in the hospital for a month with a single child while work remained in the field and the rest of their family was expecting them. Therefore, a great many of them left the feeding centre prematurely as their child's status improved. It was this pressure from the mothers that led medical personnel to start outpatient treatment for some children, albeit not without imposing a preliminary phase of hospitalization. The chief emergency physician and the nurse/nutritionist who started the programme were convinced of the need to persevere in this direction. In the use of Plumpy'nut and the outpatient programme, they saw an opportunity to improve the management of acute malnutrition not only in Niger, but also in MSF's other regions of intervention, where malnutrition frequently occurs. They hoped to avoid admitting a significant number of children by allowing mothers to administer the nutritional treatment at home. They were also counting upon this innovation to reduce the number of dropouts.

Against this background, the decision was made to continue the feeding programme in Niger. From the beginning of the programme, headquarters and the field teams knew that under-five mortality in Niger was one of the highest in the world. They were equally aware of the role played by malnutrition in this mortality. It was clear to everyone that the problem of malnutrition was a recurring one and that there were many children suffering from acute malnutrition throughout Niger. However, the objective of the programme had to be realistic. It needed to be medically reassuring (outpatient care was to be done gradually and the results measured in a precise manner) but also circumscribed in order to avoid a drift toward issues outside the organization's area of competency and clearly involving more of a development focus. The objective was therefore consciously limited to reducing the mortality associated with severe acute malnutrition among the children presented at our health facilities in Maradi. There was no question of preventing malnutrition, or of treating every child in Niger, and certainly not of decreasing under-five mortality in Maradi.

However, wider applications were being considered as soon as the programme began, even though these applications were still viewed with caution. In a report dating from the end of 2001 and addressed to the operations department, the main issues were discussed as follows:

Can MSF address malnutrition using only an emergency framework, such as conducting a few surveys, a few food security reports, analyzing the deficiencies of the aid system and the political use of hunger, all without having a long-term programme in this area? MSF is capable of conducting an "Access to Medicines" campaign. Can it include in this campaign access to "nutritional" medicines? I am starting to believe that it might be interesting to involve ourselves once again in Niger and try not only to respond medically to malnutrition—which would in itself not be easy—but also to create a link between all the different intervening actors involved in the vast subject of "food" in Niger. We might get roughed up, but we might learn a lot as well, with perhaps a decrease in mortality in the end.

However, the in-house hesitation about any excessively ambitious objectives is clearly taken into consideration, since the author concludes: "No need for worry—no commitment was made..."[3]

Developing an innovative strategy

During these three years, therefore, the programme's main objective was to develop an outpatient system of nutritional rehabilitation for children suffering from severe acute malnutrition. This was to be done to decrease the mortality linked to this disease. In concrete terms, the aim was to send home children who were so far receiving treatment inside feeding centres. For many carers, this new approach was far from being obviously right.

To avoid hospital treatment for children with the most severe forms of acute malnutrition was an ambitious objective for MSF, one which implied a radical change in medical and nutritional practices. Under the existing protocol, children with severe acute malnutrition needed significant nutritional and medical surveillance. Nutritional rehabilitation was complicated and required a strict diet based on the administration of therapeutic milk every three hours. Each child received different quantities of milk depending on his or her

[3] Internal MSF report, Niamey nutrition meeting, 2001.

weight and treatment stage. The milk did not keep longer than two hours and was prepared accordingly eight times per day. There were numerous personnel involved in the preparation and administration of the milk. Furthermore, since these children are particularly sensitive to infection, impeccable hygiene must be guaranteed—not an easy task when several hundred children and mothers are hospitalized.

With the outpatient strategy, neither medical nor nutritional surveillance could be as precise as this. The objective was to decrease the number of defaults by offering a system better suited to the constraints of the mothers, as well as reducing the risk of nosocomial infection by decreasing the number or duration of the hospitalizations. It also involved treating a higher number of children with fewer medical personnel.

The outpatient component of the programme began in January 2002 with great caution: following an initial hospitalization phase, children with a good appetite, whose associated conditions were under control, would be monitored in an outpatient setting. At this point, strong reservations were already arising among members of the combined Niger and international team. Few physicians agreed to send such severely sick children home before a complete recovery. For some Niger medical personnel, outpatient care was considered to be substandard medical care. However, even though the difficulties were significant, this did represent a first step, since the entire challenge was for children to be allowed directly into the outpatient feeding programme, without prior hospitalization. This presumed that after a simple consultation, the medical staff member would decide to send the child home and would trust the administration of all the medical and nutritional treatment to the mother. A year and a half was needed for some children to be allowed directly into an outpatient setting.[4] It was only then that the number of hospitalizations truly lessened and the number of children in the programme grew significantly. Indeed, outpatient centres require few resources; they can be relatively easily multiplied and situated nearer to the mothers and sick children. MSF pursued its efforts, to the point that, little by little, the majority of children began to receive their entire nutritional rehabilitation at home. The number of children accepted into the programme increased and the results improved every year. MSF presented these results to the public in October 2003, during a conference organized in Dublin by the NGOs Concern and Valid International.

However, another problem was plaguing this new treatment protocol. Plumpy'nut's cost had been identified from the very start of the programme as

---

[4] This involves children with marasmus with no severe medical complication or anorexia.

an obstacle to its adoption by other actors. The course of action chosen was to produce this food in Niger. In October 2003, a collaboration began among a Nigérien company, the Société de Transformation Alimentaire (Food Processing Company), and MSF. At the end of 2004, MSF withdrew from this project and Nutriset, the company holding the Plumpy'nut patent, became responsible for the quality of the food products.

The main programme objective was attained at the end of 2004. An effective model for the treatment of severe acute malnutrition was demonstrated, with more than 80% of programme participants recovering and less than 6% defaulting. In spite of this success, MSF's work remained marginal and was seen by most national and international healthcare actors as "a medical response to a social problem". Malnutrition was considered at best a problem of poverty, and at worst a cultural problem. Most NGOs still failed to treat children with malnutrition and UNICEF remained little involved in the area of nutrition. Plumpy'nut remained an unrecognized product. Only the World Food Programme (WFP) judged the nutritional situation of the country to be an emergency and decided to conduct surveys in 2005. It should also be mentioned that for the first time, malnutrition was cited in the Health Development Plan 2005–2009 as a priority health problem in Niger and as the cause of half of all under-five childhood deaths. However, no concrete measure was implemented. Intervention strategies for malnutrition were still based on educating mothers and fortifying porridge.

Under such conditions, MSF could not discontinue its programme. The only way out was for other actors to begin to treat malnutrition. Furthermore, the very high number of children treated in 2004 (9,632), in a country at peace, after three years of good harvests, greatly tested the teams and headquarters. During the previous nutritional crises in Angola in 2002 and Darfur in 2004, MSF had admitted 6,000 and 4,000 children respectively into its centres, whereas almost 10,000 were treated in Niger in 2004. In a report on his visit to Maradi, the programme officer for Niger wrote that "the situation in Maradi is not defined as a nutritional emergency situation like those MSF is used to, but in terms of the number of children that we are treating, this is an emergency situation".[5] Another challenge was the early treatment of malnutrition at a stage referred to as "moderate". Teams were confronted on a daily basis with many children with moderate malnutrition, who were showing up at screenings and yet could not be admitted to the programme since

[5] Internal MSF report, June 2004.

the criterion for admission was severe malnutrition. Since these children were not being treated under the Nigérien healthcare system, some of them were descending into severe malnutrition. MSF medical personnel were forced to explain to mothers that their children were not yet sufficiently sick to qualify for care.

While the nutritional situation was defined by the programme officer as an emergency, no real operational translation was taking place. The operational objectives for 2005 were not much different from those for 2003 and 2004. There was no clear desire to expand the programme or to provide better coverage in the region. However, MSF was still aware that as long as Niger's health policy failed to consider the treatment of severe malnutrition a priority, not only would children continue to suffer from an excessive mortality rate, but we obviously could not withdraw from the programme, either. As such, an important line of work for MSF teams consisted of raising awareness of malnutrition as a major health problem in Niger and promoting the new treatment options offered by Plumpy'nut. The issue of moderate malnutrition was then put aside, since no one had a real solution to offer for the very high number of children to be treated (at least five times more than the number of severely malnourished). The priority was still to treat severe acute malnutrition.

Although the programme in Niger was not expanded into regions other than Maradi, MSF began to use the outpatient strategy in other countries. In Darfur, in 2004, outpatient treatment seemed to be the most suitable solution for a crisis situation marked by lack of medical personnel. Despite the success of the strategy carried out in Niger, this programme was introduced in an extremely cautious manner in the Sudanese IDP camps. Children were seen in consultation every two days, even though their families were all living within a perimeter of a few kilometres around the centre, and the centre was open every day. Such caution is most probably explained by the fact that MSF teams in Darfur had never treated malnourished children in this way.

During a visit to Niger, the nutrition officer from MSF's medical department, convinced of the real prospects of treating severe malnutrition and exasperated by various actors' inertia, expressed the belief that "if we wish to deal with this reality, there is only one method. We must take our existing project, expand it, strengthen it, and publicize it, in order to pound this message into the head of not only the Ministry officers, but also UNICEF, WFP, and other local and international NGOs."[6]

---

[6] Internal MSF report, March 2004.

Crisis and shift in scale

It was in the first week of February 2005 that an increase in the number of children suffering from severe acute malnutrition was noted by our teams (fifth week of 2005: 729 admissions to the programme, as opposed to 480 in 2004). In the report on her 5 February visit, the programme officer wrote: "From discussions with peasants from the Maradi region and visits to their granaries, it seems that there are only two to three months of millet left for them, even though the next harvest is not anticipated until October 2005. Entire families have already migrated to Nigeria [...]. Seeing this year's grain shortage, exploratory missions must be conducted and outpatient care must be started in the most affected regions of Maradi, such as in all likelihood Dakoro."[7]

The FAO and WFP report on their crop and food supply assessment mission, dating from the end of 2004, to which we had paid little attention until then, initially determined the location of our operations. This report mentioned: "Following the drought and damage caused by desert locusts, Niger is acknowledging a grain shortage for 2004–2005 of an estimated 280,000 tons, or around 9% of the national requirements. Even if this shortage does not seem to be enormous at the national level, this must not obscure the extreme food vulnerability facing more than three million people living in the agro-pastoral area in the centre and north of the country."[8] According to this report, four regions were particularly affected by the poor harvests: Tahoua, Zinder, Maradi and Tillabéri. For each of these regions, the agro-pastoral area was cited as suffering from the most severe shortage. As a result, MSF initially directed its missions to assess children's nutritional status and food security in the agro-pastoral zone.

While activities were being organized in the field (assessment mission in Dakoro and Keita in February, opening of feeding centres in Dakoro in March and April, nutritional and retrospective mortality surveys in April, assessments in the Tahoua region, etc.), at headquarters a debate was taking place regarding the very existence of the crisis. Was 2005 an unusual year? We knew that malnutrition is a chronic problem, that poor harvests are common, and that the increased number of children admitted could be explained by the greater awareness of the programme on the part of mothers. However, the rate of this increase seemed to exceed normal programme growth and convinced our

[7] Internal MSF report, February 2005.
[8] FAO/WFP assessment of harvest and food availability in Niger, 21 December 2004.

teams of the seriousness of the nutritional situation. At this stage, however, we had not identified the areas and populations most affected by this problem, and we lacked a satisfactory explanation for a peculiar phenomenon. Doubts on the existence of a serious crisis would be bolstered by the result of the nutritional surveys conducted in the Keita and Dakoro districts. These surveys did in fact reveal a poor nutritional situation, but one that could be interpreted as "usual" in these regions. However, results of the retrospective mortality surveys were troubling: emergency thresholds had been crossed for children under five.

In spite of the doubts about the existence of a crisis, a press release published by MSF on 26 April 2005 mentioned for the first time a rapidly degrading situation and called on all humanitarian aid actors to mobilize in order to avoid a major nutritional crisis. This press release came out shortly after a release from the World Food Programme, which had conducted nutritional surveys in the regions of Maradi and Zinder in January 2005, and which described the situation as including "malnutrition rates observed in countries during wartime".

In spite of the divergent opinions on the existence of the crisis, a concentration of different factors pushed us to strengthen our response. First and foremost, the number of children with severe acute malnutrition presented at the centres was increasing. Next, we were in command of a nutritional rehabilitation strategy that could presumably be used on a larger scale. Finally, one of the objectives of the 2005 programme was to single out malnutrition as a major health problem in Niger, and to do this, there could be nothing so effective as treating a large number of children. As a result, in March, MSF decided to expand the feeding programme to the northern districts of Maradi and the Tahoua region.[9] MSF-Belgium was contacted in order to conduct assessments in the regions of Zinder and Tillabéri (these assessments were conducted starting in mid-April, but did not result in any programme openings, since the malnutrition rates were very low in the villages visited).

While the number of admissions continued to increase, it became urgent to understand more precisely the reasons for this phenomenon, particularly since we had no certainty at the time about which geographical areas the crisis was hitting the hardest, or which population was the most affected. This lack of awareness hampered the effectiveness of the aid (poorly conducted explora-

[9] The districts of Tessaoua, Mayahi, and Dakoro in Maradi, and those of Tahoua, Keita, Illela, Abalak, and Tchin-Tabaraden in the Tahoua region.

tory missions, belated decision to distribute food, no intervention until July in the southern districts of Zinder).

Various visits from headquarters and a researcher's report added to our understanding. Starting in April, the poor harvests in Nigeria, speculation on the price of millet available in Niger, and the inefficiency of the system implemented by the government in response to the crisis (sales of millet at moderate prices, poorly accessible to the population, and in inadequate quantities) were all identified as probable factors in the 2005 crisis. In June, the researcher dispatched by MSF discovered new explanatory factors, such as the creation of an artificial shortage, peasant families being pushed into poverty, and political choices that led to the prolonged refusal of free food aid distribution.

During June, internal and external debate concentrated on the responses to this type of crisis; food distribution was particularly covered in this debate. In our 9 June press release, we asserted that only emergency access to food aid could avoid danger for thousands of children already suffering from malnutrition.

We sharply criticized the strong reluctance of donor agencies, United Nations agencies, and the government of Niger to carry out distribution of free food, which was in our opinion the only measure capable of avoiding a degradation of the situation and a high number of deaths. Even so, it should be noted that we did not decide to organize any distribution of food supplies ourselves at that time. MSF's lack of experience in this type of food crisis and the difficulties in measuring its magnitude and in localizing it, as well as the population size, the number of villages presumably affected, and internal disagreements may all account for the fact that our targeted food distributions—in effect, a common element in MSF response to a nutritional crisis—would only be implemented belatedly.

In the beginning of July, MSF teams noted a clear difference between the numbers of admissions to the feeding centres in the region of Maradi and in the region of Tahoua. This trend, observed in July, would eventually be confirmed: in total, of the 43,000 admissions conducted in 2005, 90% occurred in centres located in the region of Maradi. But it was in the south of this region, in the agricultural area, that the contrast was most striking. Indeed, whereas the number of cases admitted started to drop in the northern areas, it continued to increase in the south. Accordingly, it was in the south that programme officers decided to strengthen treatment capacities by opening new feeding centres. Targeted food distribution[10] was also organized in the

[10] These distributions included 25 kg of enriched flour and 5 litres of oil, and were distrib-

two southern districts of Madarounfa and Guidan Roumdji, where most of the cases were concentrated.

It was also in July that internal and external debates on the existence of the crisis and how to respond no longer seemed appropriate in view of the very high number of children treated in the feeding centres and the rising number of media reports on severe malnutrition. The month of July was marked by the arrival of many NGOs (including four MSF sections) and a strengthening of the UN emergency setup. Niger adopted a protocol based on outpatient treatment and the use of ready-to-use foods. Furthermore, the authorities decided to distribute free food aid at this time.

This might have been the end of the story. Unfortunately, the free food distribution failed to target the areas most affected by malnutrition. In the same way that, in May, MSF had expanded its programme to the north of the country, the food distribution in August was targeted towards the agro-pastoral areas. According to various reports from early warning systems, these regions had experienced the most significant grain shortages. However, the nutritional crisis occurring in 2005 was especially acute in the southern districts, in the middle of the agricultural zone.

This targeting error can be explained by the lack of analysis regarding this type of nutritional crisis and the causes of malnutrition. First of all, it should be mentioned that the various early warning systems did not include malnutrition rates. Awareness took hold too late. Furthermore, general consensus on the notion that malnutrition was a structural issue, and its eradication would be achieved mainly by reducing poverty and giving information to mothers on the nutritional needs of children, was an obstacle to an emergency response. This consensus opposed free food distribution, on the grounds that this would only destabilize the market and place future development in peril. Finally, the general understanding was that if a crisis arose, this could only be the result of a sizeable deficit in cereal production. The number of malnourished children in the region called the "bread basket" of Niger, however, is evidence of the disconnection between agricultural production and incidence of acute malnutrition.

Seeing the very small amounts of food aid distributed in those districts with the highest number of admissions, we decided to speak out and issue a press release on the day before Kofi Annan's visit to Niger on 22 August. In spite of

---

uted for a period of one month to children from 6 to 59 months of age with a brachial perimeter of less than 125 mm, as well as to children under 6 months.

a rather positive reaction from him, the southern regions did not receive any additional food. Nonetheless, the press release had the benefit of starting a debate on the understanding of this type of nutritional crisis and the appropriate response to it.

The statistical data established for the entire year of 2005 demonstrated just how much the severity of the nutritional situation, subject of so much questioning at the time of the emergency, was real. The incidence of severe acute malnutrition, calculated on the basis of admissions to the MSF centres during all twelve months of the year and official population figures, was clearly the best indicator: in certain cantons, more than 20% of the children under five had suffered from severe acute malnutrition.[11] In the areas of the south, where admission rates were highest, the mortality numbers were also high: a retrospective mortality survey conducted in August by Epicentre in the district of Mirriah, south of Zinder, revealed an under-five mortality rate of 5.3 (3.9–6.7)/10,000/day during the period from 21 April to 19 August.[12]

The crisis did, however, also provide an opportunity to prove that it was possible to treat tens of thousands of children suffering from severe acute malnutrition. This change in scale was significant, since more than 40,000 children were treated, with a recovery rate of over 90%. Such success was essentially due to the therapeutic food used and the outpatient system. And to go even further, it can be said that without the outpatient system and Plumpy'nut, MSF would certainly not have been aware of the nutritional emergency. It was these new treatment options that revealed the crisis. That suggests that this type of crisis has passed by undetected several times in Niger in the past, and is likely doing so in other countries at the moment. At the time when the programme started in 2001, the situation was probably similar to that of 2005.

The objective that we set for ourselves in 2004—to mobilize other actors over the issue of malnutrition—was achieved beyond our expectations. For the very first time, the government of Niger, United Nations agencies, and donor agencies drew up a plan for 2006 to treat 500,000 children suffering from acute malnutrition. Nutritional surveillance was also integrated into Early Warning System. In addition, the government, with the support of the World Bank, has decided to offer free health care to children under five, a measure that has been applied since the spring of 2007. Finally, after their

[11] Epicentre/MSF, *Nutritional Crisis in Niger in 2005, Epidemiological Description of Admissions and Description of MSF Interventions*, January 2006.

[12] Epicentre, *The 2005 Niger Nutritional Crisis: Results of Five Nutritional and Retrospective Mortality Surveys*, Paris.

emergency mobilization, many NGOs have shown their readiness to commit themselves to the treatment of acute malnutrition in the long run. For this reason, we decided to hand over our programmes in the region of Tahoua and the north of Maradi to two of these NGOs in the autumn of 2005.

Considering this significant mobilization, MSF could have made the decision to withdraw from Niger. In fact, this option was never really considered. The excellent results achieved in 2005 showed some promise for the treatment of acute malnutrition at an earlier stage. We then saw two possible options.

Over the past several years, we had had a problem with refusing a large number of children whose malnutrition did not meet the programme criterion. It took the 2005 emergency to decide to distribute specialized food to this category of vulnerable children. Loss of immune defences is less significant in moderately malnourished children than in severely malnourished ones. Nevertheless, moderate malnutrition does increase the risk of death. As there are many more moderately malnourished children, the highest number of deaths in absolute terms occurs in this group. Until the present time, we were running up against two problems while treating this group: the high number of children and the recommended treatment, whose limits are revealed in the chapter by André Briend in this volume. The operational success of 2005 led us to consider expanding the treatment approach for severe malnutrition to the entire spectrum of acute malnutrition.

The second option was to act at an even earlier stage by distributing ready-to-use food to all children under three years of age. Since we knew that a significant proportion of children under three in the southern districts of Maradi would have an episode of acute malnutrition during the months of the lean period, it seemed both logical and feasible to prevent this from happening. This option was not exercised in 2006. At that time, we lacked a specific food that would be suitable for distribution targeting an entire age group. In addition, a number of people at MSF were still reluctant to make a commitment to a preventive approach to malnutrition.

Beyond the treatment of severe acute malnutrition

In 2006, the feeding programme consisted of treating children with ready-to-use therapeutic food (RUTF) from the moderate malnutrition stage, the programme's objective being to reduce the mortality associated with global acute malnutrition. For this objective to be attainable, the programme was redirected towards the two districts of Maradi that we considered to be the most severely affected, on the basis of the number of admissions the previous year.

Those children with moderate malnutrition were admitted to feeding centres and treated in exactly the same way as those suffering from severe malnutrition. The distinction was no longer made between moderate or severe stages of malnutrition, but rather in terms of whether or not it was necessary to admit a given child to hospital. We differentiated between complicated malnutrition—when a child refuses to feed himself or has an associated disease that requires hospitalization—and uncomplicated malnutrition, for which a child is monitored on an outpatient basis once per week. The RUTF used was the Plumpy'nut, previously intended for use only in severely malnourished children. The child was considered to be cured when his weight-to-height ratio was greater than 80% of the median on two consecutive visits. Upon leaving the programme, all children received a quantity of Plumpy'nut equivalent to a week's treatment, as well as 25 kg of enriched flour and 5 litres of oil.

In 2006, more than 65,000 children with acute malnutrition were admitted, including more than 45,000 children living in the districts of Madarounfa and Guidan Roumdji. Once again, the treatment approach allowed us to reveal the pathology's reach in this region.

58,000 moderately malnourished children and 8,000 severely malnourished children were admitted to 11 feeding centres. More than 90% of the children were treated directly in the outpatient system. The results demonstrated that the weight gain in moderately malnourished children, which was between 5.3 and 6.7 g/kg/day, was at least twice the weight gain observed when using enriched flour. The recovery rate for moderately malnourished children was more than 95%, the case fatality rate under 0.5%, and the default rate under 4%. These results demonstrated the effectiveness of RUTF in the treatment of moderate malnutrition. The high number of admissions, combined with the low default rate, showed the good adherence and active participation of the mothers in the programme. Just as in the treatment for severe acute malnutrition, the ease of use of the RUTF, as well as delegation of part of the treatment to mothers, were the pillars of the programme's success. Yet qualified medical personnel remained essential for identifying those children who could be monitored at home, as well as for the hospitalization of the most severe cases.

These results were even more promising. For the first time, there was no seasonal peak in severe malnutrition during the lean period. The weekly number of admissions remained stable, even decreasing as the year went on. These results suggested that severe acute malnutrition had been prevented through the use of RUTF.

The nutritional survey conducted in November 2006 by the government of Niger, UNICEF, and the WFP revealed a prevalence of overall acute malnutrition of 6.8% and severe acute malnutrition of 0.6% in the region of Maradi, whereas the national average was 10.3% and 1.4% respectively. For the first time, the region of Maradi, which usually suffered the highest rates of acute malnutrition, became the region where children's nutritional situation was the best at the end of 2006. The results from the national survey, as well as the fact that there was no increase in severe malnutrition during the lean period, suggested that an improvement had taken hold in the nutritional status of young children through the use of RUTFs. Furthermore, it can be reasonably concluded that this improvement had a significant impact on the mortality of all the children of this age group, even if the array of factors that influence this mortality makes it difficult to measure this impact with certainty.

The prospects suggested by this experience were however countered by arguments regarding the programme cost, which resulted from the price of RUTF and the programme's significant personnel requirements. MSF proceeded to mobilize different partners to search for a way to lower the cost of ready-to-use food. The main obstacle was the price of raw materials, primarily milk, which international aid agencies currently reserve only for those children suffering from the most serious stages of malnutrition. This action will need to be undertaken for some time, in the style of those actions carried out for general access to antiretrovirals for people living with HIV/AIDS in poor countries.

The human resources problem is another matter altogether. In August 2006 alone, more than 10,000 children were monitored in the 11 health centres run by MSF. Such a large number of patients obviously required significant medical staffing. The admissions procedure for these centres meant that an important part of the staff's work was concentrated on triaging those malnourished children who would be admitted into the programme. But the reasons why the other children were refused admission were not always understood by their mothers, and this led them to implement many circumvention strategies. This placed the teams in the absurd position of strengthening their controlling system "against" the mothers. This position was difficult to maintain and even less understandable for the mothers, because in many cases the refused children ended up being admitted a few weeks later, as they had meanwhile "fallen" into severe malnutrition. The energy expended by the mothers to have their children admitted to a centre, which was also done to receive a little supplementary food for their families, must be seen above all as proof of the precariousness of their food situation.

In addition to the triage work, another important task for the medical or paramedical personnel was the weekly monitoring of children who suffered from moderate malnutrition but did not exhibit, or no longer exhibited, any medical complications. Even if the outpatient treatment approach was much less burdensome for mothers, it still involved a weekly visit to the centre for four to six weeks. Reducing the number of centre visits is possible if mothers have food at home suitable for their children to regain weight.

During the months of the lean period, a general worsening in the nutritional status of children under three is observed. Therefore, distributing food suitable for all children of this age during these difficult months should reduce the number of malnutrition cases, while lightening the programme load for both triage and the medical monitoring of non-sick children. All of these arguments led us to reorient the programme once again in 2007. Just as was envisaged at the end of 2005, we opted for the distribution of a new ready-to-use food, called Plumpy'doz, henceforth available in small jars, given monthly to all children younger than 36 months in the district of Guidan Roumdji for the most sensitive months of the year. Only children with severe acute malnutrition (according to the WHO standards of 2006) would be monitored weekly in centres, with all other children receiving a consultation only if they are sick. Thanks to this distribution, we hope to significantly decrease the number of children experiencing an episode of acute malnutrition during the year. This new programme organization should also make it possible to treat acute malnutrition in a less human resource intensive manner, by decreasing the number of children in the centres, and concentrating medical resources on the sick.

Conclusion

The history of the MSF feeding programme in Niger shows that it was the progress achieved in treatment of acute malnutrition that revealed, year after year, a disastrous medical and nutritional situation in the southern districts of the Maradi region. As is often the case in MSF's work, it is contact with patients that enables us to understand a situation. And patients do not come to us unless the care we offer meets their expectations. So the mothers of Maradi have shown us once again.

Diagnosing these crises in a precise manner remains difficult, however. On the one hand, we must admit the intrinsic difficulty of working in an open environment. On the other hand, the tools we are using at the present time are not entirely suitable. Indeed, they have been developed primarily for refugee camps. Hence we are not able to correctly measure the phenomenon of acute malnutrition in Niger, staggered over several months and affecting children under three years of age, using a nutritional survey on prevalence in children under five years of age. In the same way, our retrospective mortality surveys are only valid during an acute event. Until now, it is the number of admissions that has best defined the nutritional situation.

Certain public health issues have been repeatedly at the heart of the debates concerning our work in Niger. Decreasing under-five mortality has been put forth as the main objective of the 2007 programme, and there were lively discussions on this. This objective was not considered achievable or as falling within our mandate. For the past ten years or so, we have worked to improve the quality of the care delivered to those who come to our healthcare facilities. At the same time, various efforts involving public health, coverage, decreasing mortality, or programme impact have been abandoned since they were deemed hardly achievable for an organization such as ours. However, it should be emphasized that over the previous years it was always the measures enabling treatment of a large number of people that both we and others around us considered to be major progress. Thanks to the notable progress achieved over previous years in treatment of the most severe diseases and development of techniques enabling treatment of a large number of patients, it seems possible now, in certain crisis settings, to once again consider decreasing mortality as a feasible objective.

Today, RUTFs are recommended as treatment for severe acute malnutrition by UNICEF, WHO, and the WFP—the three UN agencies in charge of health and nutrition issues. This consensus is already good news, since treating those children most at risk of death is of course the priority. We must now go further. Ready-to-use foods enable us to achieve more significant advances. The programme that ran in 2006 demonstrated that these types of food are a quality alternative to enriched flour for the treatment of moderate malnutrition. The results also suggest that it is possible to reduce the rates of severe acute malnutrition. The 2007 programme will attempt to demonstrate the effectiveness of ready-to-use food for prevention of the most severe stages of acute malnutrition, while at the same time treating acute malnutrition in a more economical manner in terms of human resources. If this is confirmed, the different possibilities for ready-to-use food can be easily imagined; most obviously, it could be added to family rations for general food distribution during crises.

Thanks to proper nutrition provided by ready-to-use food, associated with effective malaria treatment using artemisinin derivatives, the use of antibiotics such as ceftriaxone, vaccination against measles, and the ongoing development of other vaccines, it is reasonable to envisage achieving a real impact on childhood mortality in most African environments.

Translated from French by Eric Bullington.

9

Treating Malnutrition: New Issues and Challenges

André Briend

The issue of childhood malnutrition, like the more general issue of world hunger, is at the intersection of fundamental problems like poverty, distribution of wealth, environmental protection and demography. It is thus not surprising that the problem can be viewed in many ways and that every society—even every group within society—may understand the problem differently and understanding can change over time. This general evolution also characterizes the understanding and knowledge of malnutrition's medical and nutritional aspects, which also vary by medical specialty.[1] Thus the gaps between changes in treatment methods, scientific recommendations and practices in the field are largely the result of this varying development of knowledge, the relative isolation of various disciplines and the persistence of earlier views.

In that regard, a May 2002 Maradi field visit to evaluate MSF's strategy for treating severe malnutrition offers a revealing example and a useful introduction to this chapter. At that time, all severely malnourished children who arrived in Maradi were treated in a therapeutic feeding centre. They were pri-

---

[1] For a historical discussion of the evolution of medical and nutritional understanding of child malnutrition, see André Briend, *La malnutrition de l'enfant*, 1998: 1–15 (http://www.danone-institute.be/communication/mono06.html).

marily fed F100, a milk-based formula that must be prepared with drinking water and given only under supervision. Because of these safety requirements, children could not be treated at home. The feeding centre was overburdened and MSF logistical planners constantly sought to expand its capacity. Despite their efforts, capacities remained insignificant given the number of children who needed treatment. When the field teams learned that I was a nutritionist from Paris, they briefed me on the situation and the cultural problems responsible for the region's high malnutrition rate. When I raised the issue of families' access to nutritious food appropriate for children, I encountered a lack of understanding. My questions seemed misplaced and typical of someone unfamiliar with the local situation. Later, when I asked to visit the Maradi bakery to discuss whether it could prepare an initial batch of a nutritional food based on a recipe that was beginning to show results in Maradi, I sensed that people saw me as an eccentric nutritionist. However, the MSF nutritionist I was working with helped convince the teams to work on this project with me. In the end, I was there when the new food was first distributed to the children at MSF's centre. They liked it very much. Hurray for the Maradi bakery! However, my visit was coming to an end and I left Niger wondering whether the programme would continue. After a brief period of latency, MSF's approach to treating severely malnourished children shifted quickly, as shown by the 2005 crisis.

I mention these personal experiences to remind the reader that the current approach to treating severely malnourished children is still quite new and is still evolving. We are on the threshold of a decisive change in the treatment of childhood malnutrition that offers hope for the rapid eradication of the most severe forms of this scourge. However, many obstacles remain to treating childhood malnutrition early.

Treating severe acute malnutrition—between neglect and confusion

Children suffering from severe acute malnutrition are either emaciated or bloated from oedema and require appropriate emergency treatment. This is a major public health problem in many poor countries. According to a recent statement from the World Health Organization (WHO), UNICEF and the World Food Programme (WFP), it affects 20 million children around the world (*Community-based Management of Severe Acute Malnutrition*, June 2007). Strangely, despite occasional media attention during major food crises—when the number of emaciated children is too great to be hidden—it is often neglected. In 2003 the prestigious medical journal *The Lancet* invited leading international public health experts to write a series of articles on measures to reduce the number of children who die in poor countries every year. United Nations members had committed to such actions when they adopted the Millennium Development Goals.[2] Surprisingly, not a single sentence in the series addressed the treatment of severe acute malnutrition (Jones *et al.*, 2003).

The perception of these public health experts is not without consequences. The goal of eradicating severe acute malnutrition is technically achievable in the short term. However, it has not been the subject of international mobilization comparable to that associated with AIDS, for example, or polio. There are many reasons for this neglect. As Barbara Cooper and Benedetta Rossi show in this book, a major factor is that most cases of malnutrition occur in poor countries and among marginalized (often minority), politically powerless groups. The lack of advocacy organizations in wealthy countries—which do exist for AIDS—certainly helps explain the silence surrounding the issue of severely malnourished children. However, this is not the sole explanation. The Millennium Development Goals include reducing infant mortality as well as eradicating extreme poverty and hunger. Logically, the public health community should thus make treatment of severe acute malnutrition a central concern. However, as the *Lancet* articles illustrate, the experts addressing neglected public health problems in poor countries show little interest in severe malnutrition. This may be a result of their training, as they are more knowledgeable about medical than nutrition issues. Severely malnourished children often die from accompanying illnesses, like diarrhoea or acute respiratory infection, which are often named in inquests into causes of death. Infectious diseases are thus often considered to be the primary cause of infant mortality. However, another factor is clearly involved: severe malnutrition is often thought to fall outside the scope of public health approaches.

If a problem is to be considered a public health priority, it must affect a large number of individuals, represent a major cause of death and be amenable to large-scale preventive or treatment measures. In practice, severe acute malnutrition is often presented as failing to fulfil these criteria. First, it is often assumed that the number of severely malnourished children in the world is such that the problem is currently insurmountable. Second, treatment of

---

[2] The corresponding United Nations resolution is available at: http://www.ohchr.org/english/law/millennium.htm.

severely malnourished children is often seen as a particularly complex task and impervious to a mass-based approach. Those perceptions are mistaken.

Considerable confusion exists today regarding the extent of severe acute malnutrition, due in large part to the mass of statistics cited when issues of world hunger or malnutrition are raised. International organizations are not talking about the same phenomenon when they refer to individuals facing hunger or those who are malnourished. The FAO, the United Nations agency responsible for food and agriculture issues, is responsible for measuring "world hunger". This estimate is based on examining agricultural statistics. Broadly speaking, the FAO evaluates agricultural production, food imports and exports, non-food uses and losses at the country level, from which it determines the availability of food for each individual. After correcting for inequalities in food distribution, comparison of food availability and energy needs provides an estimate of undernourished individuals.

However, this method offers only approximations and involves major risks of error. Population statistics and agricultural production data from many developing countries should be treated with caution. WHO and UNICEF are responsible for estimating child malnutrition. However, each takes an entirely different approach. They regularly estimate the numbers of malnourished children in various countries by comparing the weight and height of children under 5 years with those of children from a supposedly well-fed reference population. Statistics obtained by estimating energy availability (as calculated by the FAO) and childhood malnutrition rates estimated using anthropometric measurement (as published by WHO and UNICEF) often conflict. Beyond the considerable bias found in these two types of measurement, children's weight is not, in general, strongly correlated with food energy availability. This discrepancy is undoubtedly explained, in part, by children's particular needs for nutrient-rich foods, as well as by intrafamilial food distribution problems.

In its reports, the FAO thus places the number of undernourished people at more than 800 million worldwide,[3] while UNICEF estimates that 150 million children are malnourished.[4] These dizzying figures could lead one to believe that the problem is insurmountable and that only a major improvement in the standard of living in all poor countries can solve the problem. There is some truth to that view; only by eliminating extreme poverty can we

[3] See FAO statistics at: http://www.fao.org/es/ess/faostat/foodsecurity/index_en.htm.
[4] See UNICEF statistics at: http://www.unicef.org/publications/files/pub_wethechildren_stats_en.pdf.

effectively eliminate malnutrition. However, when we examine these data, we must remember that they refer to individuals and children who suffer from varying degrees of malnutrition, most of which is moderate (see box). Severely malnourished children represent only a small fraction of the children whom UNICEF counts as malnourished and, to an even greater extent, of the number of undernourished individuals according to the FAO. Indeed, even in the poorest countries, it is rare that more than 2–3% of the most vulnerable children (those between 6 and 59 months) are severely malnourished (Gross and Webb, 2006). Even in the poorest countries, the extent of the problem is, thus, limited enough for effective treatment in the context of health activities to be feasible in the near future.

Forms of malnutrition: interpreting anthropometric studies

In the late 1980s the World Health Organization standardized the technique of anthropometric surveys. This involves measuring the weight and height of a sample of children under 5 years of age and comparing those data to the weight and height of well-nourished children of the same age and height. The measurements are used to calculate three primary indices:

Age-Weight: compares the child's weight to that of well-nourished children of the same age
Weight-Height: compares the child's weight to that of well-nourished children of the same height
Height-Age: compares the child's height to that of well-nourished children of the same age.

These indices represent different types of malnutrition. Children who are of low height for their age have stunting, those with a low weight-height ratio have wasting and those with a low weight-age ratio are underweight.

When these surveys are analyzed, the numbers of children who depart, to a greater or lesser extent, from the median measure among well-nourished children are counted for each index. This deviation is expressed as a standard deviation, a statistical measure of variation within a population of individuals.

Next, the percentage of children who are two or three standard deviations below the median for each index is usually presented. Children up to two standard deviations below the median are considered to be moderately malnourished. Those more than three standard deviations below are considered severely malnourished.

Severe *acute* malnutrition refers to children with a weight-height index less than three standard deviations below the median for well-nourished children.

That group also includes children with nutritional oedema, as well as those with a middle-upper arm circumference (MUAC) of less than 110 mm at between 6 and 59 months of age. That last criterion is often used to screen for children who require emergency treatment because it is easy to measure and, if left untreated, is associated with a high risk of death.

Severely malnourished children represent only a small fraction of the children defined as "malnourished" according to the other criteria. However, since 2006, the WHO recommends that new growth standards should be used to evaluate children's nutritional status. Contrary to the reference curves used previously, these standards are based on the growth of breast-fed children during the first four to six months of life. The use of these new standards, which are markedly different from the curves used previously, will reveal the number of children identified as severely malnourished on the basis of the weight-height criterion.

NOTE: The results of anthropometric surveys conducted in various countries may be reviewed at the website of the WHO's nutrition office: http://www.who.int/gdgmwho/p-child_pdf/.

Treating severe malnutrition—from yesterday to today

Children suffering from severe malnutrition have a high risk of death and require nutritional rehabilitation based on special milk-based foods enriched with vitamins and minerals. Until the last few years, experts cited two reasons for recommending that these children should be hospitalized or placed in a specialized therapeutic feeding centre (WHO, 2000). First, a medical setting is clearly preferable for treating the frequent and potentially fatal medical complications in these children. Furthermore, until recently, the preparation and storage of milk-based formulas required for the nutritional rehabilitation of severely malnourished children was a sensitive process that could be carried out only in a location where a minimum of sanitary conditions could be observed. A hospital or therapeutic nutritional rehabilitation centre seemed most appropriate. In general, milk-based formulas are excellent environments for the growth of pathogenic bacteria. Poor families cannot be expected to use them to feed children at home in a contaminated environment lacking access to potable water. In addition, distributing milk-based formulas in powder form could also create confusion around programmes promoting breast-feeding. These powdered therapeutic foods look like infant formulas, so it would be difficult to tell mothers to choose breast milk over infant formulas to feed their children, while giving powdered milk to those who need to gain weight quickly.

For a long time, the need to treat severely malnourished children in a specialized setting has limited treatment possibilities because there are far too few hospitals in the poor countries where most severely malnourished children live. Furthermore, it was observed early that hospitalizing these particularly fragile children creates a risk of nosocomial infection (one acquired in a hospital setting) (Jelliffe and Jelliffe, 1970). For all these reasons, it became the practice to admit only the most severe cases into treatment centres, which lent credence to the notion that, in general, severely malnourished children were very difficult to treat.

Conditions for treating severely malnourished children have changed dramatically with the development of ready-to-use therapeutic foods (RUTFs). These foods are derivatives of F100, the milk-based product recommended, even recently, by the WHO for rapid weight gain after the patient had completed the initial phase of treatment for complications. However, RUTFs differ from F100 products in their form of presentation. They do not take the form of powdered milk to be reconstituted with water, but are dry products with the consistency of a paste or crumbly biscuit that the child can eat directly, and they do not have to be mixed with water. This offers a considerable advantage. Because bacteria need water to multiply, they cannot proliferate in these dry foods. Of course, the child must drink water in addition to eating them. However, even if that water does not satisfy all hygienic requirements, it is much less risky to consume water and the therapeutic food separately than to mix them, because this prevents pathogenic bacteria from multiplying exponentially once water and the nutrients they require to reproduce are combined.

RUTFs were developed in the late 1990s, but several years of study and validation were required to confirm that by using them, hospitalization of severely malnourished children could be avoided in most cases. Today, those children are hospitalized only if complications are present. As a result, malnutrition treatment has been simplified considerably and can now be conducted on a large scale (Collins et al., 2006). It is currently recommended that severely malnourished children are screened through the use of a simple MUAC measurement and that those without complications are treated directly in the community with RUTFs (Prudhon et al., 2006). This approach has greatly facilitated treatment of large numbers of children.

MSF's experience in Niger provides a useful illustration of this evolution. During the 2005–6 crisis the number of children who could be treated, thanks to this new outpatient approach, was considerably greater than during any other MSF effort, as Isabelle Defourny explains in her contribution to this book.[5] The conditions required to implement large-scale programmes to eradicate severe malnutrition have now been met (Briend *et al.*, 2006).

Treating moderate malnutrition in emergency situations: pending questions

The development of foods that allow severely malnourished children to be treated at home represents unquestionable progress in the fight against malnutrition. However, it is not appropriate to wait for children to become severely malnourished before taking action. It seems logical to find ways to intervene sooner, specifically to treat those suffering from moderate malnutrition and prevent their conditions from worsening. Ideally, families would have access to nutrient-rich foods, allowing them to treat moderately malnourished children themselves. This is often impossible, particularly in emergencies, so it would be simpler to consider distributing special foods to moderately malnourished children. Paradoxically, however, less progress has been made in developing foods for treating moderate malnutrition than for severe malnutrition. More than 30 years of research on the metabolism of severely malnourished children, whose nutritional needs are relatively well known, have contributed to the development of RUTFs. The fact that these children have been admitted to hospital, and are thus available for close study, facilitated this research. In addition, treatment of moderately malnourished children faces a major cost problem. There are considerably more of them than of severely malnourished children, so distributing large quantities of foods like RUTFs to them becomes very difficult. Because these foods are produced with milk, they are fairly expensive. A reasonable approach to dealing with a small number of high-risk children becomes less reasonable when large numbers of children at moderate risk are involved.

In emergency situations, children with moderate malnutrition are usually treated with large quantities of blended flours. The principle behind these foods is simple. It refers back to the 1960s, when protein deficiencies were believed to be the leading problem in child nutrition in poor countries. It involves mixing balanced proportions of cereals, which provide medium-quality proteins because of insufficient lysine content, with legumes that provide considerable amounts of lysine, but relatively little of the sulphur-

[5] See also Tectonidis, 2006.

containing amino acids present in large quantities in cereals. The mixture provides appropriate levels of amino acids at a low price because it uses raw ingredients that are available at very low cost.

Recent developments in treating severely malnourished children have raised questions about using blended flours for moderately malnourished ones. Children who consume them show little weight gain and often need several months to recover an acceptable weight, contrary to severely malnourished children fed with an RUTF, who regain weight in several weeks. Low weight gain among children receiving these flours was long attributed to the belief that families were probably sharing the supplements the children received. This explanation had an element of truth, but why, then, would children receiving an RUTF—which would also be shared—show a markedly higher weight gain? The most likely explanation is that composite foods do not perform as well as RUTFs in the area of weight gain. A study conducted in Malawi suggests that moderately malnourished children who consume RUTFs regain weight and recover much faster (Patel et al., 2005). In 2006, MSF noted similar results in its programmes in Niger. Scientific rigour requires that these results must be confirmed by other studies to verify that they are reproducible. These preliminary observations have already revived questions regarding the efficacy of blended flours in treating moderately malnourished children.

Blended flours are generally made by using soy flour as a legume, balancing the proteins found in maize, a low-cost cereal that does not contain gluten, which is an additional advantage. Soy has interesting nutritional properties, but its use also poses problems for childhood nutrition. Soy proteins are difficult to digest and soy contains anti-nutritional factors that limit absorption of the mineral elements present in it or added. Finally, soy flour contains large quantities of indigestible carbohydrates, called fibres, that may reduce the child's appetite. These disadvantages have been known since the early twentieth century, when soy-based products were first used in infant feeding. Paediatricians had already observed that children who ate these foods had copious and foul-smelling stool (due to the effect of the fibres) and multiple deficiencies (Fomon, 2001). To ensure appropriate growth, soy-based children's foods used in wealthy countries are prepared from extracts of (very expensive) purified proteins, thus avoiding most of the problems encountered with non-refined products. Nonetheless, in general, paediatricians continue to prefer using milk-based products for infant feeding (ESPGHAN, 2006).

Blended foods used in food aid are produced with soy flour obtained directly by grinding seeds during cooking, through a mechanical process called extrusion. Some anti-nutritional factors are destroyed during this process, but it is not clear that the final product is appropriate for feeding young malnourished children. Although thousands of tons of these products have been used in food aid programmes over the last 20 years, their effect on growth has not been studied extensively and few efforts have been made to improve them. This omission is particularly surprising, given that for years, programmes using blended flours have generally been considered of limited efficacy (Beaton and Ghassemi, 1982).

Thus the treatment of moderately malnourished children in emergency operations today raises many questions. It would seem to be important to improve programme efficacy by using products that are known to be effective and that have been optimized to promote nutritional recovery. That said, the choices are not clear. Should we focus on improving the nutritional composition of blended flours currently in use, which are highly affordable? If the main problem is poor absorption of minerals required for the child's growth, the solution is relatively simple—add larger quantities of these minerals in chemical form. If, on the other hand, the basic problem is the digestion of proteins or the excessive quantities of indigestible fibres in these products, the solution is much less obvious. Using fat supplements derived from RUTFs given in small amounts could be another option. However, if they are to address the issues specific to moderate malnutrition, the formulation of products used currently in therapeutic programmes must be reviewed. For reasons of cost and to achieve programme sustainability, moderately malnourished children should, to the greatest extent possible, receive foods available within the families. Supplements should provide only those elements lacking in the diet of poor families. The issue is technically complex and tests will be required to obtain and validate a truly efficacious supplementation method.

Preventing malnutrition in non-emergency conditions: the challenges

The distinction between emergency and chronic situations is often artificial, as several of the contributions in this book show, and depends largely on the perception of both donors and local governments. Both tend to lose interest in chronic situations, even if the children's status remains precarious and should be considered urgent. In practical terms, however, this distinction has clear implications: in the absence of a perceived emergency, nutritional programmes receive the smallest share of funding and governments are not enthusiastic about programmes that involve distributing food supplements. Donors are sometimes prepared to subsidize food distribution for malnourished children, but the extent of the problem often exceeds wealthy countries' food aid programmes. In addition, massive imports of food products can have negative effects on the local economy. This approach is, thus, limited. For that reason, malnutrition prevention programmes not linked to emergency situations often concentrate on efforts to educate mothers, with the goal of helping them make the best use of foods available to them.

Relying on training mothers assumes that they have food at home to feed children, but do not know how to do so appropriately. Is that a reasonable assumption? Nutritionists may be partially responsible for the perception that malnutrition is often a question of ignorance. Until the 1960s and 70s, most nutritionists believed that the main problem facing children in poor countries was a lack of protein. According to that notion, teaching mothers which foods contained proteins would solve the problem. More than 30 years ago, we realized that that approach was mistaken (McLaren, 1974). Nutritional knowledge has evolved since the 1970s and we now know that certain nutrients that were not mentioned then—zinc, for example—are very important for children's growth and survival. These advances in nutritionists' knowledge clearly challenge the efficacy of efforts based on assumptions about mothers' ignorance, *a fortiori* when they have a limited budget. In mathematical terms, making the best use of food available in the home at the lowest cost that satisfies nutritional recommendations (by the presence of essential nutrients) involves solving a problem with as many variables as there are foods and as many constraints as there are nutritional recommendations. In practice, the problem cannot be resolved rigorously without the help of a computer (Briend *et al.*, 2003).

Suggesting that a computer be used to solve a problem that most mothers in wealthy countries manage to overcome on a daily basis would seem absurd. Suggesting it to mothers in poor countries is even more nonsensical. Mothers in wealthy countries can nourish their children more easily than those in poor countries because the former have access to food like milk (often enriched with vitamins and minerals when intended for children), meat, fruit and vegetables, which are rich in all kinds of nutrients. In practice, an infinite combination of these foods allows them to feed their children reasonably appropriately. Mothers in poor countries face much more limited food choices. Specifically, these mothers rarely have access to foods of animal origin, which are the richest in nutrients that young children need. Furthermore, using milk, the lowest-cost product of animal origin in terms of nutritional value, is risky for families who do not have a refrigerator or for whom simply boiling milk poses a problem. The use of meat and fish also poses food conservation problems. Because these families have limited buying power, they often feed their children a diet based almost exclusively on cereals, which offer inadequate nutrients.

What should be done? The limitations imposed by family poverty do not mean that educational programmes play no role. Some child feeding practices can be introduced at low cost and even no cost to families and can have an impact on survival and, to a lesser degree, children's growth. This includes early starting of breastfeeding after birth and exclusive breastfeeding during the first six months, with complementary foods introduced then and continued breastfeeding. Furthermore, where families do not live in extreme poverty, they can improve children's growth by making wiser food choices, as demonstrated recently in Peru and China (Penny *et al.*, 2005). However, when these education programmes are implemented in conditions of extreme poverty, their impact may be very limited because the mothers may simply not be able to act on the advice offered. A systematic study of food costs that shows the extent to which families can afford a balanced diet should be undertaken before assigning priority to education programmes over supplement programmes. That rarely happens. In those situations in which the lack of high-nutrient foods is a major problem—undoubtedly very common—education programmes will have little impact. Malnutrition will disappear only when the living standards of the lowest-income groups rise considerably.

Research currently under way on treating moderate malnutrition could provide solutions applicable in chronic situations. Indeed, incorporating low-fat milk powder, which is relatively inexpensive, in a paste-like food will protect it against bacteria. This technique would thus enhance poor families' access to this nutrient-rich food. In addition, all vitamins and minerals required for children's growth are now available in chemical form at a cost several times below that of providing them through the foods, and are equally effective as in their natural form. Foods in paste or powder form, or enriched and improved blended flours, that would provide a balanced diet to children in poor countries can realistically be developed at low cost, without waiting for a marked improvement in living standards. The development and sale of highly nutritional foods at affordable prices will help families at an intermediate standard of living, but will be of little use to the poorest. Only social welfare programmes will resolve the issue of the poorest families' access to food that allows them to nourish their children properly. Such programmes made it possible for wealthy countries to eliminate child malnutrition several decades ago. Much more work is required to achieve that result worldwide.

Conclusion

Simplifying the method for treating severe malnutrition means that we can reasonably foresee the short-term implementation of large-scale programmes that would transform these children's lives and avoid thousands of deaths each year that have, for too long, been considered inevitable. MSF programmes in Niger offer a fine example of achieving a major impact. From that perspective, MSF's operational response to Niger's critical nutritional situation in 2005 and the media coverage it received undoubtedly gave additional impetus to a general movement begun several years earlier. RUTFs, the outpatient strategy, improved access to rapid screening via brachial measurement and the WHO worldwide study to establish new anthropometric standards, adopted in 2006, are all key factors in a shift that required greater awareness. It is significant that since 2005, United Nations agencies (specifically, UNICEF and the World Food Programme) have shown renewed attention to the problem of severe acute malnutrition. In addition, these organizations, together with WHO, have just issued a very strong statement on the need to treat severely malnourished children.[6] UNICEF has just sponsored the launch of local production of RUTFs in Ethiopia. Let us hope that decision-makers will also gain an understanding of recent developments in treating malnutrition and quickly implement measures to eradicate the most severe forms of malnutrition. That would represent major progress.

Researchers, practitioners in the field and governments must next develop proactive methods, beginning with treating moderate malnutrition. The new methods that MSF implemented in Maradi beginning in early 2006 offer encouraging prospects in that area, too. However, they must be reproduced and adapted so that the programmes are both effective and sustainable. Additional research and genuine political will are required to overcome the many scientific, technical and financial problems and to address these issues. I have presented several approaches in this chapter, from improving supplement

---

[6] Joint declaration of the WHO, UNICEF, WFP and the United Nations Standing Committee on Nutrition. Community treatment of severe acute malnutrition. Geneva, 2007. Available at: http://www.who.int/nutrition/topics/Statement_community_based_man_sev_acute_mal_eng.pdf.

programmes targeting the most vulnerable children in emergency situations to developing low-cost nourishing foods and selling such foods at affordable prices in relatively stable settings. However, in the long term, eliminating poverty—by implementing broad social welfare programmes, if necessary— will give families access to foods with high nutritional value and remains the best way to eliminate malnutrition permanently.

Translated from French by Leah Brumer.

BIBLIOGRAPHY

Beaton, G.H. and H. Ghassemi, 1982. "Supplementary Feeding Programmes for Young Children in Developing Countries", *American Journal of Clinical Nutrition*, vol. 35 (4 Suppl), pp. 863–916.

Briend, A., 1998. *La malnutrition de l'enfant. Des bases physiopathologiques à la prise en charge sur le terrain*, Institut Danone.

Briend, A., N. Darmon, E. Ferguson and J.G. Erhardt, 2003. "Linear Programming: A Mathematical Tool for Analyzing and Optimizing Children's Diets during the Complementary Feeding Period", *Journal of Pediatric Gastroenterology and Nutrition*, vol. 36, pp. 12–22.

Briend, A., C. Prudhon, Z.W. Prinzo, B.M. Daelmans and J.B. Mason, 2006. "Putting the Management of Severe Malnutrition back on the International Health Agenda", *Food and Nutrition Bulletin*, n° 27 (3), S3–6.

Collins, S., N. Dent, P. Binns, P. Bahwere, K. Sadler and A. Hallam, 2006. "Management of Severe Acute Malnutrition in Children", *The Lancet*, n° 368, pp. 1992–2000.

ESPGHAN Committee on Nutrition, 2006. "Soy Protein Infant Formulae and Follow-on Formulae: a Commentary by the ESPGHAN Committee on Nutrition", *Journal of Pediatric Gastroenterology and Nutrition*, n° 42, pp. 352–61.

Fomon, S., 2001. "Infant Feeding in the 20th Century: Formula and Beikost," *Journal of Nutrition*, n° 131, pp. 409–20.

Gross, R. and P. Webb, 2006. "Wasting Time for Wasted Children: Severe Child Undernutrition Must be Resolved in Non-emergency Settings," *The Lancet*, n° 367, pp. 1209–11.

Jelliffe, D.B. and E.F. Jelliffe, 1970. "The Children's Ward as a Lethal Factor?" *Journal of Pediatrics*, n° 77, 1970, pp. 895–9.

Jones, G., R.W, Steketee, R.E. Black, Z.A. Bhutta, S.S, Morris and Bellagio Child Survival Study Group, 2003. "How Many Child Deaths can we Prevent this Year?", *The Lancet*, n° 362, pp. 65–71.

McLaren, D.S., 1974. "The Great Protein Fiasco," *The Lancet*, vol. 2, pp. 93–6.

Patel, M.P., H.L. Sandige, M.J. Ndekha, A. Briend, P. Ashorn and M.J. Manary, 2005. "Supplemental Feeding with Ready-to-use Therapeutic Food in Malawian Children at Risk of Malnutrition", *Journal of Health, Population and Nutrition*, n° 23, pp. 351–7.

Penny, M.E., H.M. Creed-Kanashiro, R.C. Robert, M.R. Narro, L.E. Caulfield and R.E., Black, 2005. "Effectiveness of an Educational Intervention Delivered through the Health Services to Improve Nutrition in Young Children: a Cluster-randomised Controlled Trial", *The Lancet*, vol. 365, pp. 1863–72.

Prudhon, C., Z.W. Prinzo, A. Briend, B.M. Daelmans and J.B. Mason, 2006. "Proceedings of the WHO, UNICEF, and SCN Informal Consultation on Community-Based Management of Severe Malnutrition in Children", *Food and Nutrition Bulletin*, n° 27, 99–104.

Tectonidis, M., 2006. "Crisis in Niger: Outpatient Care for Severe Acute Malnutrition", *New England Journal of Medicine*, n° 354, pp. 224–7.

WHO, 2000. *La prise en charge de la malnutrition severe: Manuel à l'usage des médecins et autres personnels de santé à des postes d'encadrement*, Geneva (available at: http://www.who.int/nutrition/publications/en/manage_severe_malnutrition_fra.pdf).

POSTCRIPT

Niger 2005: The Year of the Biscuit

Jean-Hervé Bradol

Certain catastrophes recur so regularly that society ends up seeing them as normal. And then, often unexpectedly, a new therapeutic method opens up unforeseen possibilities. From this point of view, 2005 was a noteworthy year. For the first time, Niger's health information system no longer counted only cases of malnutrition and deaths, but also a large number of children who were successfully treated.

From January to November 2005, the Médecins Sans Frontières (MSF) teams admitted more than 60,000 children suffering from severe acute malnutrition to the nutritional stabilization centres, and the result was more than 90% cured.[1] To the best of our knowledge, it is the first time that so many severely malnourished children were treated in such a short time, with such a high recovery rate. The new treatment for severe malnutrition was incorporated into the national protocol. The government of Niger implemented free treatment for children and pregnant women, even though the financial means for carrying out this policy were cruelly lacking. Access to treatment for acute malnutrition increased considerably: more than 300,000 children obtained treatment in 2006 through a network of 900 nutritional stabilization centres.[2]

---

[1] Milton Tectonidis, "Crisis in Niger—Outpatient Care for Severe Acute Malnutrition", *New England Journal of Medicine*, 2006, n° 354 (3): pp. 224–7.

[2] UNICEF, "Niger: Response to Child Malnutrition, 2006 Annual Review" (http://www.unicef.org/media/files/Niger_a_year_in_nutrition_-_2006_Annual_review.pdf).

To grasp the importance of these figures, it is necessary to understand how serious the situation was. Niger has approximately 14 million inhabitants, including 2.8 million children under the age of five. Two hundred thousand of these children die each year,[3] and half of these deaths are associated with malnutrition.[4] In 2005, the national system of prevention and response to nutritional crises, and Niger's health system, did not make it possible for those who were going to die—small children—to receive nutrition adapted to the physiological needs of a developing child. Let us say it clearly: today, no country can hide behind the excuses of extensive poverty and lack of resources to justify such carnage.

According to the World Bank, the number of children suffering from malnutrition is constantly increasing in sub-Saharan Africa. In Asia, the situation is only slightly better: the absolute number of cases is decreasing, but Asia still has both the highest prevalence and the highest number of cases.[5] Food shortages have become commonplace in the modern world and, contrary to what might be expected, they do not spare young democracies whose economies obey market laws. The main victims are children, within a specific age bracket: those under the age of two. They are scattered throughout families living in the rural world, where handicaps accumulate (low incomes, limited access to education, etc). We are far from the images of nineteenth or twentieth century famines which bring to mind entire families, starving and skeletal, roaming around public areas looking for food. Today's food shortages—not counting those caused by refugee movements or blockades due to armed conflict—do not evoke the same images, but are no less deadly. The objective of those who claim that these new situations are not famines is not to demand more accuracy in the handling of historical analogies, but to refute the existence of a serious crisis and the need for exceptional measures.

As dictated by the free market economy, the starved are referred back to their individual responsibility. If they cannot meet their own needs, the assumption is that it is their behaviour that must change, not the way society distributes the available food. Sure enough, national and international public action can most often be described as proposing a change of behaviour (having

---

[3] Cf. http://www.unicef.org/infobycountry/niger.html.

[4] Amt L. Rice, Lisa Sacco, Adnon Hyder and Robert E. Black, "Malnutrition as an Underlying Cause of Childhood Deaths Associated with Infectious Diseases in Developing Countries", *Bulletin of the World Health Organization*, 2000, 78 (10): pp. 1207–21.

[5] World Bank, "Repositioning Nutrition as Central to Development: A Strategy for Large-Scale Action", Washington DC, 2006, p. 6.

fewer children and changing feeding habits) rather than aid. Free distribution of food is reserved for the poor living in rich countries, and for populations in times of war. Outside these categories, free distribution of food triggers objections reminiscent of the "reactionary" type of discourse established by Albert Hirschman: such distributions are considered dangerous (negative economic interference), futile (the cause is attributed to the inappropriate behaviour of the poor, not to lack of food), and perverse (promotion of laziness).[6]

The appearance of a new generation of therapeutic foods made it possible to improve the recovery rate and to multiply tenfold the number of children who could be treated. A treatment that used to be administered in a hospital for cases of severe acute malnutrition evolved into a treatment taken at home, for the majority of cases. Usually, it was the mothers and the Nigérien health personnel who achieved this remarkable progress, within the framework of the national public health plan. It is important to note the lucidity of the General Health Directorate of a Ministry whose current resources do not allow it to face the scale of the problem, but which nevertheless authorizes innovative initiatives in order to pave the way for the future.

We urge that—in catastrophic situations of high prevalence of malnutrition and abnormally high juveno-infantile mortality—the chronic and repetitive nature of these crises should no longer be used as justification for inaction. In the past, the medical approach allowed many individuals to be cured in countries of the South, but the complexity of the treatment prevented it from being applied on a wide scale. Only profound economic and behavioural changes might reduce the extensive sources of malnutrition and their deadly consequences. For the first time, the development of a new category of therapeutic food made the medical approach possible on a large scale, by allowing the patient, the child, and his or her mother to be the main engine of recovery. In the Maradi region the mothers understood this well and, after the 2005 crisis, spoke frequently of the advantages of the "biscuit" (*biskit*), referring to the new therapeutic food.[7]

---

[6] Albert O. Hirschman established this classification (jeopardy, futility, perversity) with reference to the discourse which opposed progress in the matters of civil rights, citizenship, and social and economic rights; see Albert O. Hirschman, *The Rhetoric of Reaction: Perversity, Futility, Jeopardy*, Cambridge, MA: The Belknap Press of Harvard University Press, 1991. The author specifies that he uses the words "reaction" and "reactionary" without adopting the "negative connotations" which are attached to these terms. It is Hirschman's version of the term "reactionary" which is used here.

[7] "The *biskit* stimulates the appetite, opens the child's stomach, calms him, and makes him

At last, we are on a serious track which may break the association between poverty and abnormally high infant mortality caused by malnutrition in countries where poverty is frequent and resources are limited. This comes at a price, that of milk, sugar, oil, and vitamins. Is this too much to ask?

A society that does not feed all its children

In a speech to the Economic and Social Council of the United Nations, in October 2005, James Morris, then Director of the World Food Programme (WFP), declared that "Africans at war get far more attention than Africans at peace. [...] Occasionally I have thought the worst place for a hungry child to live in Africa today is a country at peace and stable, but just plain poor."[8]

The government of Niger does not contradict the WFP Director's diagnosis. UNICEF and the WHO estimate that approximately 100,000 deaths of children under five years of age can be attributed to malnutrition as the underlying cause.[9] The skeletal children of the Sahel first appeared on televisions during the famines of the 1970s, and remained there throughout the mid-1980s. After that, nothing until 2005. Twenty years of free market economics, democratization and development efforts, and yet the results are inescapable.

The epidemiological data which have been available since the early 1990s are partial and make it difficult to make comparisons from one year to another.[10] Nevertheless, they highlight certain noteworthy facts.

Chronic malnutrition is hyper-endemic. A large number of young children (44%) suffer from delayed growth caused by chronic malnutrition, half of them severely.[11] The consequences of these conditions are known: higher

---

regain weight. All the children who eat *biskit* quickly regain their health"—testimony of a mother in Maradi, quoted in LASDEL, *La crise alimentaire de 2005 au Niger dans la région de Madarounfa et ses effets sur la malnutrition infantile: approche socio-anthropologique*, Main report: M. Koné, preface by J.-P. Olivier de Sardan, May 2006: p. 68.

[8] James Morris, "Statement of the Executive Director to the ECOSOC Special Event on the Food Crisis in Africa", WFP, New York, 27 October 2005.

[9] Cf. http://www.unicef.org/french/infobycountry/niger.html and A. Rice *et al.*, "Malnutrition as an Underlying Cause of Childhood Deaths Associated with Infectious Diseases in Developing Countries", *op. cit.*

[10] Francis Delpeuch, "Evaluation du Dispositif de prévention et de gestion des crises alimentaires du Niger durant la crise de 2004–2005: synthèse concernant les aspects nutritionnels", in *Rapport de l'IRAM pour la République du Niger*, Prime Minister's Office, Food Crisis Cell; June 2006.

[11] National Institute for Statistics of Niger, UNICEF and WFP, "Enquête nutrition et survie de l'enfant", Niamey, October-November 2006.

infection rates, definite cognitive handicaps, and abnormally high juveno-infantile mortality. Individuals who do reach adulthood will have higher than average morbidity (diabetes, arterial hypertension, cardio-vascular diseases) and lower life expectancy.

Against this backdrop of permanent chronic malnutrition, an epidemic of acute malnutrition occurs each year. It reaches its peak during the season known as the "lean season" between the two harvests. Acute malnutrition causes a rapid loss of weight, which increases the probability of death in the short-term by two to twenty times, depending on the severity. It affects the youngest children the most, namely those aged six months to two years. Depending on the region, its prevalence is either severe (greater than or equal to 10%) or critical (greater than or equal to 15%), and reaches its height each year in August-September. The map depicting infant mortality does not match the one reflecting agricultural production deficits. Most undernourished children live in densely populated zones, where most of the country's agricultural production takes place.

It is important to point out that data measuring the prevalence of malnutrition give only a snapshot of the situation at one specific moment. These figures do not reflect the accumulation of cases over time—called the incidence rate. Therefore, prevalence of 3% of severe acute malnutrition calculated during one given month does not help to predict the reality of the accumulated annual cases. In the most affected districts of Maradi, MSF observed that 20% of children under five had crossed the threshold of severe acute malnutrition during 2005.[12] Only surveys that measure the number of accumulated cases of acute malnutrition over one year make it possible to compare one year with the next. These data are not available. Failing that, figures for the admissions into the nutritional stabilization centres do account for the accumulation of cases over a given period of time. But children attending a nutritional stabilization centre are not a representative sample of their age group within a given administrative unit (commune, district, department, or region). Furthermore these centres, when they exist, draw only a limited proportion of cases.

Infant malnutrition is a key public health concern because of its impact on mortality. Adult undernutrition is rarely studied. In 2006, one single source[13] showed a prevalence of 18.5% malnutrition among mothers. Probably a large

---

[12] Internal Médecins Sans Frontières report, 2005.

[13] National Institute for Statistics of Niger, Ministry of Economics and Finance: *Niger: Enquête démographique et de santé et à indicateurs multiples 2006*, Niamey, February 2007: p. 201.

segment of the adult population is poorly nourished, as suggested by many testimonies and the rare epidemiological data that are available, even though more in-depth studies are lacking.

The rate of infant mortality clearly shows how catastrophic the situation is. In the early 1990s, one child out of three did not reach the age of five. Ten years later, this was still the case for one out of four. During the 1990s, malnutrition was the underlying cause of approximately one million deaths of children under five years of age. In the present decade the situation has improved but remains serious: one child out of five dies before reaching the age of six.

Over a period of about fifteen years, the means and methods of assistance that were once used to respond to such catastrophes changed. Nutrition centres no longer provide food for children suffering from acute malnutrition. In fact, the frequency of this pathology is no longer calculated on a regular basis. Food aid decreased from 5.6 kg provided per year and per inhabitant, between 1987 and 1990, to 1.6 kg provided between 1997 and 2000.[14] By the end of the 1990s, the medico-nutritional treatment of acute infant malnutrition had become a rare phenomenon. This realization motivated the opening of nutritional stabilization centres supported by MSF in the region of Maradi in 2002.

In 2004, these nutritional stabilization centres reached a record of 10,000 admissions, made possible by implementation of a new treatment protocol. In early 2005, the situation deteriorated and the centres registered three times more admissions than the previous year during the same period. The annual epidemic of acute infant malnutrition cases started early and reached a peak on a scale rarely seen. The intense activity in the nutritional stabilization centres triggered a collective awareness of the cycle of yearly catastrophes, which until then had remained silent and invisible: these were the images of dying skeletal babies.

The impossible famine

The appearance of these images increased the pressure on different actors, in particular the leaders of the country. The statistics from the feeding centres, as well as the price of millet, which had doubled or even tripled compared with the previous year—a new record—emphasized that 2005 was a more critical

---

[14] Jean-Hervé Jézéquel: "'Ici, l'enfant n'a pas de valeur.' Sécurité alimentaire, malnutrition et développement au Niger", Report written for Médecins Sans Frontières, July 2005.

year than usual. Opposition political parties, unions and associations mobilized and organized strikes and street demonstrations against the rising cost of living. The government made concessions: it distributed free food in certain areas, lowered the price of certain foods (milk, sugar, oil) and of fuel, and finally included civil society representatives in the ad hoc committee in charge of managing the nutritional crisis.

In the spring, the Qatari television channel Al Jazeera produced a documentary that brought the crisis onto the international scene for the first time and resulted in food donations from African and/or Arabic-speaking states. The government of Morocco even sent a medical team, while King Mohammed VI visited Maradi in July. At the beginning of the summer the BBC World Service produced a series of reports, which completed the international awareness of the crisis.

The first consequence of these images was to bring about a debate on the very existence of a famine. As the word famine does not have a precise scientific definition, the answer cannot be given by experts. For the government, the issue at stake in the public debate was not only to find the correct definition of the crisis in order to adopt the most appropriate response. The leaders' obsession—and that of many development actors—was a fear that the word famine would become associated with a notion that the politics implemented during the previous years had failed. The worst-case scenario, from this point of view, was that use of the word famine would mean having to resume free distribution of food.

As Mamoudou Gazibo emphasizes in the chapter he writes in this book, Niger's head of state became very irritated at the use of the word famine.[15] Mohamed Ben Omar, Minister of Planning and spokesman for the government, stated that the situation could not be described as a famine because "there have been no adult deaths in the country, no Nigérien village has become depopulated, no shantytown has sprung up near the big urban centres (...)."[16]

The Financial Commission of the French Senate expressed its "concern at the thought that, faced with this situation, France may not have been as present as it should have been", and denounced "the irresponsible declarations of non-governmental organizations (NGOs)" in a report written by

---

[15] This was also the case when the President granted the author an interview in August 2006.

[16] Interview conducted by David Cadasse, Afrik.com, 5 October 2006 (www.afrik.com/article8844.html).

M. Charasse and A. Gouteyron. The way in which the report casts doubts on journalists can be read as an unconscious yet lucid admission of political failure: "Their reports aimed to be alarmist, yet masked the reality of the crisis in Niger: the humanitarian catastrophe they discovered has been occurring each year for decades."[17] The LASDEL Institute, on the other hand, admitted that "in spite of the media-driven excesses, the simplistic parallels between famine and infant malnutrition, or its reduction to a simple economic cause, the mobilization which MSF triggered in 2005 at least had the merit of bringing infant mortality to the forefront as a major public health issue (...)."[18]

Many of the images of emaciated Nigérien children that appeared on television in 2005 were filmed in MSF nutritional stabilization centres, because these were some of the few that existed at the beginning of that year. This brought about a confusion according to which MSF was thought to be the main instigator of the international mobilization that happened at that time. Our messages of alarm were neither earlier nor stronger than those of numerous other actors (politicians, journalists, aid workers). In fact, other actors witnessing the crisis had already sounded the alarm. As early as November 2004, the government—which was in an election campaign and under pressure from social and political groups—had sold food at reduced prices. The first appeal to donors by the UN was made the same month. In January 2005 the NGO Helen Keller International, supported by the WFP, conducted a survey that drew a very clear conclusion for the regions of Maradi and Zinder: "The situation in these two regions, and probably others as well, is comparable to that of people living in a war- or disaster-zone."[19] The European Parliament adopted a resolution entitled "Famine in Niger".[20] On 28 May Niger's Prime Minister, Hama Amadou, made an "anxious appeal" to the international community for emergency food aid.[21] On 27 July the French President Jacques

---

[17] French Senate: *Rapport d'information sur la mission d'évaluation et de contrôle du soutien français au dispositif nigérien de gestion de la crise alimentaire*, Rapporteurs: M. Charasse et A. Gouteyron, 29 September 2005.

[18] Jean-Pierre Olivier de Sardan et al.: *Analyse rétrospective de la crise alimentaire au Niger en 2005*, LASDEL (*Laboratoire d'Etudes et de Recherche sur les Dynamiques Sociales et le Développement Local*), May 2007: p. 54. This study is one of the most interesting sources for understanding how the families reacted to the crisis.

[19] Report by WFP and KHI: "Evaluation de base de l'état nutritionnel des enfants de 6 à 59 mois dans les régions rurales de Maradi et Zinder. Rapport de deux enquêtes," April 2005.

[20] Resolution P6_TA(2005)0338.

[21] www.rfi.fr/actufr/articles/066/article_36701.asp.

Chirac wrote a letter to the President of Niger, which opened with the phrase: "At this time when populations in Niger are under duress because of the famine, I would like to express the solidarity of the French people."[22]

The examples of public comment mentioned above show that the debate regarding the existence or not of a famine affected all the actors concerned, but in a confused fashion. The debate cannot be reduced to a conflict between political leaders and development actors on one side and emergency organizations on the other, with the latter prone to exaggeration in order to justify their intervention and to feed the media's well-known taste for sensational news. It should be noted that this debate also ran through MSF, reproducing the same arguments and divisions. On the use of the word famine, the BBC got the last word when, exasperated by the controversy, it asked, "How many dying babies make a famine?"[23]

Is the cure worse than the disease?

From the medical humanitarian point of view, when faced with a catastrophe, the main goal is not to change the political regime or come up with the most scientific analyses, but rather to find the most relevant strategies of intervention. Which means of providing assistance will avoid the most deaths? It is in this area—not that of producing alarm signals—that MSF's actions and public positions were the most noteworthy. We had not, in fact, understood any better than others the causes of the situation that year after year lead to the deaths of approximately 100,000 young children. But the decision, taken in 2002, to provide treatment for young children, at a time when most other actors had given up on doing so years before—as well as the empirical discovery of a new and considerably more efficient treatment protocol—placed us in an unusual position from the start of the crisis. We do not know any better than other actors why this country does not feed some of its children. However, we do know which ones die (infants under the age of two or three, for the most part), where most of them live (the agricultural regions), and which treatment to provide (the new protocol). The large numbers of children admitted into the centres, as well as the particularly high recovery rate, may provide hope, as long as more than just the usual methods are employed.

[22] http://www.elysee.fr/elysee/elysee.fr/francais_archives/interventions/lettres_et_messages/2005/juillet/famine_au_niger_lettre_du_president_de_la_republique_a_m_mamadou_tandja_president_du_niger.30868.html.

[23] http://news.bbc.co.uk/1/hi/world/africa/4139174.stm.

MSF provides free food to families that present cases of acute infant malnutrition—food that contains therapeutic elements adapted to the nutritional recovery needs of infants—and also offers free medical care for children who need it. Free distribution of food and of medical treatment are two ideas which go against the grain of twenty years of popular belief about development, all the more so because the map of this food distribution does not match the one used by the Food Crisis Unit (*Cellule de Crise Alimentaire*) which is under the authority of the Prime Minister and is supported by donors and the UN. Our efforts focused on the regions where the number of malnourished children was the highest and not those where there was a deficit in millet production, as the Food Crisis Unit does.

This unusual decision, justified for us by high mortality associated with malnutrition, aroused strong opposition. Many actors who think infant malnutrition is not due to lack of food in the families[24] find it difficult to accept the notion of free food distribution. The arguments against distributing food can be divided into three categories: "detrimental", "futile", or "dangerous". One of the first arguments used is to deny that there is any direct link between the malnutrition of a child and the availability of food, and hence to suggest that giving food to the families is useless, futile.

The correlation between infant malnutrition and availability of food within the family is an often debated yet poorly understood issue. In times of crisis, a plethora of commentators appear to question the degree to which a food shortage contributed to the appearance of malnutrition. It seems that this argument denying such a link is frequently deployed in order to explain why food distribution is not a priority, in spite of a high prevalence of malnutrition. Other risk factors, which also contribute to malnutrition, are emphasized to explain the extent of malnutrition among young children, and to reject the idea of free food distribution. These other risk factors, which are quite real, are linked to the family's behaviour (in particular the mother), its living and hygiene conditions, and the pressures caused by illnesses, in particular infectious diseases. Yet intra-family food shortages are not equal to other risk factors. Lack of food always leads to malnutrition. Nevertheless, experts and politicians are often satisfied with presenting anecdotes in which families—particularly the mothers—did have food and resources but did not use them efficiently.

---

[24] "The paradox is that, in fact, there is no direct and unequivocal link between infant malnutrition and food crises", in Jean-Pierre Olivier de Sardan *et al., Analyse rétrospective de la crise alimentaire au Niger en 2005*, LASDEL, *op. cit.*: p. 53.

To understand best whether or not the availability of food adapted to the nutritional needs of infants is an important factor, it is helpful to organize the factors that favour a return to a good nutritional condition into a hierarchy—instead of examining the risk factors for malnutrition. It then becomes obvious that, in order to treat malnutrition (whatever the cause) it is necessary, but of course not sufficient, to start by making available food which is adapted to nutritional recovery. Children who recover from malnutrition thanks to therapeutic food (nine out of ten in our cohort) are cured in the heart of their families, for whom neither the food culture nor the health and material living conditions have been significantly modified.

From a medical point of view, this debate is only interesting because of its impact on the way in which assistance is provided. In all cases, children's nutritional deficiencies require that they be given rich and expensive foods (milk, oil, sugar, minerals and vitamins) so that they can be stabilized and regain weight. In Niger, it is difficult for such food to be spontaneously available to families because of the Sahel's environment. Given the extensive poverty in Niger, it is also difficult for families to devote a significant part of the household budget to purchasing such food, even though it is indispensable to children's growth and, all the more so, to the nutritional recovery of an infant suffering from malnutrition. Two thirds of the families living in the affected rural areas are already forced to purchase more than half their food needs on the market.[25] Even though the price of millet, in 2005, was two to three times higher than the previous year, and in spite of the severity of the crisis, the suggestion to carry out wide-scale free distribution of food specifically adapted to the needs of infants encountered huge resistance, including within MSF.

One of the main arguments put forward was that the region's economic development would be jeopardized. "In Place Where the Hungry Are Fed, Farmers May Starve", read a *New York Times* headline.[26] From this point of view, deciding to distribute free food to the starving was seen not only as futile (since malnutrition has other causes) but as dangerous, since the free distribution could jeopardize the entire agricultural production and starve the farmers. The argument was that the massive and late arrival of food aid—just at the time when farmers were selling their crops—could destabilize the economy.

Those responsible for the United States' early-warning system, FEWS-Net, went even further. "Recent media coverage and NGO reports have claimed

---

[25] USAID/FEWS-Net, "Niger Livelihood Profiles", Washington, January 2005.
[26] Natacha Burley, "In Place Where the Hungry Are Fed, Farmers May Starve", *New York Times*, 22 September 2005.

famine conditions and the potential for the starvation of as many as 3.5 million people. The heavy and sensational media attention, and the possibility that more resources will be made available to treat the problem, create enormous pressures and incentives to agree with these claims, and may actually impede the market in delivering lower-cost food to those who need it most."[27]

One final argument against free distribution is that it might have detrimental side effects such as discouraging families from seeking their own means to provide sufficient resources; they would therefore become dependent on outside aid. This completes the three categories of arguments deployed. "What made the free distributions of food which were carried out in 2005 particular, from this point of view, is not that they 'injected' aid-dependence into areas which otherwise would not have encountered it, but that they increased it."[28]

In November 2005, governments in the region (those of Mauritania, Mali, Niger, Chad, Burkina Faso, Senegal, The Gambia, Cape Verde, and Guinea Bissau), international donors, and the UN gathered in Dakar, Senegal. In a press release that summarized the outcome of the conference, they expressed a strong hostility to emergency humanitarian aid. "Recognizing that humanitarian action is nothing but a temporary palliative, inappropriate and costly in this type of situation, we decided that the time had come to engage in a real dialogue among governmental, international and local partners to work towards a better future for the Sahel," said Margareta Wahlström, UN Deputy Emergency Relief Coordinator.[29]

Do rich countries also reject the concept of free distribution for themselves? One would expect that, with the help of a society's overall wealth, it would be easy for all families in rich countries to find work and therefore have revenues that would meet the food expenses necessary to the survival of the most fragile members of a family. Yet the Restaurants du Coeur (a French non-profit organization), food banks and other social services (whether public or private) distribute tens of millions of meals per year (67 million meals distributed by Restaurants du Coeur during the 2004–5 winter only). In France, 12% of the population is poor,[30] and if they had to buy specialized food for

---

[27] USAID/FEWS-Net "Niger: an evidence base for understanding the current crisis," Washington, 28 July 2005.

[28] Jean-Pierre Olivier de Sardan *et al.*, "Analyse rétrospective de la crise alimentaire au Niger en 2005", LASDEL, *op. cit.*: p. 25.

[29] "Sahel: Development Needed to Counter Food Insecurity", OCHA Press release AFR/1289 IHA/1118; Dakar/Geneva/New York, 18 November 2005.

[30] According to the definition of monetary poverty adopted by the European Union. Cf.

infants at market prices, there is no doubt that the country would face an epidemic of acute malnutrition and an abnormally high death rate. Yet nutritional self-sufficiency is exactly what the international system of aid and the governments are requiring from farmers in Niger—including self-sufficiency in the costly foods which are necessary to infants' growth—even though Niger ranks last in the UN Human Development Index.

In rich countries, great poverty associated with malnutrition has not disappeared even though the scale is not massive as was the case in Niger. Yet leaders have succeeded in disconnecting poverty from high infant mortality by relying on a network of prevention and treatment—in France, for instance, through Maternal-Infant Protection. Since it is clear that policies of social assistance can have negative side effects, these must be taken into consideration; but why do rich countries advise the poorest to adopt solutions that they themselves are incapable of implementing at home? Do the poor in Maradi have to strive for nutritional self-sufficiency, but not those in Paris?

A revolutionary treatment?

The new generation of therapeutic foods represents significant progress. The complete, ready-to-use meals greatly simplify treatment. In most cases, the child no longer needs to be hospitalized, which relieves the families from the burden linked to extended absences of the mother or other carers who had to stay with the child during hospital treatment. This usually lasted more than one month—often to the detriment of other children left at home. The advent of outpatient treatment made decentralized care possible. Setting up nutritional stabilization centres as close to the affected villages as possible diminishes the time and cost of transport for families.

The transfer of therapeutic responsibility from a group of specialized health workers to the children and their mothers is one of the most important aspects of the new products. If the child still has the strength, he or she sucks the paste directly from the packet of specialized food. If he or she is too weak, the mother administers the treatment on the tip of her fingers. The only thing the mother now has to do is tear the corner of the packet, whereas in the past she had to prepare a meal especially designed for the child using several key ingredients. Transferring a large part of the curative responsibility from the medical team to the mother and child has had a considerable overall impact.

Sarah Bouquerel and Pierre-Alain de Malleray, *L'Europe et la pauvreté: quelles réalités?*, Notes from La Fondation Robert Schuman, 2006.

Quite simply, it means that the same medical team can multiply the number of beneficiaries by ten. Furthermore, and this is a key element, the mother and child become the main crafters of the cure. Severe acute malnutrition is a heavy pathology, which is particularly lethal. Not long ago, it required hospital treatment that lasted several weeks. Who would have imagined that, thanks to a well-designed product, mothers would do better at home than doctors in a hospital?

What is in this product which results in such rapid and systematic nutritional recovery? Milk, sugar, oil, minerals and vitamins. In fact, this is milk's great comeback, enriched with energy and micronutrients. Powdered milk had been banished from public health programmes in poor countries because—contrary to the assertions of certain multinational agribusiness companies—it did not provide a safe alternative to breast-feeding, since the conditions in which the powder was reconstituted into liquid milk could be dangerous because undrinkable water was often used. It must be noted that exclusive breast-feeding remains the best way to guarantee the growth and health for an infant up to six months of age. With the new generation of ready-to-use therapeutic foods, milk is now presented in the form of a paste or a biscuit, and is enriched with energy and micronutrients. Thus, once more, it becomes the key element in the strategy to fight against juveno-infantile malnutrition.

The fact that this milk paste is enriched with additional minerals and vitamins is not a minor detail. Several decades of research were necessary in order to better understand the critical role played by deficiency of certain micronutrients. Maternal milk alone, in particular that from a mother suffering from nutritional deficiencies, cannot cover the needs during the most critical period of infancy. Starting at six months, other foods must systematically be introduced into the diet. These additions cannot be restricted to proteins and calories but must also include a multitude of micronutrients, a fact that started to be understood in the 1970s. As André Briend brings up in this book, preparing meals adapted for nutritional stabilization using basic foods available in the home would require the person in charge to calculate equations which only a computer could solve—hence the importance of a ready-to-use therapeutic food. In summary, the new generation of therapeutic food has made faster and more frequent recovery possible, and has increased tenfold the number of children admitted for a course of treatment.

Finally, the new therapeutic generation offers another perspective. Using the previous treatment protocols, individual children suffering from acute, severe or moderate malnutrition could also be cured, even if the number of cases of severe acute malnutrition that could be cared for was significantly lower than with the new protocol. Nevertheless, supplementary feeding programmes for children suffering from acute malnutrition do not reduce the prevalence of acute malnutrition among a whole population.[31]

In 2006, in two of Maradi's districts which were the most affected in Niger, Madarounfa and Guidan Roumdji, MSF started the systematic distribution of the new generation of therapeutic foods earlier than elsewhere—at the point when the children reached the stage of moderate acute malnutrition. Over 64,000 children suffering from acute malnutrition were admitted into the MSF centres; 93% of them were under three years of age and 92.5% were moderate cases. The weight gain (4.6 to 6.2 grams per kilo weight of the child at admission) must be compared with that usually obtained (2.0 to 4.0 grams[32]) using the previous generation of therapeutic foods for moderate acute malnutrition, which consisted of enriched flour and oil which were provided separately and had to be prepared. The children who received the treatment recovered nine times out of ten (seven out of ten using enriched flour).[33]

A national survey of the prevalence of acute malnutrition was carried out at the end of 2006 and showed a sharp drop in prevalence at the national level, from 15% to 10% for children under five years of age. Several regions, which often have a high prevalence, saw a significant decrease. This improvement reflects the involvement of many actors in the treatment of malnutrition since the 2005 crisis. The most spectacular results are to be found in the department of Maradi: the prevalence of acute malnutrition recorded at the end of 2006 was lower than that in Niamey, historically the lowest in the country.[34]

Weigh, measure, and ration

André Briend is right to point out that comparison of a few sets of operational statistics is not enough to establish the superiority of one treatment over

[31] Carlos Navarro-Colorado, *A Retrospective Study of Emergency Supplementary Feeding Programmes*, Save the Children UK, Emergency Nutrition Network, 2007.

[32] *Ibid.* p. 41.

[33] *Ibid.* p. 37.

[34] National Institute for Statistics of Niger, UNICEF and WFP, "Enquête nutrition et survie de l'enfant," Niamey, Niger, *op. cit.*

another with scientific certainty.[35] The same can be said for any attempt to compare the prevalence of acute malnutrition between 2005 and 2006.

As mentioned earlier, milk paste enriched with calories and micronutrients has proven its superiority in treating severe acute malnutrition.[36] This is the current scientific consensus. In practice, however, this means that the use of milk in the treatment of malnutrition is reserved for children who are on the verge of death. Apart from those—that is, for the immense majority of under-nourished children—milk is not to be provided. Those who defend continuing this situation—a rather reactionary view,[37] given the history of public health with regard to infants—put forward two main arguments: on one hand, the absence of scientific proof, and on the other, the cost.

The year 2005 marked the end of the consensus among those who opposed giving treatment for severe malnutrition. Yet a new consensus, which is no less worrisome, is incubating: to limit the access to the new generation of therapeutic foods. The plan is to provide this food to the smallest number of beneficiaries and as late as possible (once a case becomes severe acute malnutrition). Medical objections are weak and very categorical. Given the body of medical knowledge already gathered regarding the nutritional needs of infants, it is hard to imagine that a product of animal origin, namely milk, containing all the necessary micronutrients, and ready to use, could be less efficient than a product without animal origins and needing to be prepared. Furthermore, the first operational data show that the new treatment offers a clear advantage, as explained earlier.

From an operational point of view, in a region with a high prevalence of malnutrition and an abnormally high death rate among infants and children, restricting the treatment to acute cases of malnutrition is absurd. As Isabelle Defourny demonstrates in this book using the example of the MSF intervention in Maradi, this would mean waiting each year for the same particularly deadly epidemic to occur during the lean season, even though it is possible to avoid it. Not to mention that carrying out individual care, and even more so the process of identifying thousands of children within a population of hundreds of thousands, require the work of hundreds of people. The main expense

---

[35] See Chapter 9 in this book.

[36] Joint statement by WHO, WFP, SCN (UN Standing Committee on Nutrition), UNI-CEF: *Community-based management of severe acute malnutrition*; Geneva, May 2007. Available on: http://www.who.int/nutrition/topics/Statement_community_based_man_sev_acute_mal_eng.pdf.

[37] Again, in the Hirschmanian sense: cf footnote 6.

in such an operation is the payment of wages. If personnel were efficiently deployed to distribute therapeutic food to malnourished children, there would be no reason for comment. However, in practice, when such strategies are used, the main objective is no longer to administer treatment to sick children but to identify those who are in the last stage of the illness, and in this way to ration the distribution of specialized food as much as possible. The teams therefore dedicate most of their energy to *triage* and measurement (weight and height), in order to exclude the majority of children from receiving a nutritional complement—one that almost all will need during their first years of life. The teams spend the rest of their effort on individual care, which is heavy by definition, whereas systematic early treatment of children in the most vulnerable age bracket would mobilize fewer human resources, enable a larger volume of food to be distributed, and above all prevent the annual peak of acute malnutrition, which is particularly deadly. This is the gamble MSF is taking in 2007 in the Guidan Roumdji department, a region of Maradi. The preliminary results are very encouraging.[38]

It is important to note that the main objection raised by those who oppose the widespread use of the new generation of therapeutic food is economic. When it comes out of the factory, the new product costs approximately three euros per kilo. For feeding a very large number of children in need (more than half of the children in certain age brackets), the systematic distribution of a nutritional complement would be too costly. In the case of Niger, an effort to cover the needs of infants suffering from malnutrition—acute or chronic— would result in an annual expense of several tens of millions of euros in order to purchase the therapeutic food. Is it possible to include such an expense in countries' annual budgets in a sustainable way? Given the current market conditions for food products, it is impossible: the prices of some products, such as milk, have skyrocketed. Even if the public health budgets grew, it would not be enough to cover an important increase in spending in the area of nutrition. The impact of the economic factors—already very controversial in the discussions surrounding the origins of malnutrition—surfaces once again, this time as the main obstacle to the search for solutions. The question had already been raised at the time of the international launch of the Expanded Programme on Immunization (EPI), twenty years earlier. Such international interventions could never have taken place if the vaccines had to be purchased at market prices. For this reason, a group of vaccines was made

---

[38] Internal MSF reports, numbers of weekly admissions for acute malnutrition in the district of Guidan Roumdji.

available to health actors at markedly reduced prices. The same model was implemented for contraceptives. Why couldn't the same model be applied to therapeutic food to prevent malnutrition?

The situation is ripe for action, since many conditions have been met. Member states of the UN have placed mortality and malnutrition at the top of their list of development priorities. New therapeutic methods make it possible to leave the impasse in which medicine has been stuck with regard to treatment of malnutrition. The perception of the economic consequences of investing in treatment of malnutrition is evolving. Thus, the authors of the World Bank report on malnutrition emphasize that "improving nutrition increases productivity and economic growth" and "returns from programmes for improving nutrition far outweigh their costs."[39]

Yet to this day, international aid agencies, donors and governments are unwilling to take the initiative needed to eliminate the main sources of child malnutrition. We believe that humanitarian doctors must reject such an attitude. Is it too much to ask for milk, sugar, oil and vitamins for sick children?

Translated from French by Laura Brav.

---

[39] World Bank: "Repositioning Nutrition as Central to Development," *op. cit.*, p. 21.

Contributors

Jean-Hervé Bradol is a doctor and former president of the French section of Médecins Sans Frontières (2000–2008). He is currently a research director at the Médecins Sans Frontières Foundation in Paris and co-editor of a forthcoming collective essay on medical innovation in humanitarian settings.

André Briend is a doctor, nutritionist and research director at the Institut de Recherche pour le Développement (IRD). He specializes in problems of childhood nutrition in developing countries and it was he who formulated Plumpy'nut. He is involved in research on improving the treatment of severely malnourished children at community level.

Barbara Cooper is a historian, professor and director of the Center for African Studies at Rutgers University (New Jersey). She is the author of articles and books on Niger, notably on the history of Hausa women in the Maradi region.

Xavier Crombé is a research director at the MSF Foundation and teaches humanitarian issues at the Institut d'Etudes Politiques de Paris.

Isabelle Defourny is a doctor and programme manager at Médecins Sans Frontières in Paris.

Marthe Diarra is a sociologist. She works as an independent rural development consultant, focusing on gender and natural resource management.

Mamoudou Gazibo is an associate professor in the political science department at the University of Montreal. He has written several books on political institutions and democratization processes in Subsaharan Africa.

Kent Glenzer holds a PhD in anthropology and is the author of several articles on the history and anthropology of development in Sahelian Africa. He currently works with Oxfam America, where he is the Director for the Learning, Evaluation, and Accountability Department.

Jean-Hervé Jézéquel is a historian and holds a PhD in history from the École des Hautes Études en Sciences Sociales. He has taught African history at Emory University (Atlanta) for several years and recently joined the MSF Foundation as a research director.

Marie Monimart is an International Fellow with the International Institute for Environment and Development (IIED). Her work is focused on gender issues, more specifically related to equitable natural resources management, household livelihood security, and pastoralism.

Benedetta Rossi is an historian and anthropologist. Her field research and academic work have been focused on transformations of social hierarchies and the impact of international aid in the Ader region of Niger. She has been a lecturer at the LSE and SOAS in London and is currently RCUK Fellow in International Slavery at the School of History of the University of Liverpool.

Index